Beyond trade friction

T0328853

Beyond trade friction

Japan–U.S. economic relations

Edited by

RYUZO SATO and JULIANNE NELSON

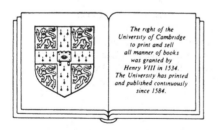

The right of the
University of Cambridge
to print and sell
all manner of books
was granted by
Henry VIII in 1534.
The University has printed
and published continuously
since 1584.

CAMBRIDGE UNIVERSITY PRESS

Cambridge

New York   Port Chester   Melbourne   Sydney

CAMBRIDGE UNIVERSITY PRESS
Cambridge, New York, Melbourne, Madrid, Cape Town, Singapore, São Paulo

Cambridge University Press
The Edinburgh Building, Cambridge CB2 2RU, UK

Published in the United States of America by Cambridge University Press, New York

www.cambridge.org
Information on this title: www.cambridge.org/9780521364676

First published 1989
Reprinted 1990
This digitally printed first paperback version 2006

A catalogue record for this publication is available from the British Library

Library of Congress Cataloguing in Publication data
Beyond trade fraction : Japan-U.S. economic relations / [edited] by
Ryuzo Sato and Julianne Nelson.
p. cm.
Papers of a symposium held in Sept. 1986, and cosponsored by the
Japan-U.S. Relations Center, International University of Japan
and the Center for Japan-U.S. Business and Economic Studies,
New York University.
Includes index.
ISBN 0-521-36467-1
1. United States – Foreign economic relations – Japan – Congresses.
2. Japan – Foreign economic relations – United States – Congresses.
3. United States – Economic policy – 1981 – Congresses. 4. Japan –
Economic policy – 1945 – Congresses. I. Sato, Ryuzo, 1931 –
II. Nelson, Julianne Beth. III. Kokusai Daigaku (Yamato-machi,
Niigata-ken, Japan). Nichi-Bei Kankei Kenkyūjo. IV. New York
University. Center for Japan – U.S. Business and Economic Studies.
HF1456.5.13B49   1989
337.52073 – dc19   88-21536
                                                                  CIP

ISBN-13 978-0-521-36467-6 hardback
ISBN-10 0-521-36467-1 hardback

ISBN-13 978-0-521-02614-7 paperback
ISBN-10 0-521-02614-8 paperback

Contents

Foreword

It is a pleasure for me to pen a brief foreword to this very special volume. As a participant in the 1986 conference on which it is based, I was able, firsthand, to hear renowned practitioners such as Haruo Mayekawa and Alan Greenspan, and a host of academic experts, expound on why both the United States and Japan must strive diligently, and in urgent terms, to take concrete action to cool the trade frictions that beset us. Their various views were perceptive and prescient then and they remain so today. If you possibly doubt this, simply begin turning the pages that follow. You will not be disappointed with what you read. Indeed, you will find it difficult to put down *Beyond Trade Friction*.

Richard R. West

Preface

In the world of modern economics and especially in the United States today, little credence is given to the concept of "economic planning." In Japan, however, not only is there a government bureau called the Economic Planning Agency, but careful planning has also been considered a virtue since time immemorial. This attitude is reflected in the Japanese language itself. The adjective *mukeikaku* (*mu* = lack, *keikaku* = plan), for example, does not simply mean that plans are absent; rather, it suggests that an action is rash, reckless, and ill-advised. A tendency to believe in the propriety of guiding and being guided in the general planning process has traditionally existed in Japan. Minor cultural differences of this kind may perhaps have some bearing on the sometimes critical reaction of many Americans to the "administrative guidance" provided by the Ministry of International Trade and Industry (MITI).

These opening remarks are not intended to lead into a discussion of the role of economic planning, but are by way of a confession. Although the choice of the two keynote speakers at our international symposium back in September 1986 and the speeches they gave on U.S.–Japan economic cooperation and the balance of trade may now appear to be the result of careful planning, at the time Dean West and I had no such master plan in mind. Of course, we did our best to invite people of the highest caliber, but we never dreamed that we would be bringing together the two men who perhaps more than anyone else today represent the leadership, past and present, of the Japanese and American financial worlds.

On that September day in Tokyo, sitting together on the same platform at Keidanren Hall, the headquarters of the Federation of Economic Organizations, one of the most influential economic bodies in Japan, were Haruo Mayekawa, the former governor of the Bank of Japan, whom we might call the Japanese Paul Volcker, and Alan Greenspan, who did not know – or at least did not let on that he knew – he would one day become Volcker's successor as chairman of the Federal Reserve Board.

Anyone who is unaware that these choices had been made without any of the long-term planning that is traditionally a Japanese forte will take one look at this book and say, "Mayekawa and Greenspan! What foresight to invite those two – that really was good planning."

Be that as it may, the appearance in book form of this collection of lectures by some of the most sought-after experts in the field today has an almost symbolic significance. Frankly speaking, I feel slightly embarrassed that the result of a random deviation arising from a typically American lack of planning might be mistakenly praised as an example of Japanese-style planning. But that feeling does not diminish one iota my pleasure and pride in being an editor of this book.

Recently I was invited to speak on the topic of the "new Japan" at a symposium entitled "U.S.–Japanese Competition and Cooperation," which was sponsored by the Japan Society of Boston with support from the Japanese Consulate General.

I sincerely believe that in order for there to be a new Japan, there must be a new America. If the new America must free itself from its twin budget and trade deficits and regain its competitiveness under a stable dollar, its mirror image, the new Japan, must reduce its enormous trade surplus and improve the nation's standard of living by stimulating demand in the domestic marketplace. But if we look at what is actually happening, money from Japan's trade surplus is being excessively concentrated on Tokyo. The result is inflation and soaring prices for land and equities there, with excessive consumption of Japanese goods, domestic unemployment, and industrial decline here. Thus, distortions in the economic activities of Japan and the United States are causing damage and suffering in both countries. Yet few people seem to have fully grasped this cause-and-effect relationship.

This book, of course, has no ready answers to these pressing problems. It should nevertheless prove a valuable guide to anyone attempting to understand the proper relationship between the United States and Japan.

As a single glance through the pages of this book makes abundantly clear, the authors of the essays collected here constitute an impressive company. Scholars who have made significant contributions in their various academic specialties have been brought together into what can only be called in Hollywood terms "an all-star cast" of the economic world.

The overview written by my coeditor, Julie Nelson, is also an outstanding achievement that thoroughly summarizes the rich content of this book. My only fear is that she has done her job all too well and that readers will be so completely satisfied with what was intended to be an appetizer that they may be tempted to forego the essays that form the main course.

In conclusion, I would like to take this opportunity to express my deep gratitude to Sohei Nakayama, the founder and chancellor of the International University of Japan, and to the Japan–U.S. Relations Center there, which cosponsored the September 1986 symposium that formed the basis for this book; to Saburo Okita, the university's president; and to Chihiro Hosoya, director of the center. My heartfelt thanks go as well to Dean Richard West of New York University, who kindly took time from his busy schedule to help me organize this symposium. Last, but not least, I wish to thank all the members of my staff at the Center for Japan–U.S. Business and Economic Studies, who, in addition to their regular duties, willingly assumed the onerous task of preparing the conference proceedings for publication. Without their assistance this book would never have been possible.

Ryuzo Sato
New York

Contributors

JAGDISH BHAGWATI   Arthur Lehman Professor of Economics, Columbia University, New York, NY 10027

WILLIAM H. BRANSON   Jacob Viner Professor of International Economics, Princeton University, Woodrow Wilson School of Public & International Affairs, Princeton, NJ 08544

ALAN H. GREENSPAN   Chairman, Board of Governors, Federal Reserve System, Washington, DC 20551

KALA KRISHNA   Associate Professor of Economics, Harvard University, Littauer Center, Cambridge, MA 02138

HARUO MAYEKAWA   Advisor, The Bank of Japan, 2-2-1 Hongoku-cho, Nihonbashi, Chuo-ku, Tokyo, Japan

JULIANNE NELSON   Assistant Professor of Economics, Stern School of Business, New York University, New York, NY 10006

TOSHIYUKI OTSUKI   Professor of Economics and Statistics, Graduate School of International Management, International University of Japan, Niigata, Japan

RYUZO SATO   C. V. Starr Professor of Economics and Director, The Center for Japan–U.S. Business and Economic Studies, Stern School of Business, New York University, New York, NY 10006

NORIYOSHI SHIRAISHI   Assistant Professor, Graduate School of International Management, International University of Japan, Niigata, Japan

TOSHIO SHISHIDO   Chairman, Research Institute of Construction and Economy (Kensetsu Keizai Kenkyusyo), Tokyo, Japan, and Professor, Toyo Women's College, Tokyo, Japan

INGO WALTER   Dean Abraham L. Gitlow Professor of Economics and Finance, Stern School of Business, New York University, New York, NY 10006

RICHARD ZECKHAUSER   Frank P. Ramsey Professor of Political Economy, John F. Kennedy School of Government, Harvard University, Cambridge, MA 02138

CHAPTER 1

Beyond trade friction: an overview

JULIANNE NELSON

Economic relations between Japan and the United States in the 1980s
have been marked by frictions over macroeconomic policy coordination,
trade practices, and financial market integration. Perceptions of the frictions have differed with location and over time. A 1987 telephone poll
indicated that 55 percent of Japanese labeled relations between the two
countries as unfriendly, whereas only 19 percent of Americans did so.[1] In
contrast, a similar poll conducted in 1986 revealed that as few as 29 percent of Japanese and 8 percent of Americans felt this way.[2] These tensions led to demonstrations by both public figures and private citizens:
In the summer of 1987, members of the U.S. House of Representatives
smashed a Toshiba radio on the steps of the Capitol;[3] in the fall of the
same year Japanese farmers in Hokkaido demolished an effigy of President Reagan.[4]

   The essays in this book review the causes of these frictions and propose
ways to avoid them in the future. With one exception, earlier versions of
these papers were presented at a symposium entitled "Beyond Trade Friction" held in Tokyo on September 1 and 2, 1986. The symposium was
sponsored jointly by the Center for Japan–U.S. Business and Economic
Studies of New York University and the Center for Japan–U.S. Relations
of the International University of Japan. The remaining paper by Kala
Krishna reflects the same concerns as those that inspired the symposium
and is therefore included as a complement to the conference proceedings.

1   Macroeconomic policy issues

The 1980s have witnessed a growing awareness of economic interdependence worldwide. In his paper, written before his appointment as chairman of the Federal Reserve Board of Governors, Alan Greenspan argues

I would like to thank Tom Pugel for his comments on an earlier draft. I would also like to
thank Jackie Urra and Raju Kalyani for their help in finding references for this article.

1

that this interdependence was inevitable given the structure of the international economic system. He calls attention to the growing U.S. trade deficit during the 1980s, particularly the bilateral deficit with Japan. Tables 1.1a and 1.1b summarize this trend. Greenspan notes that the United States has also been accumulating external debt during this period. Table 1.2 reviews sales of U.S. securities abroad. Greenspan reasons that an increasing unwillingness of U.S. trading partners to hold dollar-denominated liquid assets would force a depreciation of the dollar and an increase in foreign direct investment in the United States. Tables 1.3 and 1.4 confirm his hypothesis. By the end of 1987, the dollar had depreciated against the yen in particular and against a trade-weighted basket of foreign currencies in general. From 1985 to 1987 foreign direct investment in the United States, particularly by the Japanese, also climbed rapidly. Greenspan believes that U.S. fiscal policy (i.e., efforts to deal with government budget deficits) and increasing competition between Japan and Korea for U.S. markets could create conditions that would foster increasing economic integration in the 1990s.

Haruo Mayekawa, former governor of the Bank of Japan, focuses on the need for change in Japan in the face of the growing economic integration of the 1980s. He reviews the recommendations of the Mayekawa Report issued in April 1986 by the Committee on Economic Adjustment, of which he was chairman: The report indicated that one method of reducing the Japanese trade surplus would be to expand domestic demand, but that this required political support. Mayekawa points out several impediments to this expansion: the government budget deficit, rising land prices, an export-oriented Japanese economy, and Japanese import restrictions. He also notes the importance of exchange rate stability for the Japanese economy.

By the end of 1987, it was clear that some progress had been made toward the goals cited in the Mayekawa Report. The economic slump of 1986, labeled *endakafukyo* or high-yen recession, forced manufacturers to cut costs and reorganize production by closing plants and exporting jobs.[5] In addition, the government had made a variety of expansionary policy adjustments. Table 1.5 indicates the decreases in the discount rate offered by the Bank of Japan to commercial banks. In the wake of this policy change, interest rates declined and Japanese building began to boom.[6] Implicit and explicit subsidies to farmers were cut back: The Japanese government lowered by 5 percent the price it paid farmers' cooperatives for rice, and relaxed import restrictions on some agricultural products. Personal income tax cuts went into effect in 1987, and the government abandoned the goal of ending government bond sales by 1990 and increased public works spending for the first time since 1982.[7] The result was a

Table 1.1a. *U.S. trade in goods and services*[a]

	1980	1981	1982	1983	1984	1985	1986	1987(I)	1987(II)	1987(III)
Export of goods and services	344,667	372,892	348,324	332,201	362,021	358,498	372,807	98,511	102,225	101,887
Merchandise exports	223,966	236,254	211,217	200,257	219,916	214,424	224,861	57,201	61,644	61,717
Import of goods and services	(333,888)	(361,813)	(351,502)	(365,113)	(457,965)	(461,191)	(498,501)	(128,963)	(141,211)	(147,544)
Merchandise imports	(249,308)	(264,143)	(247,606)	(261,312)	(334,023)	(338,863)	(368,700)	(93,940)	(101,273)	(104,231)
Balance on goods and services	10,779	11,079	(3,178)	(32,912)	(95,944)	(102,693)	(125,694)	(30,452)	(38,986)	(45,657)
Merchandise balance	(25,342)	(27,889)	(36,389)	(61,055)	(114,107)	(124,439)	(143,839)	(36,739)	(39,629)	(42,514)

[a] Millions of $US.
Source: U.S. Department of Commerce Survey of Current Business.

Table 1.1b. *U.S. bilateral trade with Japan*[a]

	1980	1981	1982	1983	1984	1985	1986	1987(I)	1987(II)	1987(III)
Export of goods and										
services to Japan	29,074	32,019	30,519	31,427	33,579	32,792	40,203	9,606	10,616	11,420
Merchandise exports	20,806	21,796	20,694	21,677	23,240	22,145	26,361	206	79	37
Import of goods and										
services from Japan	(37,755)	(46,050)	(46,199)	(49,710)	(71,227)	(78,059)	(96,422)	(23,928)	(25,991)	(26,465)
Merchandise imports	(31,217)	(37,598)	(37,685)	(41,307)	(60,211)	(65,653)	(80,764)	(19,574)	(21,131)	(21,314)
Balance on goods and										
services with Japan	(8,681)	(14,031)	(15,680)	(18,283)	(37,648)	(45,267)	(56,219)	(14,322)	(15,375)	(15,045)
Merchandise balance	(10,411)	(15,802)	(16,991)	(19,630)	(36,971)	(43,508)	(54,403)	(19,368)	(21,052)	(21,277)

[a] Millions of $US.
Source: U.S. Department of Commerce Survey of Current Business.

Table 1.2. *Sales of U.S. securities*[a]

	Net foreign purchases of U.S. corporate securities	Net foreign purchases of U.S. bonds[b]
1980	5,427	5,461
1981	5,827	5,043
1982	3,901	1,451
1983	5,410	903
1984	−2,980	12,897
1985	4,941	44,132
1986	18,719	50,650
1987	25,933[c]	25,872[c]

[a] Millions of $US.
[b] Includes state and local government securities, and the securities of U.S. government agencies and corporations.
[c] Figures for January–October.
Source: Federal Reserve Bulletin.

Table 1.3. *Exchange rates*

	Market rate (¥/$)[a]	Nominal effective $US exchange rate[b]
1980	203.0	100.0
1981	219.9	112.7
1982	235.0	125.9
1983	232.0	133.2
1984	251.0	143.7
1985	200.5	150.2
1986	159.1	122.5
1987	123.5	100.0

[a] End of period rates. Based on International Financial Statistics, line ae for Japan.
[b] Trade-weighted (MERM) index of exchange rates (units of foreign currency per U.S. dollar). Based on International Financial Statistics, line amx for the United States.

demand-led recovery: The Organization for Economic Co-operation and Development (OECD) placed Japan's real economic growth at 3.5 percent in 1987 and predicted continued growth at the same rate in 1988.[8]

Nevertheless problems remained. Table 1.6 indicates the increases in property values at the time. The government budget deficit continued to

6   **Julianne Nelson**

Table 1.4a. *Aggregate direct investment*[a]

	Net direct investment abroad by U.S., increase (−)	Net direct investment by foreigners in U.S., increase (+)
1980	(18,546)	10,854
1981	(8,691)	21,301
1982	3,008	10,390
1983	(4,881)	11,299
1984	(4,503)	22,514
1985	(18,752)	17,856
1986	(28,047)	25,053
1986I	(11,460)	1,846
II	(8,771)	4,536
III	(6,222)	6,077
IV	(1,594)	12,594
1987I	(9,826)	7,726
II	(5,439)	9,486
III	(7,288)	8,941

[a] Millions of $US.
Source: U.S. Department of Commerce Survey of Current Business.

Table 1.4b. *Aggregate direct investment*[a]

	Net direct investment by U.S. in Japan, increase (−)	Net direct investment by Japan in U.S., increase (+)
1980	(24)	726
1981	(506)	2,662
1982	42	1,744
1983	(1,050)	1,706
1984	69	3,469
1985	(1,131)	3,081
1986	(1,884)	4,098
1986I	(484)	(141)
II	(743)	503
III	(111)	1,161
IV	(546)	2,575
1987I	(355)	1,518
II	(769)	1,604
III	(223)	1,204

[a] Millions of $US.
Source: U.S. Department of Commerce Survey of Current Business.

Table 1.5. *Discount rates: Japan*

1985I	5.0
II	5.0
III	5.0
IV	5.0
1986I	4.0
II	3.5
III	3.5
IV	3.0
1987I	2.5
II	2.5
III	2.5
IV	2.5

Source: International Financial Statistics.

Table 1.6. *Percentage changes in Japan's property values*

	1981	1982	1983	1984	1985	1986	1987
Tokyo residential land							
Annual	12.3	5.8	3.9	3.2	3.9	10.0	76.8
Cumulative	12.3	18.8	23.4	27.4	32.4	45.6	157.4
All residential land							
Annual	11.4	8.3	5.1	3.0	2.2	2.2	7.6
Cumulative	11.4	20.6	26.8	30.6	33.5	36.4	46.8
Tokyo commercial land							
Annual	9.3	6.3	5.5	9.3	12.4	22.3	76.2
Cumulative	9.3	16.2	22.6	34.0	50.6	84.2	224.5
All commercial land							
Annual	6.7	5.8	4.0	3.5	3.8	5.1	13.4
Cumulative	6.7	12.9	17.4	21.5	26.1	32.6	50.3

Source: Adapted from the *Economist,* October 3, 1987.

grow: In January 1988, the Japanese cabinet approved a $447.5 billion draft budget for the fiscal year beginning in April 1988, essentially continuing the policies implemented in 1987. The projected $69.75 billion deficit was to be financed by the sale of bonds and government-owned stock in the Nippon Telephone and Telegraph Corporation.[9] At the local level, Japanese farmers lobbied their many representatives in Parliament and staged demonstrations to protest proposed further reductions in agricultural subsidies.[10]

William Branson of Princeton University reviews the problems inherent in achieving Mayekawa's goal of exchange rate stability through policy coordination. Branson argues that joint efforts in support of target exchange rates are eventually doomed: Exchange rate targets imply restrictions on domestic monetary policy that may be politically unpalatable and economically unwise. He argues that monetary policy alone cannot counteract "real" economic changes that affect exchange rates, and that the lack of consensus on the linkages between fiscal policy and exchange rates render formal multinational agreements virtually impossible. He illustrates his point through the appreciation of the dollar during the early 1980s. He finds that exchange rate changes had a significant negative effect on U.S. manufacturing employment and that an increase in the U.S. government budget deficit necessitated an increase in real interest rates and the appreciation of the dollar.

Exchange rates continued to have an impact on U.S. manufacturing production in the late 1980s. The depreciation of the dollar (see Table 1.3) initially led to lower profit margins on goods imported into the United States but eventually encouraged worker recalls and increased capacity utilization in late 1987, particularly in the paper, textile, and aerospace industries.[11] The politics of policy coordination continued to present seemingly intractable problems. In an essay published in early 1988, Gottfried Haberler wrote, "The drive for policy coordination has in practice become largely a sparring match between the United States on one hand and Germany and Japan on the other; we demand that they stimulate their economies; they admonish us to cut our budget deficits."[12]

2   Trade policy issues

In the 1980s, trade friction between Japan and the United States periodically manifested itself in the form of U.S. demands for greater access to Japanese markets and U.S. threats to limit the Japanese penetration of domestic markets. For example, in 1987 a dispute settlement panel of the General Agreement on Tariffs and Trade (GATT) supported a U.S. claim that Japanese quotas on ten agricultural product groups violated international trade agreements.[13] Japan was then faced with a choice between lifting agricultural trade restrictions (and thereby incurring the wrath of politically powerful domestic farmers), or facing U.S. claims for compensation under GATT rules. Efforts to resolve this dispute were overshadowed by negotiations for the removal of 100 percent tariffs that the

United States had imposed earlier on a limited number of Japanese electronic goods and for policy changes that would enable U.S. firms to bid on major Japanese public works projects.

Echoes of these quarrels were heard in Europe after Spain and Portugal joined the European Economic Community (EEC). As these Iberian nations opened up domestic markets to Japanese imports, they also sought to increase their exports of agricultural products to Japan. The failure to reach an agreement led to threats of higher tariffs on Japanese electronics, while the number of antidumping investigations against Japanese manufacturers continued to grow.[14]

The essays in Part II of this book place these recent tensions in a historical context and explore the implications of some of the methods used to resolve the disputes. Jagdish Bhagwati of Columbia University argues that these disputes are similar to those that occurred in the 1930s. In both instances, Japan's economy in general, and its export sector in particular, grew faster than the economies of its trading partners. Bhagwati notes, however, that recent events are distinguished by popular demands for reciprocity in trade liberalization and by deeper resentment among workers in the shrinking U.S. traded goods sector. On an industry level, he traces the source of the disputes not to "unfair" trade practices but to differences in social institutions and product quality. He concludes that Japan must adapt to the trend away from GATT-style multilateral trade agreements, and that Japan's future prosperity depends upon increased direct foreign investment and a variety of bilateral discriminatory trading partnerships.

In the 1980s, negotiated trade agreements between Japan and the United States were used to resolve a variety of trade disputes. Kala Krishna of Harvard University compares the economic implications of tariffs and voluntary export restraints (VERs). She argues that VERs provide a means of circumventing the express GATT prohibitions on quotas and may be preferred to tariffs by producers in both countries. The voluntary acceptance of such trade limitations allows foreign producers as a group to precommit to a low level of sales in a given country. This promise could serve to reassure existing domestic producers and encourage them to accommodate entry. VERs could also facilitate efforts by domestic manufacturers to raise or maintain high prices at home. Finally, a VER effectively establishes a foreign cartel controlled by the agency administering the program.

Krishna finds that the incentives of foreign and domestic producers to lobby for VERs depend upon whether imported goods are used in combination with or instead of domestic products. When foreign and domestic products are complementary, she argues, both tariffs and VERs lead to fewer imports and higher import prices in equilibrium. Either of these policies would limit the market for domestic goods and harm domestic producers. Under these circumstances, domestic producers would seek neither policy action. When foreign and domestic products are complements in demand, foreign producers clearly prefer a VER to a tariff, since the former allows them to keep revenues that would otherwise go to the domestic government. Compared with free trade profits, however, VERs provide foreign producers few benefits, if any: Price increases on imported goods lead to reduced sales of domestic goods and a shrinking market for imports. Incentives change substantially when imports are substitutes for domestic products. In this case, both foreign and domestic producers have the incentive to lobby for VERs: The ability to restrict output and increase prices enables both sets of producers to reap monopoly profits. In contrast, tariffs benefit only domestic producers (and their government).

The early history of VERs on Japanese exports of automobiles to the United States nicely supports Krishna's hypothesis. Robert Crandall[15] estimates that in 1984 and 1985, VERs increased the average price of Japanese cars by about $2,500 and provided Japanese manufacturers with an extra $10 billion in revenue. At the same time, the reduced competition from foreign imports allowed U.S. car manufacturers to collect an extra $16.6 billion in revenue. When President Reagan released the Japanese from the agreement in 1985, they unilaterally continued the restriction, albeit at a slightly higher volume.

Trade friction in the semiconductor market illustrates other points that Krishna makes. The pact signed in July 1986 set minimum prices for Japanese microchips in all markets. A year later, U.S. computer manufacturers complained of higher chip prices and the production cutbacks encouraged by the Ministry of International Trade and Industries (MITI) as it sought to enforce the agreement. Although the pact benefited U.S. producers of substitute chips, it injured U.S. computer manufacturers as producers of a complementary product: Since the computer industry uses chips in production, semiconductors are effectively a complement to computers. The pact also offered some benefit to Japanese chip manufacturers, allowing them to curtail price wars driven by excess production capacity.[16]

Joint ventures and international mergers provided other means for resolving trade disputes in the 1980s. Ryuzo Sato of New York University and Richard Zeckhauser of Harvard University review the justifications given in theory and in practice for domestic and international mergers and acquisitions. Examining management explanations for 72 nonbank mergers between 1983 and 1985, Sato and Zeckhauser find that a salient motive for mergers in the United States was the desire for growth and

economies of scale. In contrast, they note that international mergers, particularly between U.S. and Japanese firms, were often motivated by efforts
to circumvent protectionism, by a search for technological innovations,
and by the need to imitate the behavior of rivals. Sato and Zeckhauser
find that product diversification incentives, price-earnings arbitrage, and
corporate raiders had little impact on international mergers.

The most recent liberalization of capital controls in 1980 made it easier
for foreign companies to acquire majority interest in existing Japanese
firms and facilitated the overseas investments discussed by Sato and Zeckhauser. For example, mergers and joint ventures provided foreign firms
more immediate access to Japanese markets: In 1983 Merck acquired a
4–5 percent share of the Japanese pharmaceutical market by purchasing two local manufacturers;[17] in 1987 a multinational consortium was
awarded a license to land and operate a trans-Pacific telecommunications
cable in Japan;[18] in 1988 U.S. construction companies were invited to
form partnerships with Japanese firms to gain experience in competing
for Japanese public works contracts.[19]

Joint ventures and direct investment also limited the effectiveness of
protectionist policies. For example, production in Canada and the United
States by Japanese automobile manufacturers undermined the long-run
impact of VERs. Although shipments of cars to the United States were
below agreed-upon levels in 1987, the scale of North American manufacturing operations led to an increase in the actual availability of Japanese
automobiles.[20]

The technology transfer cited by Sato and Zeckhauser as an incentive
to merge sometimes led to political tensions. In 1987 the U.S. government blocked a proposed merger between Fujitsu and Fairchild Semiconductor on national security grounds.[21] National security arguments
were also blamed for keeping the United States out of joint research ventures sponsored by MITI: U.S. companies did not have the laboratory
facilities necessary to comply with the MITI requirement that research
it sponsors be conducted in Japan.[22]

The style of international mergers could change in the 1990s as some
Japanese companies begin to adopt U.S. corporate strategies. By the second half of the 1980s, Japanese firms had started to consider the acquisition of existing firms as a viable alternative to de novo entry: In 1987 reported Japanese acquisitions in the United States totaled $5.9 billion, up
from $26.3 million in 1986.[23] Not all of these takeovers were amicable: In
1987 Dainippon Ink and Chemicals acquired Reichhold Chemicals Inc.
through a hostile tender offer. This strategy was described as an effort "to
reach economies of scale for materials and marketing that will make it a
low-cost producer globally."[24]

3   Financial integration issues

During the 1980s, Japan came to play an increasingly important role in world financial markets, both as an intermediary and as a source of investment capital. The chapters in Part III of this book review the changes in Japanese investment policies and financial institutions.

As Toshio Shishido of the International University of Japan notes, Japan held 25 percent of international banking assets by the end of 1985, relegating the United States to second place with only an 18 percent share. Shishido cites the high rate of savings in Japan and its accompanying current account surplus as the underlying cause of this change in the world financial system. He attributes the specific form of the shift to the liquidity of world financial markets, the regulation of Japan's domestic financial markets, the change to a market value accounting standard for Japanese banks, and the mass psychology of Japanese investors. Table 1.7 documents the parallel shift in the position of the United States as an international financial intermediary. By 1985 the United States had become a net creditor and by 1986 even long-term investment by foreigners in the United States overshadowed long-term investment by the United States abroad.

Shishido argues in favor of a shift in the composition of investments that Japan used to recycle its surplus in the early 1980s. He recommends a movement out of portfolio investment and into direct investment in manufacturing as a means of avoiding trade friction and stimulating the U.S. economy in the 1990s. He notes that direct investment would allow Japanese corporations to circumvent trade barriers, would facilitate technology transfers to the United States, and would provide a useful role model for U.S. business management.

It is clear that Shishido's goal requires an adjustment in both the level and the type of direct investment. Some progress had been made by 1987: Table 1.4b documents the growth in the level of Japanese direct investment in the United States. However, the composition of this investment was not necessarily conducive to revitalizing U.S. manufacturing directly. Table 1.8 provides a breakdown of Japanese direct investment in 1986, both by geographical region and by purpose. It indicates that 75.9 percent of Japanese foreign direct investment in 1986 went into service sectors rather than manufacturing. Nevertheless, improvements in infrastructure in the United States and elsewhere could eventually increase U.S. productivity and stimulate demand for U.S. products.

Ingo Walter of New York University analyzes competitive strategies in the financial markets needed to allocate both portfolio and direct investment. He proposes a framework that can be used to study the increased

Table 1.7. *United States as international financial intermediary*[a]

	1980	1981	1982	1983	1984	1985	1986
U.S. holdings of foreign assets							
Cash[b]	26,756	30,075	33,957	33,748	34,933	43,185	48,516
Short-term investment[c]	121,014	166,157	218,281	236,525	239,837	239,820	270,340
Long-term investment:	459,320	523,603	572,690	603,637	621,319	666,364	749,031
Private total	397,297	456,402	499,806	525,840	538,451	580,554	660,437
Direct investment abroad	215,375	228,348	207,752	207,203	211,480	229,748	259,890
Portfolio[d]	181,922	228,054	292,054	318,637	326,971	350,806	400,547
Government[e]	62,023	67,201	72,884	77,797	82,868	85,810	88,594
Total foreign assets	607,090	719,834	824,927	873,910	896,088	949,369	1,067,886
U.S. liabilities to foreigners							
Short-term "deposits"[f]	277,059	311,070	359,456	397,987	427,956	458,417	558,021
Long-term "deposits":	223,771	267,626	328,596	386,322	464,495	602,836	773,431
Direct investment in United States	83,046	108,714	124,677	137,061	164,583	184,615	209,329
Portfolio[g]	140,725	158,912	203,919	249,261	299,912	418,221	564,102
Total foreign liabilities	500,830	578,696	688,052	784,309	892,451	1,061,253	1,331,452
"Net worth"	106,260	141,138	136,875	89,601	3,637	(111,884)	(263,566)
Liabilities & net worth	607,090	719,834	824,927	873,910	896,088	949,369	1,067,886

Table 1.7. *(cont.)*

	1980	1981	1982	1983	1984	1985	1986
Memoranda							
United States as net creditor	106,260	141,138	136,875	89,601	3,637	(111,884)	(263,566)
Short-term position[h]	(129,289)	(114,838)	(107,218)	(127,714)	(153,187)	(175,412)	(239,166)
Long-term position	235,549	255,976	244,093	217,315	156,824	63,528	(24,401)

[a] Millions $US.

[b] Gold, SDRs, convertible currencies, U.S. reserve position in the International Monetary Fund.

[c] U.S. government currency holdings and short-term assets plus 50 percent of U.S. claims on unaffiliated foreigners reported by nonbanks and 50 percent of U.S. claims reported by U.S. banks not included elsewhere.

[d] Private holdings of foreign securities plus 50 percent of U.S. claims on unaffiliated foreigners reported by nonbanks and 50 percent of U.S. claims reported by U.S. banks not included elsewhere.

[e] U.S. government international loans and other long-term assets abroad.

[f] Foreign official assets in the U.S. plus $\frac{2}{3}$ of U.S. liabilities to unaffiliated foreigners reported by U.S. nonbanks and $\frac{2}{3}$ of U.S. liabilities reported by U.S. banks not included elsewhere.

[g] U.S. government securities held by foreigners plus $\frac{1}{3}$ of U.S. liabilities to unaffiliated foreigners reported by U.S. nonbanks and $\frac{1}{3}$ of U.S. liabilities reported by U.S. banks not included elsewhere.

[h] U.S. short-term claims on foreigners minus foreigners' short-term claims on the United States.

Source: U.S. Department of Commerce Survey of Current Business. Definitions suggested by Holgar Engberg of New York University.

Table 1.8. *Japanese direct investment*

	Amount ($US billion)	Share (%)
Area		
North America	6.79	46.8
Latin America	3.07	21.2
Asia	1.51	10.4
Middle East	0.03	0.2
Europe	2.26	15.6
Africa	0.20	1.4
Oceania	0.64	4.4
Type		
Manufacturing	2.48	17.1
Commerce	1.20	8.3
Finance, insurance	4.70	32.4
Transport	1.25	8.6
Property	2.60	17.9
Other services	1.26	8.7
Others	1.02	7.0
Total	14.5	

Source: Economist, February 20, 1988. Estimates by Stephen Thompson, published by the Royal Institute for International Affairs.

interaction between Japanese financial institutions and those of Europe and the United States. He notes that conditions in a given market (as defined by client type, product type, and geographical location) depend upon the concentration and market power of suppliers and clients, available product substitutes, and a variety of entry barriers. He argues that a particular firm is more likely to behave aggressively in a given market if both of the following conditions are satisfied: (1) either the stakes are high or the firm has market power, and (2) either relations among competitors are poor, or competition in the market constitutes a zero-sum game.

The 1980s clearly witnessed changes in the competitive structure of world financial markets. In 1986, the Federal Reserve Bank of New York for the first time included two of the "Big Four" Japanese brokerage firms (Nomura Securities and Daiwa Securities) in the list of primary dealers in U.S. government securities. The Industrial Bank of Japan was also included in the list by virtue of its purchase of an existing dealer.[25] By the middle of 1987, Japanese banks held 9 percent of U.S. banking assets, more than double the share they held in 1980.[26] Japanese banks and insurance companies bought minority positions in U.S. brokerage houses:

In 1986, Sumitomo Bank purchased 12.5 percent of Goldman, Sachs and Company; in 1987 Nippon Life Insurance purchased 13 percent of Shearson Lehman Brothers; and the Yasuda Mutual Life Insurance Company bought 25 percent of Paine Webber.[27]

At the same time, U.S. financial institutions began to penetrate a variety of Japanese domestic markets. In early 1987, Citicorp announced plans to share automated teller machines with Dai-Ichi Kangyo.[28] By the end of 1987, nine U.S. investment banks had been allowed to purchase seats on the Tokyo Stock Exchange, and a U.S. commercial bank had obtained a seat on the Tokyo exchange by acquiring the London-based owner.[29] A 1987 policy change by Japan's Ministry of Finance allowed U.S. commercial banks in general to establish Japanese securities subsidiaries in conjunction with off-shore nonbank partners. The U.S. commercial banks that applied for these securities licenses were thereby able to circumvent some of the Glass–Steagall restrictions on their securities market activities in the United States and were granted privileges not then available to Japanese commercial banks.[30]

Pressure to further deregulate Japanese financial markets nevertheless persisted. In 1987, foreign banks accounted for only 3 percent of banking assets in Japan.[31] Michael Sesit described the regulatory environment in Japan at the time: "Commissions on most stock transactions are fixed. There is no commercial paper market and, effectively, no Treasury bill or repurchase-agreement markets. Options are prohibited, and a new equity futures market is considered incomplete."[32] Stock markets in Japan and the United States differ in several other respects as well: (1) trading on the Tokyo Stock Exchange is suspended if a stock price rises or falls more than a certain percentage; (2) specialists do not trade for their own accounts in Tokyo; (3) programmed trading is absent in Tokyo; and (4) there is a limit on margin trades in Tokyo that depends on market conditions.[33] In June 1987 the Japanese Finance Ministry announced a timetable for future financial market liberalization and left market participants contemplating the next round of negotiations.

Toshiyuki Otsuki and Noriyoshi Shiraishi analyze the relative efficiency of stock markets in the United States and Japan during these deregulation efforts. They review the theoretical literature on market efficiency, and discuss three market efficiency hypotheses commonly found in empirical work: the weak form (efficient with respect to information found in past prices); the semistrong form (efficient with respect to current public information); and the strong form (efficient with respect to all existing information). Otsuki and Shiraishi also review the literature on the efficiency of Japanese capital markets and argue that these studies are not generally directly comparable with tests of U.S. markets.

Table 1.9. *Market fundamentals*

	January 1987[a]	January 1988[a]
Price/earnings		
Tokyo	49.4	55.6
New York	16.2	14.0
London	14.3	12.3
Price/cash flow[b]		
Tokyo	14.2	15.7
New York	8.2	6.8
London	8.5	7.5

[a] End-of-period observations.
[b] Earnings plus depreciation.
Source: "Boom Time in Tokyo," *Economist,* February 6, 1988. Data from Morgan Stanley International.

In their own comparison of the New York Stock Exchange (NYSE) and the Tokyo Stock Exchange (TSE), Otsuki and Shiraishi find evidence to suggest that trading on both exchanges has become more efficient over time: In their samples from the NYSE and the TSE, more stock price changes in 1974–83 could be described as white noise than in 1964–73. They also found evidence to suggest that trading on the NYSE was more efficient than trading on the TSE: A higher proportion of stock price changes on the NYSE than on the TSE could be described as white noise over both nine-year intervals.

Otsuki and Shiraishi also found that the capital asset pricing model (CAPM) was less successful in explaining variations in the monthly prices of stocks traded on the TSE than on the NYSE. Furthermore, the "goodness of fit" of the CAPM for the TSE stocks was lower for the period 1974–83 than for 1964–73.

Table 1.9 provides other evidence of the differences in stock market "fundamentals" between New York, London, and Tokyo. The higher price-earnings ratios for TSE stocks have been explained by the fact that investors tend to treat Japanese stocks like discounted corporate bonds: The stocks pay low and stable dividends while accumulating (tax-free) capital gains.[34] This institutional difference, along with recent changes in the industrial structure of Japan, could help explain Otsuki and Shiraishi's CAPM results: These characteristics would make the market "beta" less stable over time in Japan than elsewhere.

4   Conclusion

The essays in this volume provide the reader with a set of clear policy goals for the late 1980s and the 1990s: macroeconomic policy coordination, the reduction and recycling of Japan's current account surplus, and financial market integration. The authors recommend measures designed to help the United States and Japan realize these goals. Only history will tell if the two countries can successfully move beyond friction to cooperation.

Notes

1 C. Haberman, "U.S. and Japan: Attitudes Shift," *New York Times*, June 5, 1987. The poll was conducted jointly by the *New York Times*, CBS News, and the Tokyo Broadcasting System. Calls were made to 1,343 randomly selected telephone numbers in the United States and visits were paid to 1,358 people in Japan randomly chosen by resident card.

2 C. Haberman, "Japanese Favor a Global Role, A Survey Finds," *New York Times*, May 3, 1986. Additional statistics provided directly by CBS News.

3 M. Tolchin, "'Japan-Bashing' Becomes a Trade Issue," *New York Times*, February 28, 1988.

4 S. Chira, "Bitter Trade Battle Tests Japan's New Leader," *New York Times*, December 8, 1987.

5 "Japan Brief," *Economist*, September 12, 1987; and B. Wysocki, Jr., "Battling a High Yen, Many Japanese Firms Shift Work Overseas," *Wall Street Journal*, February 2, 1987.

6 D. Darlin and M. Kanabayashi, "Japan's Consumers Go on a Spending Spree, and Economy Booms," *Wall Street Journal*, January 5, 1988.

7 P. Maidment, "A Yen for Growth," "The Next Task," and "Unique, They Call It," *Economist*, December 5, 1987.

8 "A High-Yen Boom," *Economist*, January 16, 1988.

9 "Japan: Steady She Goes," *Economist*, January 30, 1988; C. Haberman, "Japan to Increase Spending by 4.8%," *New York Times*, December 29, 1987; and M. Kanabayashi and A. Sato, "Japan to Raise Outlays by 4.8% in Coming Year," *Wall Street Journal*, December 24, 1987.

10 S. Chira, "Bitter Trade Battle Tests Japan's New Leader," *New York Times*, December 8, 1987.

11 A. Murray, "Aided by Weak Dollar, Factor Output Leads Economy Once Again," *Wall Street Journal*, January 26, 1988.

12 As quoted by L. Clarke, Jr., in "Why Economic Coordination Won't Work," *Wall Street Journal*, February 24, 1988, a review of *International Monetary Cooperation*, a festschrift published by Princeton's International Finance Section to honor Henry Wallich.

13 The groups included processed milk and cream, canned pineapple and non-citrus fruit juices, processed cheese, lactose, dairy preparations, sugared food preparations, processed beef, and tomato juice, tomato sauce, and ketchup.

E. Lachica, "Japan Prepares to End Quotas on Farm Goods," *Wall Street Journal,* November 11, 1987.

14 "Euro-European Trade: Full-Bodied Whine," *Economist,* May 30, 1987; and "EEC–Japan Trade: Japan-Bashing Catches On," *Economist,* July 29, 1987.

15 R. W. Crandall, "Detroit Rode Quotas to Prosperity," *Wall Street Journal,* January 29, 1986.

16 P. Waldman and S. Kreider Yoder, "U.S., Japan Microchip Firms Still at Odds," *Wall Street Journal,* November 6, 1987.

17 "A Japanese Market Ready for a Dose of Foreigners," *Economist,* July 18, 1987.

18 "International Corporate Report: Cable & Wireless Venture Gets Japan Phone License," *Wall Street Journal,* December 1, 1987.

19 E. Lachica, "Tokyo to Offer U.S. Firms Better Access to Japan's Huge Public Works Market," *Wall Street Journal,* January 13, 1988. This invitation represented one of many offers in a sequence of negotiations over eligibility to bid on public works projects in both Japan and the United States.

20 M. Kanabayashi, "Japan Expected to Keep Quota on Cars to U.S.," *Wall Street Journal,* January 19, 1988.

21 D. Sanger, "Chip Dispute: Reading between the Lines," *New York Times,* March 30, 1987. A "technology licensing exchange" nevertheless allowed the trade in information to occur.

22 S. Kreider Yoder, "Americans Spurn Japan's Research Offer," *Wall Street Journal,* December 30, 1987.

23 Michael Sesit, "Japanese Acquisitions in U.S. Jumped to $5.9 Billion in '87; Strong Yen Cited," *Wall Street Journal,* January 21, 1988.

24 D. Darlin and M. Kanabayashi, "Dainippon Ink Takes Another Bold Step," *Wall Street Journal,* June 29, 1987.

25 M. Sesit and T. Herman, "Three Big Japanese Enter Ranks of Primary Dealers Despite Opposition," *Wall Street Journal,* December 12, 1986.

26 M. Sesit, "Japan's Banks Become Ever-Bigger Lenders to American Business," *Wall Street Journal,* January 28, 1988.

27 J. Sterngold, "Japanese Buying a Place on Wall Street," *New York Times,* April 12, 1987; and L. Wayne, "Japan Moves Gingerly on Wall Street," *New York Times,* December 3, 1987.

28 J. Treece, "Soon, Citicorp 'Branches' Could Be All Over Japan," *Business Week,* January 19, 1987.

29 E. Berg, "Japan Lets 4 U.S. Banks Underwrite Securities," *New York Times,* June 4, 1987.

30 M. Sesit and E. Rubinfein, "Japan Signals Entry for Banks into Securities," *Wall Street Journal,* June 4, 1987.

31 M. Sesit, "How Slow Can You Go?" *Wall Street Journal,* September 18, 1987.

32 Ibid.

33 S. Chira, "Japan's Different Stock Market," *New York Times,* December 7, 1987.

34 "Boom Time in Tokyo," *Economist,* February 6, 1988.

PART I

Macroeconomic policy issues

CHAPTER 2

Japan and the United States: the need to prosper together

ALAN H. GREENSPAN

In seeing the extraordinary growth that has occurred in Japan, American economists are able to learn a good deal about the way an economy should function. In fact, we would like to see the American economy do more of what the Japanese economy has done. Indeed, I suspect that the pressures now evident in world markets are going to force the American and Japanese economies to integrate substantially.

In a sense, we are being pressured to move ever closer together largely because of our key positions in the world trading system and also because of the growing accumulation of dollar-denominated assets by Japan's government institutions, its private financial institutions, and its citizens. If there continues to be, as we all seem to expect, a sizable accumulation of external assets by Japan and a correspondingly sharp deterioration in the external position of the United States, it is inevitable that Japan's accumulation of dollar-denominated assets will be very large. With an annual accumulation on the order of $50 billion, an increasing amount is bound to be direct investment, even though a substantial part continues to be portfolio investment, either in U.S. treasury securities or in private issues. I suspect that as Japan's involvement in the United States economy grows, Japan will have as much difficulty integrating its economic system into the United States as we in the United States had in managing our substantial direct foreign investments, which we initiated in Europe and throughout the rest of the world in the 1960s and early 1970s.

There is very little we can do to avoid this particular process if, in fact, we are looking toward our mutual prosperity. What probably will be required is an understanding of how best to manage what is going to be one of the most extraordinary economic integrations in the history of the world. There are several fundamental economic forces that seem to make this almost certain. The first is the persistent and seemingly irreversible trade deficit in the United States, matched by a trade surplus in Japan. The key element on both sides of that equation is the significant bilateral trade surplus and deficit in the Japanese and American accounts, respectively.

There also appears to be little evidence that this situation is going to change significantly in the years immediately ahead. In August 1986, the American government released data indicating a trade deficit in excess of $18 billion overall for the United States for July 1986. In part, these data can be explained as a statistical aberration, but only in part. Even after one makes all of the adjustments for the inadequacies of the data, the lags in the recording of imports and exports, and the large flows of non-monetary gold between Japan and the United States, the figures that were published for July 1986 remain discouraging. They are discouraging in the sense that they indicate a starting point for U.S. economic improvements that involves a much higher trade deficit than we had originally contemplated.

The basic problem is in part the exchange rate, but not entirely. We saw a dramatic rise in the value of the dollar vis-à-vis the major currencies in the early 1980s, largely because real interest rates on assets denominated in dollars were higher than those on assets denominated in the other major currencies. There also appeared to be an improving political and regulatory environment in the early 1980s for foreign investment in the United States, and that in turn created a significant excess demand for dollars relative to other currencies. It was the phenomenal rise in the value of the dollar relative to the major trading currencies that obviously generated the break in America's trade position. As the dollar strengthened, we saw a significant deterioration in our competitive positions abroad. As the competitive position of our exports deteriorated, we also saw a sharp rise in imports, and, what is more important, a sharp rise across the American industrial structure in the share of imports as a percentage of aggregate demand in the United States.

Two consequences of the appreciation of the dollar were the large trading deficit and the beginning of a deterioration in our overall current account balance. We subsequently began to reduce what had been a fairly large net asset position with the rest of the world (i.e., an excess of U.S.-owned assets over liabilities) and found that not only was our merchandise trade deteriorating, but also that our services surplus, which had been so significant for so long, was under pressure. As the dollar continued to strengthen, we eventually ran into a large current account deficit and a major change in the net asset position of the United States, relative to the rest of the world. We have since experienced a sharp deterioration in the value of the dollar.

This decline is likely to continue. The reason is basically that even though we have seen a substantial deterioration in the exchange value of the dollar relative to the yen, the deutsche mark, and other European currencies, we are not likely yet to see a significant turnaround in America's trade accounts. Here, the major reason is that the six months of the considerable strengthening of the dollar (i.e., the latter months of 1984) were characterized not by a decline in import prices denominated in dollars (which is what theory would tell us would occur), but rather by a large increase in the profit margins on goods imported into the United States. As a consequence, when the dollar peaked in the early months of 1985, it did so during a period in which the profit margins on imported goods were at an all-time high. That situation enabled exporters to the United States, when confronted with the sharp reversal in the value of the dollar, to avoid increasing dollar prices in the United States and instead to contract profit margins and endeavor to maintain market shares in the U.S. economy. Throughout 1985, as the dollar weakened pretty much across the board against the major currencies, we saw little in the way of increased dollar-denominated prices on goods imported into the United States and, therefore, only a small shift in the ratio of imports to domestic production. It is, of course, not the exchange rate that matters, but the prices of imported goods, and they are not tied exactly to the exchange rate, except obviously over an extended period of time.

As a result, we have seen a substantial contraction in the profit margins on imported goods, little increase in dollar prices as far as overall imports are concerned, and little indication of a major turn at this moment. Furthermore, as costs in terms of yen, deutsche mark, and other major European currencies rose in the United States, the fact that both the Canadian dollar and the Korean won remained relatively stable created an atmosphere in which an increasing proportion of U.S. imports came from Canada and particularly from Korea. This shift in the mix of imports reduced the extent to which the weakening dollar vis-à-vis the major trading currencies affected the trade balance. What we are seeing now in the United States, and are likely to continue to see, is a trade deficit of substantial proportions that is being aggravated by an unforeseen factor only partly related to the exchange rate: the dwindling agricultural surplus on the trade accounts of the United States.

In the past, our trade balance had been positively affected by our high agricultural productivity; only recently have we been running an agricultural trade deficit. This portion of the general trade deficit obviously reflects in part the overall impact of the exchange rate. However, the extraordinary improvement in agricultural practice worldwide, such as improved crop fertilization and general agronomy, have greatly increased foodstuff production throughout the world, especially in those areas where the United States was formerly a major supplier. For example, the People's Republic of China has doubled its production in little more than four years. There have also been sharp increases in grain production in the Indian subcontinent, and even the Soviet Union seems to be coming back from a period of exceptionally poor harvests. Although we still do not know the full impact of the Chernobyl nuclear incident on the grain supplies of the Soviet Union, the presumption is that it is not a major issue in the long run.

This suggests that, under existing commodity price relationships and bilateral exchange rates, we are going to continue to see a significant accumulation of external debt by the United States, and corresponding increases in the net dollar-denominated assets held by the major countries of the world, with Japan in this instance being in the forefront. This situation is essentially unsustainable. It is not possible to project indefinitely into the future the accumulation of external debt in the magnitudes that we now observe. The basic problem here is portfolio diversification. As the claims against the United States accumulate, and as the level of those claims denominated in dollars begins to weigh heavily in the portfolios of the world's investors, there will inevitably be an attempt to diversify out of the dollar, at least in part. In fact, this very process turned the dollar from a strong currency in the early months of 1985, to what is in late 1986 clearly a weak one. More important, it is difficult to imagine this process turning around, because what we are observing is obviously an increase in the rate of foreign accumulation of dollar claims on top of an already large pool of existing debt denominated in dollars. As a consequence, we have to expect some form of deterioration in the exchange rate.

The alternative to trade adjustments through exchange rate deterioration is some mechanism that would induce investors in Japan and elsewhere to continue the current rate of accumulation of claims in dollars. This mechanism would presumably be a significant increase in the yield spread between dollar-denominated investments and those denominated in yen or deutsche marks. If this does not happen, then the foreign exchange markets will force a downward adjustment in the value of the dollar relative to the yen and the deutsche mark. Since the United States economy appears to be quite weak at the moment, and since there is little sign of any significant change in net capital investment or any other aspect of the American economy that would accelerate our growth, a significant rise in dollar-denominated interest rates seems to be a particularly improbable event. Since the lower limit on interest rates in trading partners such as Japan or West Germany is obviously zero, there is limited room for the interest rate spread between dollar-denominated assets and yen- or deutsche mark-denominated assets to widen. Therefore until and unless we can reduce the flow of dollar-denominated claims abroad, there will be continued pressure on exchange rates leading to a stronger yen and deutsche mark. It is this situation that creates the extraordinary period ahead for the United States and Japan.

Presumably a number of alternatives can occur in this particular context, but it is difficult to imagine any great material change. We do know that it will take a while for the existing imbalances in the international arena to fully work themselves out. This would lead me to conclude that the yen still has a way to increase in value, as indeed the deutsche mark has against the dollar. Eventually, I think the solution is going to be not so much an extraordinarily strong yen, but rather some significant improvement in America's ability to compete. We are already beginning to see a considerable improvement in unit costs of American manufacturing. To a large extent, this improvement is a consequence of the heavy investment in manufacturing facilities undertaken as America's manufacturers endeavored to compete with goods manufactured in Japan and, to an increasing extent, Korea and other newly industrialized countries.

As a result of the fairly extensive investment in United States manufacturing, unit costs have come down in those companies that survived the onslaught of competition from abroad in the early 1980s. Even though these lower costs are reflected in improved profitability for American manufacturers, it is fairly obvious – when you make allowances for a large recent asset write-down, inventory losses, and other forms of adjustments – that underlying profit margins are finally beginning to improve. This suggests that the adjustment process of bringing the trade deficit down in the United States need not be entirely an exchange rate adjustment. Unfortunately, at the moment capital investment has turned weak for reasons of excessive debt and other problems in the United States. However, over the long run, such investment will be crucial to the competitive positioning of the United States in world markets.

We have looked at great length at potential American governmental policy initiatives to alter this particular problem. Although there are policy initiatives that can be helpful at the margin, recent changes in the world financial markets are going to make it exceptionally difficult to stabilize the dollar against any of the major currencies in the short run. The basic reason is largely that we have built up a huge stock of dollar-denominated external claims: The underlying portfolio of claims denominated in various currencies is so unbalanced that it is going to be extremely difficult to prevent the recent instability in exchange rates from continuing. The European monetary system has been able to hold cross-rates among the major European currencies in a relatively narrow band. However, no such stabilization is likely to be initiated soon for any of the major currencies relative to the U.S. dollar. The principal obstacle is the extraordinarily large stock of U.S. dollars held in international currency portfolios, or the approximately 2.5 trillion dollars in international bank claims on nonresidents, more than two-thirds of which are denominated in dollars. Moreover, about three-fourths of international bond issues are denominated in dollars as well.

Despite Japan's dramatic rise as an international financial power, international claims denominated in yen remain a small fraction of those denominated in dollars. When there are relatively small amounts of cross-border claims in foreign currencies, and hence little in the way of financial assets held in other domestic currencies, the demand for foreign exchange tends to mirror intercountry demand for goods and services. Under those conditions, markets generally tend to arbitrage the currencies toward levels consistent with purchasing power parity; that is, they tend to equalize what currencies can purchase in the way of goods and services originating in various countries. The fact that such conditions exist, more or less, among the European currencies is a major reason for the relative success of the European monetary system in maintaining exchange rate stability. When substantial cross-border holdings of financial claims exist, however, the demand for one currency relative to another is the combination of demand for transaction and investment purposes. In recent years, it has become ever more obvious that investment demand is virtually swamping transactions demand in all dealings with respect to the dollar. This is due to the extraordinary buildup of dollar-denominated financial assets in world markets, the demand for which changes sufficiently rapidly to overwhelm changes stimulated by shifts in the underlying purchasing power of the U.S. dollar relative to other currencies.

This is not the case with other currencies, even such strong currencies as the yen and the deutsche mark. One reason why it is so difficult to reach the "right" value of the dollar relative to major U.S. trading partners is that the very size of the dollar-denominated investment holdings implies that relatively small random changes in the propensity to hold dollar-denominated assets will create flows that swamp shifts in transactions demand. Such shifts obscure pressures on the value of the currency stemming from changes in purchasing power parities. The limited supply of alternative currencies means that any moderate change in the propensity to hold dollars will create a disproportionately large change in demand for yen or deutsche mark securities relative to the available stock of such securities. This demand shift leads to major changes in the relevant bilateral exchange rates with the dollar. As a result, markets are likely to overwhelm policy in the short run.

A partial solution would be to encourage large external claims denominated in yen. This, of course, might dampen the yen–dollar rate fluctuations, although the volatility of the yen and the dollar with respect to other currencies around the world will continue under those conditions.

The ultimate solution to this whole process is not to find the yen–dollar exchange rate at which the balance of payments deficit of the United States will be zero. That number implies a yen value too high for the existing economic structure of Japan to sustain. A country's fixed capital assets obviously reflect exchange rates in the international market to some extent. However, although exchange rates can fluctuate very rapidly, it is very difficult to adjust productive capacity to the vagaries of domestic and export demands. As a consequence, should we find that the yen strengthens enough to shut off a further accumulation of dollars by Japan and others, we will probably also find an exchange rate that does considerable damage to the capital asset structure of not only Japan, but also the United States and other countries as well. Hence, an adjustment in the competitive structure of the United States will be a crucial element in resolving this situation.

Any long-term solution will have to confront the implications of the balance of trade problem between Korea and the United States. This new situation poses a problem not only for the United States, but also for Japan. As long as the Korean won continues to be relatively stable against the American dollar, the existing expansion of facilities in Korea devoted to the American market will continue.

One difficult problem that the United States economy is going to have to resolve is the extraordinary buildup in both public and private debt that has occurred in our country. Unlike the Japanese system, which has been able, over the decades, to accommodate a significant leveraging of debt against equity, the American system is really ill-suited to a situation in which the balance sheets of private U.S. corporations are excessively debt ridden. The best measure of this problem is the recent increase in fixed costs in general, and interest payments in particular, as a percentage of gross operating profits. That number has risen substantially in the last 10 or 15 years, and is now at a point where American manufacturers are reluctant to take on new debt burdens to finance new manufacturing facilities for the purpose of reducing unit costs. This means that not only does the United States have to move toward a lower cost of capital, but it has to do so relatively quickly. The Federal Reserve has endeavored to lower short-term American interest rates with some success. It has also attempted to get both the Bank of Japan and the German central bank to follow suit, largely because of concern about the spread between dollar-denominated interest rates and those denominated in yen and deutsche marks. As of late 1986, the results have been mixed. Nonetheless, long-term interest rates are more crucial than short-term interest rates in the

United States. These rates have turned out to be, not unexpectedly, quite resistant to the policies of the Federal Reserve designed to bring interest rates down. The reason is that inflation premia embodied in long-term American interest rates remain high. They will come down only if the American budget deficit is finally brought under control.

At the moment, we have optimistic projections of large declines in the budget deficit, but the actual data show the deficit still at record levels. Unlike Japan, which has a large savings resource to finance its central budget government deficits, we in the United States do not. As a result, American economic policy must be designed to bring these deficits down, bring interest rates down, and enable U.S. manufacturers to invest in new plant and equipment in order to reach a cost structure that will bring our balance of payments into equilibrium, without extraordinarily large changes in bilateral exchange rates.

The world economy is pulling Japan and the United States closer initially as competitors but ultimately as integrated economies. That we allow this to happen is essential for our mutual prosperity, given the extraordinary market forces that are currently at work, and that governmental policies are unlikely to deflect. Protectionism in the United States or in Japan will not succeed in protecting markets over the long run, except at increasingly prohibitive costs.

There are many short-term problems confronting the world economy, specifically United States–Japanese economic relationships. However, we will have to learn that, unless we coordinate our policies and endeavor to prosper together, neither of us will prosper separately.

CHAPTER 3

Internationalization and restructuring of the Japanese economy

HARUO MAYEKAWA

This chapter outlines my recommendations for the internationalization and restructuring of the Japanese economy. Many of these suggestions can be found in the Mayekawa Report submitted to Prime Minister Nakasone in 1986. I begin by reviewing Japan's external imbalance and economic structure.

1   Japan's external imbalance and economic structure

After reaching a virtual equilibrium in 1981, following two rounds of oil price hikes, Japan's balance of payments has posted sharply widening surpluses – \$20.7 billion in 1983, \$35.0 billion in 1984, \$49.1 billion in 1985, and \$36.0 billion in 1986.

The increasing external imbalance has led some economists to ask whether Japan's balance of payments surplus is cyclical or structural. Around 1985, it was generally recognized that the "export-prone" nature of the Japanese economy is responsible for the persistent external surplus.

In general terms, Japan's export-oriented economic structure can be seen as the historical product of the 40 years since World War II, and also of the even longer period since the abandonment of isolationism in 1867. This structure reflects Japan's lack of natural resources (including oil) and the consequent efforts of corporate and government policy to reinforce the economy through international commerce.

However, some more specific reasons for this orientation can be found in the recent past. Among the factors affecting Japan's recent balance of payments, the most important form a causal chain that has been built into the Japanese economy:

> First, faced with the deteriorating terms of trade after two oil shocks, Japan inevitably increased export volume in an effort to overcome oil deficits. This was partly due to the fact that in order to maintain production levels, Japanese enterprises had to rely upon exports to compensate for the decrease in

31

domestic absorption. This decline in absorption stemmed from the income leakage abroad associated with the substantial deterioration in the terms of trade.

Second, corporations have had more recourse to exports. This fact is frequently cited as a major source of the balance of payments surplus. Nevertheless, this tendency is not so much a root cause as a phenomenon arising from the flexible shift of Japanese industry into fields where the income elasticity of demand was high worldwide. It should also be pointed out that the tendency of Japanese industry to retrench and rationalize production processes and to concentrate on high value-added areas that have a low propensity to use imported raw materials has kept import elasticities at low levels. As a result, Japan's trade structure has come to be characterized by high export-demand elasticities and low import-demand elasticities.

Third, the protracted period of a strong dollar (or a weak yen) in the early 1980s conspicuously biased the pattern of technological development in Japan and thus changed corporate behavior in favor of export-oriented activities. These activities, in turn, rendered export-related sectors more competitive, thereby enlarging the balance of payments surplus. It should be emphasized that the macroeconomic policies of the United States also had a significant impact on Japan's industrial structure and accentuated Japan's tendency to export more and import less.

Given this sequence of events, Japan's external imbalance became increasingly structural in nature as the export-oriented policy of Japanese corporations became more firmly entrenched. These events culminated, in October 1985, in the establishment of the Committee on Economic Structure Adjustment for International Harmony – an advisory committee to the prime minister. The committee drafted a report proposing various medium- and long-term policy measures designed to transform the economy's export-oriented structure into one led by domestic demand. This is the report that is often called the Mayekawa Report.

I am pleased to find that the report has been quoted often and that it has raised expectations both at home and abroad. However, it is not a panacea, although I am confident that its various prescriptions can tell us what we should do.

2   The Mayekawa Report focus

The Mayekawa Report places considerable emphasis on expanding domestic demand. The report takes the view that the disparity between external and domestic demand, the export/import structure, and the previously weak yen account for Japan's substantial external surplus. Domestic demand, in particular, must be stimulated if Japan is to achieve external equilibrium and improve the standard of living in the course of structural adjustment.

Second, the report draws attention to the time horizon required for economic restructuring. This goal cannot be achieved quickly, yet we cannot wait for restructuring efforts to take effect before improving the balance of payments situation. Thus, various policy proposals in the report are designed to tackle the problem from a medium-term (about 5-year) perspective.

The third major concern of the report is implementation. After the report was finalized in April 1986, the government decided to set up, within the cabinet, a promotion council for economic restructuring (Government-Ruling Party Joint Headquarters for the Promotion of Economic Structural Adjustment) comprising concerned ministers and officials of the ruling Liberal Democratic Party. Prime Minister Nakasone was the chairman of this council.

3   Progress toward medium-term structural adjustment

Consider now the progress that has been made in the direction of structural adjustment in the first year after the publication of the Mayekawa Report.

(1) When I say that a key ingredient of the report is its emphasis on the medium-term perspective, please do not think that I am making excuses. The government has made clear its desire to implement the recommendations of the report without delay. In fact, some measures have already been adopted, so that there is no scarcity of examples to indicate conspicuous changes in the production and export structure in Japan.

I expect that efforts in this direction will be made continuously from a long-term perspective. Note, for example, that the Special Committee on Economic Restructuring was set up in September 1986 within the Economic Council of the Government as a follow-up to the Mayekawa Report. I have been asked to chair this committee, and am planning to produce a final report shortly. Although it is still under discussion, this report is expected to include various recommendations for a comprehensive package of consistent medium- and long-term economic restructuring policies that would respond to significant changes in Japan and overseas, with a view to promoting international harmony and ensuring a better standard of living and economic stability.

(2) My second point relates to the recent progress of the balance of payments and structural adjustment. Although the yen has appreciated 41 percent, from ¥238 per dollar in 1985 to ¥168 per dollar in 1986, the

current balance of payments surplus in dollar terms increased by 75 percent, from $49 billion in 1985 to $86 billion in 1986. This was the result of the J-curve effect associated with the yen's appreciation and a 43 percent reduction in crude oil prices, which accounted for about 30 percent of Japan's total imports.

However, the balance of payments in terms of yen recorded a much more moderate surplus in 1986, mainly because of the conspicuous 16 percent reduction in yen-denominated export receipts (from ¥41 trillion in 1985 to ¥34 trillion in 1986), a mainstay of Japan's economic growth in the recent past.

As for the real balance of payments, it has already shown some improvement, with export volume declining by 1.3 percent in 1986 as a result of the sharp and substantial appreciation of the yen. Therefore, in 1987, Japan's balance of payments surplus should decrease even in dollar terms, because of the virtual completion of a round of J-curve effects and rebounding oil prices. However, if the recent surge in the value of the yen continues, another round of J-curve effects would occur.

(3) The other side of this positive aspect of the yen's appreciation is the significant short-term deflationary impact that it has had on domestic economic expansion. This is one of the two major problems that Japan's economy is now facing, the other one being medium-term structural adjustment. Although these problems appear to be closely related, they are essentially different. Now that Japan is attempting to transform its industrial structure, with the stronger yen as the catalyst, something should be done in the medium term about its fundamentally "export-prone and import-sluggish" nature for its own sake, regardless of the exchange rate.

Unfortunately, the deflationary impact is being more keenly felt than the beneficial impact, especially by the manufacturing sector: The higher the dependence on exports, the more severe the deflationary effect of the stronger yen, in the form of production cutbacks, the curtailment of fixed investment, and employment adjustment.

Businesses are now voicing concern about the uncertainties stemming from the yen's appreciation and are emphasizing the importance of exchange rate stability as a prerequisite for sustained economic growth via the stimulation of domestic demand.

4   Need to expand domestic demand

In view of these circumstances, Japan needs to expand domestic demand, and I, for one, support, without any hesitation whatsoever, the implementation of measures that would spur domestic demand. However, if these measures are implemented with disregard for their implications in the medium term, they could run counter to Japan's goal of industrial restructuring. Any such measures must therefore be compatible with the medium-term goal of structural adjustment.

How, then, can expanded domestic demand pave the way for the medium-term restructuring of the Japanese economy? For one thing, it would help the Japanese economy become less dependent on exports. For another, it would mean a better quality of life for the Japanese people. In the short run, such expansion would also make up for the slowing economic momentum associated with the yen's appreciation.

However, it would be a mistake to rely solely on measures that would spur domestic demand to reduce the external surplus, which now stands at an annual rate of $80–90 billion. Only limited success could be expected in the present situation, because the surplus is so large. According to economic simulations, the rate of economic growth would have to approach 33 percent per year to reduce the surplus in the balance of payments. All in all, I believe that increased domestic demand is indispensable to the restructuring of the Japanese economy and to the improvement of the quality of life of the Japanese people, although it cannot be expected to do too much in the way of reducing the external surplus.

5   Importance of exchange rate stability

The exchange rate must be stabilized if the domestic economy is to experience the full play of dynamic activity. There are two sound reasons for this view:

1. Japan's economy essentially depends upon international commerce and therefore exchange rate stability is vital.
2. In the opinion of many economists, it would be counterproductive to rely solely on exchange rate changes to correct the external imbalance.

During the course of the appreciation of the yen since the Plaza Agreement in 1985, the Japanese people have come to realize that industrial restructuring requires urgent attention in order to adjust the external imbalance. Even stubborn nationalists accept this argument.

No one can deny that the exchange rate should play an important role in the process of adjustment. Unfortunately, however, the yen has appreciated more substantially and more rapidly than expected since the Plaza Agreement. As a result, efforts in this area have been overshadowed, as indicated earlier, by the pervasive deflationary impact of the strong yen on the economy. To make matters worse, entrepreneurs have found it extremely difficult to forecast future yen rates. This has adversely affected the business outlook and has had a restraining influence on future plans.

Hence, the reason for insisting on exchange rate stability. At this juncture, exchange rate stability would help to further the adjustment process, as it would allow domestic demand to expand steadily and would promote the investment needed for structural adjustment.

It is therefore strongly hoped that cooperation among industrial countries will go a long way toward achieving exchange rate stability. However, note that when I refer to exchange rate stability, I do not mean that the rate needs to be fixed at a particular level.

What measures, then, are needed to stabilize exchange rates? Perhaps what is most important is to see whether these measures reflect underlying fundamentals in relation to trading partners.

In the case of the yen/dollar exchange rate, it was affirmed early in 1987, in both multilateral and bilateral forums, that the rate of the yen was "broadly consistent with underlying economic fundamentals."

In my view, exchange rate stability can be ensured only by encouraging major industrial countries to coordinate their basic economic policies. There have been promising signs in this respect since the Tokyo Summit in 1986, at which participants agreed to intensify multilateral surveillance. In January 1987, for example, the United States and Japan issued a joint declaration on exchange rates; and in the February Louvre Agreement these two countries, together with other major countries, reaffirmed their intention to "closely cooperate to foster exchange rate stability around current levels."

Since there is practically no alternative to the existing floating rate regime, it behooves governments to strive for exchange rate stability based on the recognition of their respective international roles.

6   Measures for domestic demand expansion

A second great policy concern is how Japan can expand domestic demand, something which is easier said than done. In view of the sluggish contribution of external demand, a primary policy objective of the government since 1986 has been to expand domestic demand.

The rate of GNP growth has decelerated from an average annual rate of about 4 percent in the early 1980s to 2.5 percent in 1986, which is lower than the government's 3.0 percent growth target for fiscal 1986. Nevertheless, the domestic demand component has grown at an annual rate of 4 percent, which more than offsets the 1.4 percent decrease in exports. This was in marked contrast to 1985, when the economy grew at a rate of 4 percent and net exports accounted for a positive 1 percent.

The top priority of the Japanese government at present is to spur domestic demand. Unfortunately, its efforts have been hampered by several problems:

1. The budget deficit
2. High and still rising land prices, which constitute the major impediment to the promotion of important components of domestic demand, including housing and social capital
3. Japan's existing export-prone industrial structure, in which production equipment, as well as corporate strategy, tend to become oriented toward exports
4. Various impediments to the possible expansion of imports, including regulations in the area of agriculture.

These budgetary constraints stem not only from the fiscal consolidation program, but also from the present stalemate in Diet deliberations over the fiscal 1987 budget and the tax reform bills. With regard to the fiscal consolidation program, the government in 1981 decided to initiate medium-term fiscal consolidation in the hope of eliminating the deficit in the general account current expenditures of the central government by fiscal 1990. This decision was motivated by the conspicuous deterioration in the fiscal position: First, the proportion of outstanding government debt to GNP is the highest among major industrial countries (52 percent compared with 36 percent for the United States and 21 percent for West Germany); and second, in fiscal 1979 the general account deficit hit a peak equivalent to 22 percent of total expenditures. Hence, although expenditures have been restrained in recent years, the general account deficit is still at a high level (about 10 percent). It is therefore hoped that efforts to eliminate the general account deficit will be pursued further so that fiscal soundness and flexibility can be restored. Although the government's various efforts to use active and flexible fiscal policy are now constrained to a certain extent by the framework of fiscal consolidation, Japan has taken some steps to enhance the efficiency of government expenditures; for example, it is facilitating the introduction of private funds into public works in order to save government funds.

In addition, the government has proposed a tax-reform bill to the Diet in an attempt to review and rationalize Japan's revenue structure. The aim of this tax reform is to reduce direct taxation and increase indirect taxation. Hence, income and corporate tax cuts will be compensated for by a new indirect tax similar to a value-added tax. Although the reform is not designed to achieve a net tax reduction, there is some possibility of tax relief. However, the proposal has met with mounting criticism from opposition parties, and both this bill and the budget bill are now stalled in the Diet. Thus, corporate groups and individuals remain uncertain as to when, and in what form, the bill will clear the Diet. Despite these difficulties, the government intends to take stimulative measures as soon as the bills are passed.

The second difficulty in promoting domestic demand is that *land prices,* which were already extremely high by international standards, are rising, particularly in large cities, such as Tokyo and Osaka. Such hikes, usually originating in commercial areas, are now spreading to residential areas. Anticipating continued increases in the value of land, fewer owners are willing to sell at current prices. As a result, the effective supply of land is diminishing. An effective measure to contain land prices is long overdue. In fact, various measures, combined with steps for urban redevelopment, have already been proposed, to cope with the rising land prices in large metropolitan areas in particular. To implement these proposals, however, the government will have to deal with several other problems at the same time, including land ownership, the environment, the infrastructure, and local autonomy, but this will give rise to political problems.

The third difficulty in promoting domestic demand has to do with Japan's existing *export-oriented industrial structure.* Under this structure, plant and equipment, as well as corporate strategy, tend to have recourse to exports, and hence tend to adapt themselves to changing exchange rates.

Recent developments in Japan's balance of payments reflect an increasing shift to overseas production by large, medium, and small manufacturers; imports of finished and semifinished products have increased from an annual average of 26.7 percent in 1980–85 to 41.1 percent in fiscal 1986.

These tendencies have been accentuated by the rapid appreciation of the yen in recent years. Although exports have declined as a result of the shift to overseas production and imports have not yet increased on a large scale, recent changes in the export/import structure of the Japanese economy have, in the transition, pushed unemployment up and domestic production down. These are the main features of the deflationary impact of the rising yen at present. In particular, industries that process raw material, which used to be the mainstay of the Japanese economy, have started to cut production, abandon plant and equipment, and reduce employment. Processing industries have also been affected by the structural changes now taking place in Japan. The automobile industry is finally cutting back domestic production, as are structurally ailing industries such as shipbuilding (down 70 percent), coal mining (down 50 percent), and steel (down 30 percent). Aluminum refining has been terminated completely.

The fourth problem in increasing domestic demand relates to various impediments to imports. The trade surplus cannot be reduced without a substantial increase in imports. To be sure, the potential growth of imports of raw materials and crude oil has been constrained to some extent by the deflationary impact of the strong yen. Nonetheless, the real problem is that, despite the decline in import prices associated with the strong yen, imports have not increased dramatically. Although efforts have been made to open up Japanese markets, progress has been slow, which has invited criticism from abroad.

In my view, Japan should take measures to lift regulations as early as possible, in keeping with the Action Program that the Japanese government announced in 1984. The government has already placed the structural reform of agriculture high on its agenda. Such action would not only have great bearing on the previously mentioned supply of land, but would help to increase imports and to narrow the price disparity between Japan and overseas.

It is now widely recognized in Japan that the country's agricultural problem needs to be addressed without delay. Our report proposes several remedial measures, but unfortunately, limited progress has been made so far, because the problem has political overtones, as it does in foreign countries.

7   Conclusion

Japan has committed itself to structural adjustment in an effort to promote harmony between the Japanese economy and the rest of the world, and to eliminate the obstacles that now stand in the way of these efforts. The substantial external surplus Japan faces at present has had various adverse effects on the world economy, and thereby has jeopardized the free trade system.

Everyone agrees that the current situation is unsustainable. Thus, various medium- and long-term measures have been adopted with a view to restructuring Japan's economy. It should be emphasized, however, that Japan alone cannot hope to reduce the surplus in its balance of payments. As indicated in the Tokyo Summit declaration in 1986, almost all major countries are now facing various structural problems. All means available should be used to cope with the external imbalances of the leading countries of the world. A major part of Japan's external surplus is ascribed to her surplus with the United States. Conversely, a significant portion of the U.S. balance of payments deficit stems from its trade with Japan.

Much attention has already been given to the diagnosis of and prescriptions for, the so-called twin deficits of the United States, so that I need not dwell on them here. Suffice it to point out that the various structural problems of the United States, particularly the fiscal deficit, are extremely important factors to consider in determining how to eliminate the external imbalance existing between the United States and Japan. As described in the Louvre Agreement in February 1987, the solution to the external imbalance lies in positive efforts and policy coordination among the major countries.

I believe that the leading economic powers of the free world share common goals, and that nations on either side of the Pacific will increasingly work together to overcome short- and long-term problems.

Needless to say, whether or not we can establish a dynamic complementary – not confrontational – relationship in the future hinges on governmental policies and, more importantly, on the ingenuity and vitality of private enterprises. Thus, mutual understanding and efforts to create a better environment for cooperation are of utmost importance. Let me emphasize that we do not have to be too pessimistic. Instead, we should commit ourselves to the future and make the necessary efforts on each side in search of an even closer U.S.-Japan relationship, in line with the changing world environment.

CHAPTER 4

The limits of monetary coordination as exchange rate policy

WILLIAM H. BRANSON

Introduction: The argument outlined

Proposals for coordinating monetary policy in order to stabilize nominal or real exchange rates, or to target monetary policy on the nominal exchange rate, assume, explicitly or implicitly, that (a) exchange rate fluctuations are, on balance, harmful to the economy, and that (b) monetary policy can productively reduce the amplitude of these fluctuations. The main objective of this chapter is to examine the analytical basis and empirical evidence for these assumptions. The conclusion is that both hold only some of the time. This means that a coordination agreement would have to define *when* the assumptions hold, a difficult task, indeed. Further, proposals for a formal international conference to implement a coordination agreement – a "new Bretton Woods" – assume that this is at least politically feasible. Toward the end of the chapter I argue that this is not the case, and that the failed World Economic Conference of 1933 is a more apt metaphor than Bretton Woods.

Movements in the real exchange rate of the dollar have had substantial effects on employment and output in U.S. manufacturing industries. At the level of all manufacturing, the elasticity of response of employment to the real exchange rate (up is appreciation) is −0.14. Thus a real appreciation of the dollar of 60 percent from 1980 to 1985 reduced manufacturing employment by 8.4 percent, or 1.7 million jobs. However, even this magnitude of job loss in manufacturing is not a net loss to the economy because the real dollar appreciation was part of an equilibrium reaction to the shift in the structural budget position in the early 1980s. The real appreciation facilitated the foreign financing of a significant fraction of the combined U.S. fiscal deficit and domestic investment. In assessing

This paper appeared as "The Limits of Monetary Coordination as Exchange Rate Policy" in the March 1986 issue of the *Brookings Papers on Economic Activity*. Reprinted with permission.

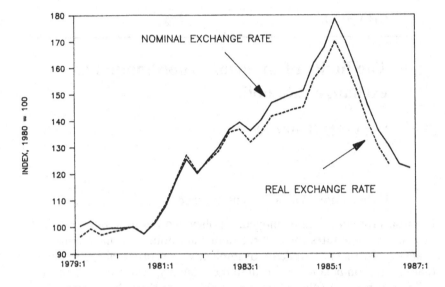

Figure 4.1 Effective dollar exchange rates, 1979–86, nominal and real indexes, quarterly data. The nominal exchange rate index is the geometric weighted average nominal exchange value of the U.S. dollar against currencies of the Group of Ten industrial countries, based on the weights used by the Board of Governors of the Federal Reserve System. The real rate is adjusted for changes in consumer prices. A rise in either index is an appreciation of the dollar against foreign currencies.

the impact of the dollar appreciation, this effect would have to be set off against the employment effects in manufacturing.

Movements in the real exchange rate can have their sources in real disturbances, such as a fiscal shift or an oil price change, or in financial or monetary disturbances. The latter move the nominal exchange rate, a quickly adjusting variable, relative to relative goods prices. Thus, undesirable fluctuations in real exchange rates can come from real or monetary disturbances. Monetary coordination can remove the latter, but not the former.

An example of the limits to monetary coordination is provided by the appreciation of the dollar in real terms from 1981 to 1984. This was in large part an equilibrium reaction to the fiscal shift that began in 1982. The *real* appreciation was achieved mainly via a *nominal* appreciation (see Figure 4.1), as U.S. prices moved roughly in line with foreign prices. A monetary policy that would have attempted to hold the nominal exchange rate against this pressure would have required a substantially higher growth of money – essentially a monetizing of the shift in the deficit. This would presumably have resulted in higher inflation in the United States and would have yielded a real appreciation via inflation instead of the nominal exchange rate. In this case it seems preferable to achieve the real appreciation by permitting the nominal rate to move.

The difficulty in incorporating equilibrium movements of real exchange rates into an agreement on monetary coordination is compounded by the fact that we do not have an analytical consensus on the causes of fluctuations in the equilibrium real exchange rate. For example, the relationship between the shift in the U.S. structural fiscal deficit and the real appreciation of the dollar is in dispute. My analysis in this chapter follows a crowding-out line that requires the trade balance to do its share to make room in full-employment GNP for the shift in the budget. This position is attacked from one side by Keynesians who argue that the *real* appreciation was due to tight money, and from the other side by monetarists who argue that there is no relationship between shifts in the budget position and the real exchange rate. With this range of disagreement on economic analysis, how are the negotiators to reach agreement? The topic is one for the National Science Foundation (NSF), not a new Bretton Woods!

If the economic-analytical problems in defining the links – from the losses caused by exchange rate fluctuations to their partial elimination by monetary coordination – are quickly solved with the aid of the NSF, we are still faced with the political problems inherent in a call for a new international monetary conference. The conference at Bretton Woods in 1944 had 44 signatories. They essentially ratified an agreement that had been negotiated between the United States (Harry Dexter White) and the United Kingdom (John Maynard Keynes) on the basis of a general economic-analytical consensus. No such agreement exists today; the analytical basis is not even in place. In addition, the number of countries has more than doubled, and there are several significant economic actors plus a seeming infinity of potential blocking coalitions. So in addition to the underlying economic problems, a conference would find agreement extremely difficult to achieve on political grounds. Quiet cooperation among a few central banks may be a better solution. The rest of this chapter provides the evidence and analysis that support the argument just presented. First, estimates of the effects of fluctuation in the real exchange rate of the dollar on U.S. nonagricultural employment, and the relation of movements in nominal and real exchange rates are summarized.[1] Then the analysis of the effect of a shift in the fiscal deficit on the equilibrium real exchange rate is presented. Finally, the analog between the "new Bretton Woods" and 1933 is briefly explored.

The real exchange rate and employment

In a recent paper coauthored with James P. Love, I reported the results of an empirical study of the effects of fluctuations in the dollar's real exchange rate on employment and output in manufacturing industries in the United States.[2] These effects are presumably a major source of the unhappiness with the movement of the dollar, concern about its "misalignment," and pressure to stabilize it. The results for employment are summarized by two-digit manufacturing industry and by state in the appendix. Here I show the results for all nonagricultural employment, to illustrate the differential effects of the dollar appreciation on the manufacturing sector.

The estimates of an equation explaining fluctuations in employment by major nonagricultural sectors are shown in Table 4.1. The estimated equations are linear in logarithms, so the coefficients in the table are elasticities. The dependent variables are total employment by sector; the independent variables are a trend, the real exchange rate represented by the International Monetary Fund's relative unit labor cost index (up is appreciation), a cyclical variable represented by the overall unemployment rate, and the price of energy relative to the CPI. The estimation period is quarterly, 1963I-85I. The equations were estimated to include an adjustment for serial correlation "rho." For details, see the appendix.

The coefficients under LRELULC in the table show the elasticity of output by sector to movements in the real exchange rate. Employment in the mining sector is most responsive to movements in the dollar, with an elasticity of -0.387. Durable manufacturing is second, with an elasticity of -0.206. All manufacturing has a highly significant elasticity of -0.140, as mentioned earlier. The service sectors, beginning in Table 4.1 with transportation and public utilities, all have insignificant coefficients, except for government. It seems that a decrease in government employment coincided with the appreciation of the dollar.

The results in the Branson and Love study are consistent with the hypothesis that fluctuations in the real exchange rate have serious effects on employment in manufacturing, particularly the durable goods producers. This is one major source of concern about overvaluation, or misalignment of the dollar.

Real and nominal exchange rates

Tables 4.4 and 4.5 in the appendix show the effects of fluctuations in real exchange rates on employment in manufacturing. With nominal exchange rates moving flexibly relative to sluggish goods prices, movements in the

Table 4.1. *Explaining employment fluctuations by sector*[a]

	RHO	TREND	SIG	LRELULC	SE	SIG	LURT	SIG	LRL-ENGY	SIG
All nonagriculture	0.966	0.0067	0.000	−0.062	0.018	0.001	−0.112	0.000	−0.013	0.398
Mining	0.537	−0.0049	0.000	−0.387	0.086	0.000	−0.133	0.025	0.569	0.000
Construction	0.940	0.0075	0.000	0.058	0.085	0.496	−0.228	0.000	−0.063	0.418
Manufacturing	0.868	0.0028	0.000	−0.140	0.028	0.000	−0.218	0.000	−0.041	0.085
Durable	0.759	0.0033	0.000	−0.206	0.027	0.000	−0.297	0.000	−0.025	0.274
Nondurable	0.951	0.0021	.000	−0.034	0.030	0.269	−0.103	0.000	−0.061	0.023
Transportation and public utility	0.808	0.0039	0.000	−0.026	0.033	0.440	−0.106	0.000	0.002	0.955
Wholesale & retail trade	0.961	0.0085	0.000	−0.033	0.024	0.185	−0.080	0.000	−0.033	0.164
Finance, real estate	0.976	0.0083	0.000	0.023	0.024	0.346	−0.046	.000	0.024	0.290
Service	0.949	0.0106	0.000	−0.002	0.018	0.910	−0.067	0.000	0.042	0.008
Government	0.991	0.0075	0.000	−0.165	0.042	.000	−0.023	0.207	−0.070	0.040

[a] Constant Trend LRELULC(0,6) LURT(0,4) LRL-ENGY(0,4).

SIG = Probability that the true value of the coefficient is zero. SE = Standard error. RHO = First-order serial correlation coefficient. TREND = Log-linear (exponential) rate of growth. LRELULC = Log of IMF real exchange rate index, deflated by relative unit labor costs. LURT = Log of unemployment rate. LRL-ENGY = Log of the relative price of energy (CPI for energy divided by CPI for all items). (0,4) indicates variable is lagged from $t − 0$ to $t − 4$. (0,6) indicates variable is lagged from $t − 0$ to $t − 6$. AR1(METHOD = MAXL) indicates the regression uses the Beach–MacKinnon maximum likelihood procedure to correct for first-order serial correlation. See C. Beach and J. MacKinnon, "A Maximum Likelihood Procedure for Regression with Autocorrelated Errors," *Econometrica*, vol. 46, no. 1 (1978), pp. 51–8. Dependent variable is the natural log of employment by sector. Model: AR1 (Method = MAXL); period 1963I to 1985I. Degrees of freedom: 70.

real exchange rate are dominated by movements in the nominal rate. This was documented early by Jacob Frenkel; recent evidence for the U.S. dollar is summarized in Figure 4.1, which shows the nominal and real effective rates calculated by the Federal Reserve Board.[3] The correlation between the two effective rates from 1979–84 is clear.

The point of the evidence in Figure 4.1 is that movements in the nominal exchange rate *may* have been reactions to equilibrium adjustments in real rates. In this case, a monetary intervention that attempted to stabilize the nominal rate would frustrate the movement of the real rate in the short run and shift the adjustment to relative prices in the longer run. This is one way in which a monetary policy that stabilized the nominal exchange rate would be counterproductive. We now turn to the analysis that indicates that the swing in the real exchange rate of the dollar in the 1980s was precisely such an equilibrium reaction.

Fiscal policy and the real exchange rate

To establish the relationship between real disturbances and the equilibrium adjustment of the real exchange rate, I summarize a short-run "fundamentals" model of fiscal policy and the real exchange rate.[4] The model is a framework for analysis that integrates goods markets and asset markets to describe the simultaneous determination of the interest rate and the exchange rate. It is a short-run model in the sense that we take the existing stock of assets as given. It is a fundamentals framework because it focuses on the underlying macroeconomic determinants of movements in rates, about which the "market" will form expectations. The framework is useful because it permits us to distinguish between external events such as shifts in the budget position (the "deficit"), shifts in international asset demands (the "safe haven effect"), and changes in tax law or financial regulation by analyzing their differing implications for movements in the interest rate and the exchange rate. We begin with the national income, or flow-of-funds, identity that constrains flows in the economy, then turn to asset-market equilibrium that constrains rates of return, and finally bring the two together in Figure 4.2.

The national income identity that constrains flows in the economy is generally written as

$$Y = C + I + G + X = C + S + T,$$

with the usual meanings of the symbols, as summarized in Table 4.2. Note that X here stands for *net* exports of goods and services, the current account balance. All flows are in real terms. We can subtract consumer expenditure C from both sides of the right-hand equality and do some rearranging to obtain a useful version of the flow-of-funds identity:

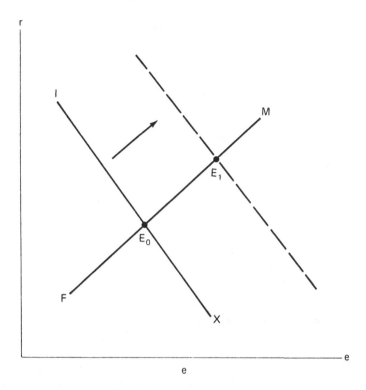

Figure 4.2 Equilibrium r and e.

$$G - T = (S - I) - X. \tag{1}$$

In terms of national income and product flows, equation (1) says that the total (federal, state, and local) government deficit must equal the sum of the excess of domestic private saving over investment less net exports.

Let us now think of equation (1) as holding at a standardized "full-employment" level of output, in order to exclude cyclical effects from the discussion. This allows us to focus on shifts in the budget at a given level of income. If we take a shift in the full-employment deficit $(G-T)$ to be external, or exogenous to the economy, equation (1) emphasizes that this shift requires some endogenous adjustment to excess private saving $(S-I)$ and the current account X to balance the flows in income and product. In particular, if $(G-T)$ is increased by \$200 billion, roughly the actual increase in the "structural" deficit, a combination of an increase in $S-I$ and a decrease in X that also totals \$200 billion is required.

Standard macroeconomic theory tells us that for a given level of income, $(S-I)$ depends positively on the real interest rate r, and X depends

Table 4.2. *Definitions of symbols*

National income flows (all in real terms)
Y = GNP
C = Consumer expenditure
I = Gross private domestic investment
G = Government purchases of goods and services
X = *Net* exports of goods and services, or the current account balance
S = Gross private domestic saving
T = Tax revenue
NFI = Net foreign investment by the United States
NFB = Net foreign borrowing = −NFI

Prices and stocks
r = Real domestic interest rate
i = Nominal domestic interest rate
i^* = Nominal foreign interest rate
e = Real effective exchange rate (units of foreign exchange per dollar); an increase in e is an appreciation of the dollar
$\hat{e}$ = Expected rate of change of e
$\hat{p}$ = Expected rate of inflation
ρ = Risk premium on dollar-denominated bonds
B = Outstanding stock of government debt

negatively on the real exchange rate e (units of foreign exchange per dollar adjusted for relative price levels). So the endogenous adjustments that would increase $S - I$ and reduce X are an increase in r and e. Some combination of these changes would restore balance in equation (1), given an increase in $G - T$.

We can relate this national income view of the short-run adjustment mechanism to a story involving foreign borrowing and capital flows by noting that net exports X is also net foreign investment from the balance of payments identity. Since national net foreign investment is minus national net foreign borrowing (NFB), the flow-of-funds equation (1) can also be written as

$$(G-T) = (S-I) + \text{NFB}. \tag{2}$$

This form of the identity emphasizes that an increase in the deficit must be financed by either an increase in the excess of domestic saving or an increase in net foreign borrowing (decrease in net foreign investment).

The actual movements in the government deficit, excess domestic saving $(S-I)$, and net foreign borrowing, and the associated movements in the real short-term interest rate r and the real exchange rate e (indexed to 1986 = 100) are shown in Table 4.3. The total budget deficit was roughly

Table 4.3. *Savings and investment flows, interest rates, and exchange rates, United States, 1979:1–1986:2[a]*

Period	Net foreign investment[b]	Excess domestic savings[c]	Total budget surplus[d]	Federal budget surplus (% of GNP)	Real interest rate for 20-year Treasury bonds (%)[e]	Real exchange rate index (Jan 85 = 100)[f]
79 :1	5.8	−15.0	20.7	−0.4	−1.3	62.7
79 :2	−1.9	−20.6	18.6	−0.2	−5.4	64.0
79 :3	4.5	−3.6	8.1	−0.8	−4.8	62.8
79 :4	−2.6	−1.1	−1.4	−1.1	−2.0	63.6
80 :1	0.1	12.3	−12.1	−1.4	−4.7	65.4
80 :2	12.1	54.2	−41.9	−2.4	−4.7	64.3
80 :3	27.9	76.5	−48.6	−2.7	3.2	63.7
80 :4	6.7	42.2	−35.5	−2.4	1.3	65.7
81 :1	16.3	30.9	−14.6	−1.6	1.7	69.1
81 :2	4.9	19.7	−14.8	−1.6	3.9	73.5
81 :3	5.5	31.7	−26.2	−2.0	2.6	77.2
81 :4	11.2	74.2	−63.0	−3.1	8.3	74.4
82 :1	7.3	83.3	−76.0	−3.5	10.9	77.7
82 :2	16.5	94.3	−77.7	−3.6	7.5	79.4
82 :3	−12.3	110.3	−122.5	−5.0	5.2	83.4
82 :4	−15.4	151.4	−166.8	−6.3	9.9	83.3
83 :1	−2.1	147.2	−149.2	−5.7	11.1	82.5
83 :2	−27.7	98.3	−126.0	−5.1	5.7	84.4
83 :3	−46.7	79.5	−126.2	−5.1	6.9	87.7
83 :4	−57.4	55.5	−112.9	−4.8	8.4	88.1

Table 4.3. (cont.)

Period	Net foreign investment[b]	Excess domestic savings[c]	Total budget surplus[d]	Federal budget surplus (% of GNP)	Real interest rate for 20-year Treasury bonds (%)[e]	Real exchange rate index (Jan 85 = 100)[f]
84 :1	−73.7	13.8	−87.5	−4.2	7.7	88.3
84 :2	−92.1	1.9	−93.9	−4.4	8.7	90.1
84 :3	−92.7	12.0	−104.8	−4.5	8.5	95.0
84 :4	−104.3	15.7	−119.9	−4.9	8.8	98.2
85 :1	−83.8	12.8	−96.6	−4.1	9.1	100.8
85 :2	−112.0	43.6	−155.6	−5.4	6.3	98.8
85 :3	−121.2	16.7	−138.0	−4.9	7.8	92.9
85 :4	−143.8	11.3	−155.1	−5.3	6.6	88.5
86 :1	−128.6	−3.6	−131.6	−4.7	7.9	83.6
86 :2	−143.0	30.3		−5.6	8.6	80.9

[a] Billions of dollars unless otherwise specified.
[b] Net foreign investment in the national income accounts summed with the national capital grants received by the United States.
[c] Gross private domestic savings minus gross private domestic investment, adjusted for statistical discrepancy.
[d] Combined federal, state, and local government budget deficits.
[e] 20-year Treasury bond yield less current CPI inflation.
[f] M. Feldstein and P. Bacchetta, "How Far Has the Dollar Fallen?" Business Economics, Vol. 22, no. 4 (1987), pp. 35–9.

zero at the beginning of 1981. It expanded to a peak of $167 billion at the bottom of the recession in the fourth quarter of 1982, and then shrank in the recovery. But the shift in the *federal* budget position left the total government deficit at $150 billion in late 1985, after two years of recovery. Initially the deficit was financed mainly by excess domestic saving, which also peaked at the bottom of the recession. But since 1982 the fraction financed by net foreign borrowing has risen; by 1983 most of the government deficit was financed by foreign borrowing. Japan has provided about 40 percent of U.S. net foreign borrowing since 1983.[5]

The movements in the real interest rate and the real exchange rate roughly reflect this pattern of financing. The real interest rate jumped from negative values to over 10 percent in 1982, fell during the recession, and rose in the recovery; it has stayed above 6 percent since mid-1983. The real exchange rate shows an initial jump of 17 percent in 1981, followed by a more gradual increase. The standard lags in adjustment of net exports to changes in the exchange rate can explain the slow reaction of net exports (net foreign borrowing) to the dollar appreciation.

The relationship between r and e that is imposed by financial market equilibrium can be seen by considering the returns that a representative asset holder in the United States obtains on domestic and foreign assets of the same maturity. The return on the domestic dollar-denominated asset is i in nominal terms, and $r = i - \hat{P}$ in real terms, where $\hat{P}$ is the (exogenous, from our point of view) expected rate of inflation in the United States. The return on the foreign asset is $i^* - \hat{e}$ in nominal terms, where $\hat{e}$ is the expected rate of change in the exchange rate. In real terms, the U.S. asset holder's return would be $i^* - \hat{e} - \hat{P}$. In equilibrium, the difference between the two returns must be equal to the market-determined risk premium $\rho(B)$. Here it is assumed that dollar-denominated bonds are imperfect substitutes for foreign exchange–denominated bonds, so that the risk premium on dollar bonds increases with their supply: $\rho'(B) > 0$. The equilibrium condition for rates of return in real terms is then

$$r - (i^* - \hat{e} - \hat{P}) = \rho(B). \tag{3}$$

Next, we need to relate the expected rate of change of the exchange rate to the actual current rate. If we denote the perceived long-run equilibrium real rate that sets the full-employment current account balance at zero as $\bar{e}$, one reasonable assumption is that the current rate is expected to return gradually toward long-run equilibrium. We can write this as a proportional adjustment mechanism:

$$\hat{e} = \Theta(\bar{e} - e). \tag{4}$$

If e is below the long-run equilibrium, it is expected to rise, and vice versa. If we put expression (4) into the equilibrium condition (3), and rearrange slightly, we obtain the financial market relationship between e and r:

$$e = \bar{e} + \frac{1}{\theta}[r - (i^* - \hat{P}) - \rho(B)]. \tag{5}$$

This condition says that for given values of the bond stock B, inflation $\hat{P}$, the foreign nominal interest rate i^*, and the long-run equilibrium real exchange rate $\bar{e}$, an increase in r requires a rise in e to maintain equilibrium in financial markets. Why? If the home interest rate rises, equilibrium can be maintained for a given foreign interest rate only if the exchange rate is expected to fall. From (4), this means that the actual current rate must rise to establish $\hat{e} < 0$. In terms of market operations, the rise in the domestic interest rate r causes sales of foreign assets and an increase in e until equilibrium is reestablished. This is essentially what happened in 1981 with the announcement of a path of future deficits. This did not substantially change the long-run $\bar{e}$ that would balance the current account, but it did move r and e.

We can now join the flow equilibrium condition (1) and the rate-of-return condition (5) to form the short-run framework for simultaneous determination of r and e. Let us rewrite equation (1) to show the dependence of S and I on r, and of X on e:

$$G - T = S(r) - I(r) - X(e). \tag{6}$$

For a given level of the full-employment budget, the trade-off between r and e that maintains flow equilibrium is given by the negatively sloped IX curve in Figure 4.2. For a given budget deficit $G - T$, an increase in r, which reduces $(S - I)$, requires a decrease in e, which increases X, to maintain flow equilibrium. An increase in the deficit $G - T$ will shift the IX curve up or to the right, requiring some combination of a rise in r and e to maintain flow equilibrium.

The rate-of-return condition (5) gives us the positively sloped FM curve in Figure 4.2, for given B, i^*, $\hat{P}$, and $\bar{e}$. Its slope is θ, the speed-of-adjustment parameter for expectations. An increase in the risk premium ρ, due to a rise in the supply of U.S. bonds B, will shift the FM curve up and to the left, requiring an increase in r for any given value of e.

In the short run, equilibria r and e are reached at the intersection of IX and FM in Figure 4.2; there, both equilibrium conditions are met. For the purposes of this analysis, we assume that initially $e = \bar{e}$, with no *expected* movement in exchange rates. This is taken to represent the equilibrium around 1980, before the surge in interest rates and the exchange rate that we are trying to explain.

A shift in the full-employment, or structural, budget toward deficit shifts the IX curve up, as shown by the dashed IX curve in Figure 4.2. The real interest rate and the real exchange rate rise, as described earlier. The composition of these movements is determined by the slope of the FM curve, representing financial market equilibrium. The movement of r and e from E_0 to E_1 raises excess domestic saving $(S-I)$ and reduces net exports X by a sum equal to the shift in $G-T$. This also produces the short-run equilibrium financing of the shift in the deficit by domestic saving and foreign borrowing. The shift in $G-T$ gives rise to the movements in excess domestic saving and foreign borrowing, and in r and e (see Table 4.2). The change in the deficit was financed mainly by excess domestic saving until the end of 1983. Since then, the major source of finance has been foreign. The real interest rate and real exchange rate increased sharply beginning in 1981. The lag in the shift to foreign financing corresponds to a typical empirical lag of about two years for adjustment of trade to a change in the exchange rate. Thus the framework of Figure 4.2 roughly captures the movements of r and e from 1981 to 1985.

The point here is to show that a shift in fiscal policy, much like the one that began in 1982, will generate an equilibrium adjustment in the real exchange rate as part of the financing process. This movement is probably being reversed now, as the Gramm–Rudman legislation brings real interest rates and the exchange rate down. A monetary policy that attempted to frustrate this movement probably would be a mistake now, as well as in 1982. It would not productively reduce the fluctuations in the nominal exchange rate.

Any agreement on coordination of monetary policy or on targeting monetary policy in the nominal exchange rate would have to allow for the effects of real disturbances such as shifts in fiscal policy on the equilibrium real exchange rate. Given the current lack of consensus on the analysis of these effects, it would be extremely difficult to write the real disturbance proviso into the agreement. The analysis here places the responsibility for the *real* appreciation of the dollar squarely on the shift in fiscal policy. This analysis is not agreed to by diverse groups who (a) emphasize the importance of tight money in the U.S. for the real appreciation, or (b) claim that the fiscal shift had no effect on the dollar. Consequently, a meaningful formal agreement on monetary coordination seems to be impossible. A loose form of central bank coordination may be useful to smooth out the *volatility* of exchange rates. But coordination on targeting is not going to eliminate the broad swings in equilibrium real rates that have been labeled "misalignment," nor should this be attempted.

A new Bretton Woods?

The Bretton Woods conference in 1944 essentially ratified an agreement between the United States and the United Kingdom on monetary coordination. Its 44 signatories met in a context of analytical consensus and agreement on the need to stabilize exchange rates to prevent a repeat of the competitive devaluations of the 1930s. No such consensus about analysis or objectives exists today, and a conference would have twice as many members.

A better example for a new monetary conference might be the World Economic Conference of 1933, where objectives were in conflict, and the analytical understanding of the relationship between exchange stabilization and national objectives was at best limited. That conference failed owing to a conflict between American and European objectives. The analysis has been summarized by Kenneth A. Oye:[6]

At the Conference, Roosevelt considered a joint French and British proposal for temporary currency stabilization, and instructed the American delegation to seek agreement on ever higher dollar/sterling rates. When one of the American offers was accepted, Roosevelt simply withdrew the offer.

Why did the United States reject the joint proposal? The concessions offered were simply not commensurate with the concession sought, a currency stabilization that Roosevelt believed would vitiate domestic reflation. In fact, rumors of the impending stabilization agreement had triggered a sharp decline in stock and commodity prices. This may have reinforced Roosevelt's views on the desirability of further dollar depreciation.

In view of the similar lack of analytical consensus and conflict of economic interests now, a major monetary conference is likely to fail. Let the central banks do the coordination and the NSFs of the world finance research on the analysis.

Appendix: Estimates of the sensitivity of employment to the real exchange rate

Initial results from an empirical investigation of the relationship between movements in the real exchange rate and employment and output for manufacturing industries are reported in a recent working paper by Branson and Love. Here I summarize the employment results. In this research, we have not modeled each industry or region individually or taken into account the special demand shocks and price effects that may be important. We have therefore constructed rather general reduced-form models that apply to each disaggregated sector or region.

The dependent variables in the regressions are the natural logarithms of employment. The independent variables include a constant, the natural logarithm of an index to measure the real U.S. trade–weighted exchange (LRELULC) rate (up is appreciation), and three variables to capture secular and cyclical changes in demand. These include time (TREND), the natural logarithm of an index to measure the real price of energy (LRL-ENGY), and the natural logarithm of the overall unemployment rate (LURT). We considered including a foreign demand variable, but found that deviations from trend growth in foreign demand were so highly correlated with changes in U.S. demand that no additional explanatory power came from foreign demand.

The data are quarterly. The equations are estimated over an interval beginning in 1963 to the first quarter of 1985, with 89 observations. The exchange rate variable LRELULC includes the current value plus six quarters of lags. The real energy price LRL-ENGY and the unemployment rate LURT both include the current value plus four quarters of lags. The estimates employ the Beach–MacKinnon maximum-likelihood procedure for correcting first-order autocorrelation.[7]

The source of the data on employment is the Bureau of Labor Statistics (BLS) *Employment and Earnings.* The dependent variable for the employment equations is the natural logarithm of the number of employed workers. In the regional equations, we use the number of workers employed in manufacturing industries, disaggregated by the 50 states plus the District of Columbia. In the industry classifications, we use the number of workers employed in each of the two-digit SIC manufacturing classifications (SIC codes 20 through 39). To test how sensitive the estimates are to changes in the level of aggregation, we have estimated equations for all of the three- and four-digit manufacturing codes that are included in the BLS Establishment Survey tape. This includes 125 three-digit industries and 176 four-digit industries.

The real exchange rate index is the International Monetary Fund's (IMF) measure of the weighted foreign exchange value of the dollar, adjusted for movements in relative unit labor costs. This is reported in the relative cost tables in *International Financial Statistics,* and is taken to represent movement in U.S. costs relative to those of major competitors. An increase in the index represents a real appreciation of the U.S. dollar.

The results are reported in Table 4.4 for two-digit SIC industries and Table 4.5 for states. The state results are sorted by size of exchange rate coefficient. The tables report the value of the first-order autocorrelation coefficient RHO, the coefficients for each of the independent variables (except for the constant), and a significance statistic. When independent

Table 4.4. Explaining employment fluctuations by industry[a]

	SIC	RHO	TREND	SIG	LRELULC	SE	SIG	LURT	SIG	LRL-ENGY	SIG
Employment in nondurable goods industries											
Food and kindred products	20	0.085	−0.0004	0.602	−0.048	0.056	0.396	−0.097	0.017	0.003	0.946
Tobacco manufactures	21	0.030	−0.0034	0.015	−0.112	0.108	0.302	−0.037	0.628	−0.020	0.826
Textile mill products	22	0.959	0.0005	0.777	−0.166	0.081	0.043	−0.093	0.025	−0.173	0.024
Apparel and other textile products	23	0.653	0.0021	.000	−0.107	0.038	0.006	−0.120	0.000	−0.161	0.000
Paper and allied products	26	0.827	0.0033	0.000	−0.018	0.042	0.675	−0.121	0.000	−0.099	0.006
Print and publishing	27	0.782	0.0047	0.000	0.115	0.021	0.000	−0.135	0.000	0.050	0.005
Chemicals and allied products	28	0.971	0.0025	0.087	−0.096	0.067	0.152	−0.137	.000	0.003	0.956
Petroleum and coal products	29	0.325	−0.0004	0.597	−0.218	0.065	0.001	−0.067	0.143	0.075	0.166
Rubber and miscellaneous plastics products	30	0.695	0.0121	0.000	−0.095	0.058	0.105	−0.206	0.000	−0.218	0.000
Leather and leather goods	31	0.942	−0.0086	0.002	−0.235	0.135	0.087	−0.111	0.096	0.022	0.855

Employment in durable goods industries

Industry											
Lumber and wood products	24	0.355	0.0033	0.000	0.004	0.056	0.937	−0.107	0.007	−0.063	0.172
Furniture and fixtures	25	0.725	0.0072	0.000	0.016	0.043	0.703	−0.195	0.000	−0.174	0.000
Stone, clay, and glass products	32	0.240	0.0025	.000	−0.176	0.048	.000	−0.140	.000	−0.108	0.008
Primary metal industries	33	0.819	−0.0004	0.758	−0.576	0.096	0.000	−0.303	0.000	−0.172	0.037
Fabricated metal products	34	0.873	0.0050	0.000	−0.279	0.053	0.000	−0.319	0.000	−0.147	0.002
Machinery, except electrical	35	0.832	0.0036	0.000	−0.434	0.046	0.000	−0.363	0.000	0.055	0.192
Electrical and electronic equipment	36	0.817	0.0049	0.000	0.024	0.053	0.648	−0.352	0.000	0.064	0.137
Transportation equipment	37	0.422	0.0010	0.120	−0.184	0.047	.000	−0.387	0.000	0.056	0.153
Instruments and related products	38	0.932	0.0040	0.000	−0.168	0.049	0.001	−0.275	0.000	0.161	.000
Miscellaneous manufacturing industries	39	0.017	0.0031	0.000	−0.270	0.036	0.000	−0.154	0.000	−0.183	0.000

[a] Constant trend LRELULC(0,6) LURT(0,4) LRL-ENGY(0,4).
Dependent variable is the natural log of employment. Model: AR1 (Method = MAXL); period: 1963I to 1985I. Degrees of freedom: 70. SE = Standard error. SIG = probability that the coefficient is zero.

Table 4.5. Explaining employment fluctuations by state

State	RHO	TREND	SIG	LRELULC	SE	SIG	LURT	SIG	LRL-ENGY	SIG
North Dakota	0.848	0.0185	0.030	-0.832	0.199	.000	0.114	0.552	-0.535	0.121
Wyoming	-0.328	-0.0158	0.002	-0.640	0.087	0.000	-0.267	0.020	0.660	.000
West Virginia	0.247	-0.0046	0.001	-0.587	0.030	0.000	-0.213	0.000	-0.065	0.161
Nevada	0.548	0.0167	0.000	-0.580	0.059	0.000	-0.386	0.000	0.067	0.446
Alaska	-0.033	-0.0255	0.247	-0.546	0.483	0.266	-0.114	0.833	1.174	0.138
Idaho	0.260	0.0145	0.000	-0.540	0.070	0.000	-0.022	0.767	-0.379	0.001
Louisiana	0.366	-0.0101	0.000	-0.513	0.042	0.000	-0.336	0.000	0.399	0.000
Kansas	0.684	0.0057	0.030	-0.496	0.064	0.000	-0.264	.000	-0.032	0.744
Iowa	0.549	0.0019	0.368	-0.469	0.049	0.000	-0.216	0.000	-0.099	0.186
Michigan	0.303	0.0071	.000	-0.449	0.041	0.000	-0.335	0.000	-0.349	0.000
Texas	0.496	-0.0042	.000	-0.405	0.023	0.000	-0.327	0.000	0.425	0.000
Oregon	0.122	0.0052	0.130	-0.378	0.077	0.000	-0.229	0.009	-0.064	0.592
Illinois	0.323	-0.0045	.000	-0.359	0.027	0.000	-0.271	0.000	-0.007	0.863
Wisconsin	0.181	0.0037	0.041	-0.354	0.040	0.000	-0.224	0.000	-0.065	0.294
Oklahoma	0.471	-0.0076	0.000	-0.351	0.030	0.000	-0.370	0.000	0.489	0.000
Ohio	0.572	0.0004	0.794	-0.331	0.041	0.000	-0.276	0.000	-0.124	0.047
Washington	0.114	0.0014	0.426	-0.330	0.041	0.000	-0.325	0.000	0.219	0.002
Kentucky	0.514	0.0039	0.008	-0.330	0.034	0.000	-0.240	0.000	-0.164	0.003
Indiana	0.479	0.0022	0.205	-0.325	0.040	0.000	-0.299	0.000	-0.156	0.015
Mississippi	0.509	0.0051	0.004	-0.308	0.042	0.000	-0.181	.000	-0.151	0.015
Rhode Island	0.058	-0.0004	0.832	-0.304	0.039	0.000	-0.253	0.000	0.034	0.584
South Dakota	0.290	0.0119	0.000	-0.292	0.050	0.000	-0.078	0.144	-0.100	0.200
Montana	0.297	0.0026	0.505	-0.268	0.093	0.007	-0.152	0.125	-0.079	0.578
Nebraska	0.363	0.0005	0.661	-0.247	0.028	0.000	-0.247	0.000	0.047	0.277
New Mexico	0.234	0.0110	0.000	-0.235	0.041	0.000	-0.109	0.017	-0.149	0.026
Pennsylvania	0.267	-0.0086	0.000	-0.227	0.017	0.000	-0.268	0.000	0.166	0.000
Vermont	0.694	0.0000	0.993	-0.219	0.055	.000	-0.333	0.000	0.270	0.001

Utah	0.360	0.0091	0.000	-0.211	0.046	.000	-0.222	0.000	0.051	0.465
Arkansas	0.563	0.0046	0.051	-0.201	0.055	0.001	-0.222	.000	-0.048	0.561
South Carolina	0.339	0.0002	0.838	-0.197	0.026	0.000	-0.195	0.000	0.049	0.211
Alabama	0.244	0.0011	0.323	-0.159	0.024	0.000	-0.193	0.000	0.047	0.221
Tennessee	0.470	0.0003	0.830	-0.152	0.036	.000	-0.228	0.000	0.030	0.582
Colorado	0.503	0.0039	0.039	-0.149	0.044	0.002	-0.317	0.000	0.228	0.001
Minnesota	0.062	0.0058	0.001	-0.138	0.036	0.001	-0.252	0.000	-0.005	0.937
California	0.103	0.0029	0.023	-0.126	0.028	.000	-0.287	0.000	0.199	.000
Missouri	0.037	0.0025	0.003	-0.114	0.017	0.000	-0.241	0.000	-0.064	0.024
Maine	0.598	-0.0029	0.178	-0.071	0.052	0.181	-0.178	0.001	0.222	0.006
New Hampshire	0.784	0.0054	0.051	-0.070	0.072	0.340	-0.311	0.000	0.111	0.289
Maryland	0.202	-0.0038	0.001	-0.057	0.023	0.019	-0.199	0.000	0.093	0.012
Connecticut	0.303	-0.0022	0.032	-0.049	0.024	0.049	-0.275	0.000	0.155	.000
Hawaii	0.049	-0.0088	0.113	-0.034	0.122	0.779	-0.028	0.833	0.287	0.146
North Carolina	0.644	0.0005	0.737	-0.027	0.037	0.470	-0.183	0.000	0.096	0.079
New York	-0.126	-0.0071	0.000	-0.025	0.016	0.127	-0.258	0.000	0.173	0.000
Georgia	0.316	0.0013	0.231	-0.016	0.024	0.510	-0.245	0.000	0.100	0.010
Virginia	0.227	0.0006	0.522	-0.003	0.022	0.888	-0.150	0.000	0.065	0.062
New Jersey	0.121	-0.0051	0.000	-0.002	0.018	0.911	-0.244	0.000	0.154	0.000
Massachusetts	-0.086	0.0002	0.698	0.007	0.011	0.524	-0.299	0.000	0.137	0.000
Arizona	0.903	0.0069	0.010	0.015	0.090	0.865	-0.459	0.000	0.307	0.003
Delaware	0.265	-0.0014	0.528	0.037	0.050	0.468	-0.229	.000	0.103	0.187
Florida	0.758	0.0044	0.067	0.081	0.064	0.220	-0.359	0.000	0.211	0.022
District of Columbia	0.602	-0.0050	0.103	0.271	0.073	0.001	-0.117	0.100	0.108	0.323

Dependent variable is the natural log of employment. Model: AR1 (Method = MAXL); period 1972I to 1985I. Degrees of freedom: 34. SE = standard error. SIG = probability that the coefficient is zero.

variables are lagged, the coefficient represents the sum of all lagged coefficients. The significance measure (SIG) is the probability that the true value of the coefficient is zero, using a two-tailed t test. The coefficient for the time variable TREND is the estimated exponential rate of growth or decline in employment (wages, or output) that occurs owing to secular changes in tastes, comparative advantage, or technology. The coefficients on the real exchange rate, the real price of energy variable (LRL-ENGY), and the unemployment rate (LURT) can be interpreted as elasticities.

In Table 4.4, the coefficient of the real exchange rate variable LRELULC is negative for 16 of 20 industries and significant at the .05 level for 11 industries. Within the nondurable goods industries, textile mill products (SIC 22), apparel and other textile goods (SIC 23), and petroleum and coal products (SIC 29) are negative and significant at the .05 level. Somewhat less significant but showing important negative effects are chemicals and allied products (SIC 28), rubber and miscellaneous plastic products (SIC 30), and leather and leather goods (SIC 31). The coefficient for the print and publishing industry (SIC 27) is significant and positive.

The durable goods sector has seven industries with a negative coefficient for the real exchange rate that is significant at the .01 level, including stone, clay, and glass products (SIC 32), primary metal products (SIC 33), fabricated metal products (SIC 34), nonelectrical machinery (SIC 35), transportation equipment (SIC 37), instruments and related products (SIC 38), and miscellaneous manufacturing (SIC 39). Coefficients for lumber and wood products (SIC 24), furniture and fixtures (SIC 25), and electrical and electronic equipment (SIC 36) are positive, but small and not statistically significant.

The results by state are shown in Table 4.5, sorted by the size of the exchange-rate coefficient. The coefficient is significant at the .01 level for 37 states. The sign is negative for all states where it is significant at the .05 level, and for 46 of the 51 states. The elasticity of employment with respect to the real exchange rate in the "Rust Belt" states runs from $-.45$ in Michigan to $-.28$ in Pennsylvania. There are four states at the bottom of the list with insignificantly positive coefficients. The service-oriented District of Columbia has the only significantly positive coefficient.

Notes

1 Further details on the effects of fluctuations in the real exchange rate on the employment rate by manufacturing sector and by state are given in the appendix.
2 W. H. Branson and James P. Love (1986), "The Real Exchange Rate and Employment and Output in U.S. Manufacturing 1974–85," photocopy, March 1986.

3 J. A. Frenkel, "Flexible Exchange Rates, Prices, and the Role of 'News': Lessons from the 1970's," *Journal of Political Economy,* vol. 89, no. 4 (August 1981), pp. 665–705.

4 The model is laid out in detail in W. H. Branson, "Causes of Appreciation and Volatility of the Dollar," in Federal Reserve Bank of Kansas City (ed.), *The U.S. Dollar – Recent Developments, Outlook, and Policy Options* (Kansas City, 1985), pp. 33–52. The rational expectations extension is in W. H. Branson, A. Fraga, and R. A. Johnson, "Expected Fiscal Policy and the Recession of 1982," National Bureau of Economic Research Working Paper no. 1784, December 1985.

5 Data are presented in U.S. Department of Commerce, *Survey of Current Business,* Table 10 in the quarterly balance of payments article.

6 K. A. Oye, "The Sterling-Dollar-Franc Triangle: Monetary Diplomacy 1929–37," *World Politics,* vol. 37, no. 1 (October 1985), p. 186.

7 See C. Beach and J. MacKinnon, "A Maximum Likelihood Procedure for Regression with Autocorrelated Errors," *Econometrica,* vol. 46, no. 1 (1978), pp. 51–8.

PART II

Commercial policy issues

CHAPTER 5

A giant among Lilliputians: Japan's long-run trade problem

JAGDISH BHAGWATI

1   Introduction

The U.S.–Japan "trade problem" is acute. The media in the United States constantly report on Japan's failure to open its markets and on the invisible and inscrutable trade barriers that successfully keep imports out of Japan despite low tariffs. Japan Inc. is the issue.

This chapter is concerned with three aspects of the problem: (1) its origins; (2) the validity of the complaints against Japan; and (3) some policy options for Japan in light of these complaints.

2   Japan's long-run trade problem

The first point to note is that Japan has always had problems with its trade relations, principally with respect to its exports. During the 1930s, for example, Japan faced serious complaints and extensive trade discrimination directed at its exports. The resulting policies were similar to the voluntary export restraints (VERs) that are placed on its exports today. Although the trade barriers prior to 1932 were directed at trade in general – in part because of the world depression and in part because of attempts by developing countries to restrict imports in general – after 1932 (especially during 1934 and 1935), one country after another resorted to high tariffs and import quotas, and even VERs, directed *specifically* against Japan (Uyeda, 1936).

This problem persisted despite Japan's trade deficits with many of the countries that practiced such discrimination. The problem was precipitated largely by Japan's rapidly expanding market penetration in several sectors, which reflected Japan's rapid growth and high import dependence. These factors in turn forced Japan to expand its exports.

This is an updated version of the paper presented at the Japan–U.S. symposium, "Beyond Trade Friction," September 1–2, 1986, Tokyo, under the auspices of the Center for Japan–U.S. Business and Economic Studies, New York University, and the Center for Japan–U.S. Relations, International University of Japan.

Thus, regardless of whether Japan has a trade surplus or a trade deficit, it will have a trade problem because its economy and volume of trade have grown too fast for a relatively sluggish outside world to absorb. The resulting trade penetration in specific sectors has given rise to worldwide protectionist demands that Japan stop these trade advances.

As long as Japan experiences relatively rapid growth and its industries and economy in general remain dependent on imports, it cannot avoid creating waves in the outside world. The reaction in specific sectors – for example, textiles, pencils, electric lamps, tuna fish, potteries, and matches in the 1930s; and automobiles, TVs, VCRs, electronics, and steel in the 1970s and 1980s – is simply going to be a fact of life for Japan. It is the problem of a giant operating in a Lilliputian world, as it were.[1]

However, the problem today differs from those that Japan has faced since the 1930s in two respects:

1. The resentment against Japan's exports is more deep-seated because the degree of adjustment required in specific import-competing sectors has been compounded, in recent years, by Japan's bilateral trade *surplus* with the United States and with the world at large, and by the fact that the United States has also had to adjust to the expansion of trade by the newly industrialized countries (NICs) and to the relative contraction of its trade sector. This contraction has been necessitated by the overvaluation of the U.S. dollar resulting from the fiscal extravagance of the United States.
2. Instead of simply imposing VERs and other protectionist measures on specific export sectors in Japan, the United States (and the European Economic Community, to some extent) has reacted by seeking to open up Japan, in a throwback to Commodore Perry! Therefore the Japanese trade problem has spread like a disease to its import sector as well. Why?

This new development can be traced to the notion of "level playing fields" or (full) "reciprocity" that has emerged in recent years, especially in the United States. The United States, unlike Great Britain – which for nearly 60 years after the repeal of the Corn Laws in the nineteenth century was a proponent of unilateral free trade – has never supported this stance. The United States has always believed in reciprocity in tariff bargaining and in its trade relations. The General Agreement on Tariffs and Trade (GATT) also embodies this view in two major respects: (1) all of its members have symmetric rights and obligations, and (2) tariff reductions are expected to be undertaken in a similar spirit, thereby ensuring what I have called first-difference reciprocity, that is, reciprocity at the margin.

In the past, however, the United States looked the other way in a spirit of leadership, and permitted certain countries not to reciprocate: the Europeans during the 1950s when they were working their way toward convertiblity, and the developing countries, when they were accorded differential treatment under the provisions of Part IV of the GATT.

It was only a matter of time before the United States sought fuller reciprocity from GATT members. The declining position of the United States in the world economy – although it continues as the force majeure – and the resulting "diminished giant" syndrome have accentuated and accelerated this turn of events, as have the overvaluation of the dollar and the resulting pressures on the U.S.-traded sector. Nevertheless, it is important to note that the demand for reciprocity, or for open markets abroad and at home, is part of the *original* U.S. conception of a desirable trading order and cannot be expected to change (Bhagwati and Irwin, 1987).

In the context of the recent surge in protectionist sentiment, fed by macroeconomic distress and the previously overvalued dollar, there has also been a tactical reason for the U.S. executive to focus on markets abroad as an antidote to the pressures to close markets at home. This is a diversionary tactic that aims at creating "countervailing power" for free trade and against protectionism in a pluralistic political system (Bhagwati and Irwin, 1987).

3   Is Japan unfairly closed?

Although considerable attention has been given to reciprocity as a result of strong short-run and trend factors, and hence to opening up external markets, there is also a general sense that Japan has been unfairly closed while enjoying (despite extensive VERs and protectionism) greater access to markets abroad.

Admittedly, the fact that Japan has a surplus is widely cited in support of this contention. However, you don't have to be a very sophisticated economist to know that this is a fallacy. It is also a mistake to suppose that the Japanese surplus or the U.S. deficit can be attacked through trade policy, whether U.S. protection or Japan's lowering of alleged trade barriers: These surpluses and deficits reflect basic macroeconomic factors.

However, it is true that given macroeconomic factors, a lowering of foreign trade barriers will make it easier for the traded sector to adjust in a country that has to contract the traded sector owing to the "overvaluation" of its currency. Given any external deficit or surplus that reflects macroeconomic factors, a lowering of foreign trade barriers will, all things being equal, increase a country's traded sector relative to its nontraded sector. Thus, it will ease the adjustment problems in its traded sector.

The key question, therefore, is whether Japan does have these invisible, inscrutable barriers to imports. Those who believe that this is the case use two approaches to prove their claims: (1) regression analysis; and (2) anecdotes and interviews.

(1) Although the *regression* approach appears more scientific, it is quite unconvincing, in my view. Consider, for example, Bela Balassa's (1986) recent work in which he examines Japan's import-to-GNP ratio on a cross-country basis. He finds it too low. But, despite his many adjustments, his argument is unconvincing. These ratios are admittedly difficult to interpret: The numerator relates to gross values and the denominator to value added. However, there are alternative ways of defining the ratios (see the recent work of Padma Desai, 1984). Regressions run by Hollis Chenery and others showing that the ratio declines as per capita income increases suggest that these ratios should decline over time in each country. In fact, they have risen dramatically in many countries over the last two decades. More compellingly, an excessively low import-to-GNP ratio equally implies an excessively low export-to-GNP ratio. Are we to conclude, then, that Japan is exporting too little? If trade shares are low, it may be that Japan is being constrained by VERs to low export levels, which in turn cause imports to decline, so that the explanation of this alleged phenomenon may well be U.S. and EEC protection rather than Japanese protection!

Similar regressions have been tried on U.S.–Japan third-market shares, which have been compared with U.S.–Japan shares in Japan itself. The assumption again is that if the United States has a significantly lower share in Japan than in third markets, compared with corresponding shares for Japan, then Japanese markets are not open. In general, this too is questionable since the relative sales efforts in different markets, for instance, may be not commensurate.

(2) More compelling therefore are the micro or sector-level arguments based on empirical and anecdotal evidence that has accumulated as the conflict with Japan has simmered in the last few years.

However, I must confess that here, too, I feel puzzled and unconvinced. This argument is largely cultural and institutional; opening Japan to rapidly escalating imports clearly runs into difficulties. An analogy would be instructive. It is quite easy for visitors to the United States to barge into American homes, be invited there, dress freely, and so on. By contrast, Japan is a more subdued and ritualized society in which visitors cannot quite expect to be accepted in the same way. A compulsory reading by frustrated American businessmen of Tanizaki Junichiro's classic essay, *In Praise of Shadows,* would perhaps be more relevant here. The inability of businessmen to appreciate that instant results, based simply on price differences, are not possible is certainly an important source of the friction.

The corresponding inability to adapt to different styles of responsible behavior is also a key factor. Casual empiricism suggests that the U.S. approach is typically that of caveat emptor or "buyer beware." The average seller takes little responsibility for courteous and accommodating behavior toward the buyer once the sale is completed. By contrast, the Japanese approach (and the European too, in large degree) is for the seller to continue being responsible for customer satisfaction. Thus, it is not difficult to see why so many of us prefer to deal with Japanese rather than with U.S. suppliers; and it is equally evident why the Japanese would vastly prefer to deal with their own suppliers, insofar as it is reasonably possible.

This is essentially the message that sociologists studying Japan (such as Herbert Passin and Ronald Dore) and even economists (such as Hugh Patrick and Gary Saxonhouse) seem to be conveying by bringing both empathy for Japan and a refined sensitivity to the problem.[2]

Historically, another parallel can be found in the ease with which Japan's trade partners have assumed that its export successes were based on unfair trading practices. Today they assume that their own failures in the Japanese market must be the result of Japan's unfair trading practices as well. Note, for example, the Curzons' (1987, p. 147) observations on Japan's treatment at the GATT:

Japan has never had the privilege of being a "normal" GATT member. In 1955, when the United States sponsored her accession, fourteen contracting parties, including all the major West European countries with the exception of Italy and Germany, refused to take part in the negotiations and invoked Article XXXV of the GATT. This Article, entitled "Non-application of the Agreement between Particular Contracting Parties," was added to the General Agreement in 1948 when the conditions for the accession of new contracting parties were changed from unanimous consent of existing members to consent by two-thirds majority, in order to encourage the accession of new member. As a result of this accelerated-accession procedure, the situation could arise that certain countries might find themselves bound by the GATT to give most favoured-nation treatment to a country with which they had no wish to develop trade ties. At the time, the provision was designed to permit India to discriminate against South Africa. But the Europeans must have been delighted to re-discover Article XXXV when the question of Japan's accession arose: Japan could by all means become a member of the GATT – but she should not expect most-favored-nation treatment!

How did these fourteen countries justify their discriminatory attitude? James Meade (1956), one of the fathers of the GATT, put it this way:

[The United Kingdom] was influenced by memories of the nineteen-thirties when many existing lines of trade and production were disrupted by a sudden incursion of cheap Japanese products, sold in many cases by means of questionable commercial devices which misled customers about origin, content or quality of the goods, which relied upon the copying of other traders' designs and which involved export subsidies of one kind or another.

Whereas the Europeans sheltered behind the convenient Article XXXV, the United States proceeded in its own way to reduce the ease of access to its markets for Japanese products. In 1955 it asked Japan to "exercise restraint" in the export of cotton textiles, at the time, Japan's principal export product.

The United States, probably quite rightly, saw the invocation of Article XXXV by most major trading countries as one of the reasons why it had to bear the full "burden of Japanese competitiveness" (Curzon and Curzon, 1987, p. 163).

Unfortunately, therefore, Japan has to deal in realities that have been shaped by unshakable misperceptions of unfairly closed Japanese markets. These notions have been reinforced by anecdotal evidence that is so compelling at times that Japan ought to weed out the offending practices: The negative fallout from them is greater than anything it can gain from the practices in question. Thus, I was told by an EEC expert from the Netherlands that Holland exports tulip bulbs to over a hundred countries but not to Japan. Why? The Japanese inspect the bulbs for health control by cutting the stems vertically in two! Even the Japanese, with all their ingenuity, cannot put the bulbs together after such inspection! The Japanese government must ask: Is this worth it?

4   Japan's response

Aside from weeding out such provocative practices, with their disproportionate impact on the volatile climate today, and undertaking the expansionary steps that would ease the present current account surplus that has exacerbated the Japanese trade problem by providing a handle to protectionists, what *can* Japan do in response to this Japanophobic attitude and corresponding demands?

4.1   *Fixed-rule versus fixed-quantity approaches: the growth of VIEs*

One option for Japan, which its increasingly militant trading partners in the West appear to be tilting toward, is to "demonstrate results" by increasing imports of specific items from specific sources. In other words, the trade regime should shift from the GATT-embodied, most favored nation (MFN), nondiscriminatory, "fixed-rule" approach to a bilateral, discriminatory, "fixed-quantity" approach. Elsewhere I have pointed out that the resulting demands that Japan import specific items from the United

States such as beef and semiconductors imply the growth on the trade scene of voluntary import expansions (VIEs) (Bhagwati, 1987; and World Bank, 1987). These match, on the import side, what VERs do on the export side: They get your trading partner to assume specific fixed-quantity outcomes in their trade with you. They contrast with the fixed-rule approach, which instead specifies the rules of trade and lets the quantities emerge as a consequence of competition among the trading partners, subject to these rules.

The growth of VIEs, and the fixed-quantity approach more generally, is also evident in recent U.S. trade policy with countries other than Japan. In the Korean insurance case under Section 301 of the U.S. Trade Act, the United States was placated, not by liberalizing the insurance trade for all, but by giving two U.S. insurance firms a larger share of a cartelized allocation of business (Cho, 1986). In the semiconductor industry, it is now known that the United States had negotiated with Japan for increased penetration of the Japanese market by U.S. manufacturers, widely believed to be 20 percent of the Japanese market, by certain target dates. Indeed, Japan's failure to provide this quantity outcome was a major reason behind President Reagan's decision to impose punitive tariffs on Japanese exports of computers, tools, TV sets, and the like in April 1987.

No serious international economist is likely to approve of such VIEs, since they also imply market-sharing arrangements and can interfere with the play of market forces beyond their duration. One fears that this is possibly happening with VERs already. How can such imports be guaranteed without some form of cartelized arrangement that parcels out the imports and their added costs to specific users or import-competing producers, or the like? In fact, this is one more example of ingenious governments providing the economist with yet more problems to study!

I feel that this aspect of the problem is most unfortunate, and not of Japanese origin, but rather must be blamed on the United States. It is doubly unfortunate because the United States should be providing the leadership on the issue in favor of the fixed-rule rather than the fixed-quantity approach. The focus on quantity outcomes in dealing with Japan also strengthens the forces within GATT (chiefly within the European Economic Community and some developing countries) that have always been in favor of "managed trade" rather than the "rule of law."

On the other hand, there seems to be little that Japan can do except point out these implications as forcibly as possible in its bilateral and multilateral negotiations, and then prudently put up with them if necessary in light of international pressures to accept quantity outcomes with respect to imports.

4.2   *Quid pro quo direct foreign investment abroad*

Opening up Japan in this fashion is only one aspect of Japan's response to its trade problem. Japanese industry has also wisely decided to use direct foreign investment (DFI) as a policy tool to contain the Japanophobia and to keep the foreign markets as open as possible.

Thus, a number of DFIs, including joint ventures such as the Toyota-GM venture, have been designed essentially to coopt U.S. corporations and/or labor unions into opposing, rather than supporting, demands for protection against Japanese imports into the United States. It is thus evident that GM was "paying off" Toyota for the joint venture and a share in the profits from Toyota's greater comparative advantage in small cars by breaking ranks with the other U.S. automakers when it opposed the renewal of VERs.[3] That breaking away was the quid pro quo for the joint venture by Toyota.

This class of DFIs, in which the more competitive foreign producer undertakes a DFI in the importing country to help defuse the protectionist threat, is what I have recently christened the Quid Pro Quo DFI (Bhagwati, 1986).[4] It may have helped moderate the protectionist sentiment in the U.S. Congress and persuade firms and possibly unions faced with import competition not to persist with protectionist demands.

However, do such Quid Pro Quo DFIs create other difficulties, such as the fear that the Japanese will wind up owning our industry? Yes, sometimes. But there is little evidence that this reaction is widespread or intense in the United States. It certainly pales in comparison with the hostility that imports tend to arouse.

Concluding remarks

It is not clear that these policy responses will satisfy the United States or the European Economic Community, for that matter. If not, Japanese policy makers will have to find solace by praying to the Shinto gods for help and, if they do not respond, by maintaining the great Buddha's equanimity and equilibrium while the barbarians rave and rant, and bark and bite.

Notes

1 That Japan's trade problem with the outside world is independent of whether it runs a surplus or a deficit is evident not merely from the historical evidence of the 1930s, but also from recent experience. See the excellent analysis of the true behavior of the Japanese current account balance and its presumed behavior in the last two decades in Curzon and Curzon (1987, pp. 159–61).

2 The detailed review by Rachel McCulloch (1986) of the economic studies of the issue of access to Japan's markets is also in general agreement with the conclusion that Japan is not unfairly closed.
3 For a detailed statement of these kinds of trade-offs or quid pro quos, see Bhagwati (1986).
4 This is what Toshio Shishido (1986) describes as "political" investment. However, a better term would be "political-economy-theoretic" investment since economically it can be readily adapted to incorporate the defusing of protectionist threats as an explanatory factor. See, for example, the two-period theoretical analysis of quid pro quo foreign investment in a perfectly competitive framework in Bhagwati et al. (1986) and in a market-structure framework in Dinopoulos and Bhagwati (1986), Dinopoulos (1987), and Wong (1987).

References

Balassa, B. (1986) "Japan's Trade Policies." Paper presented at the conference, "Free Trade in the World Economy: Towards an Opening of Markets." Kiel Institut für Weltwirtschaft, 24-6 June.

Bhagwati, J. (1985) "Protectionism: Old Wine in New Bottles." *Journal of Policy Modelling,* vol. 7, pp. 23-34.

(1986) "Investing Abroad." Esmee Fairbairn Lecture, University of Lancaster, U.K., November, photocopy.

(1987) "VERs, Quid Pro Quo DFI and VIEs: Political-Economy-Theoretic Analyses." *International Economic Journal,* vol. 1, no. 1 (Spring), pp. 1-14.

Bhagwati, J., and D. Irwin (1987) "The Return of the Reciprocitarians: U.S. Trade Policy Today." *World Economy,* vol. 10, no. 2 (June), pp. 109-30.

Bhagwati, J., R. Brecher, E. Dinopoulos, and T. N. Srinivasan (in press) "Quid Pro Quo Foreign Investment and Welfare: A Political-Economy-Theoretic Model." *Journal of Development Economics* (Symposium Issue).

Cho, Y. J. (1986) "U.S.-Korea Disputes on the Opening of Korean Insurance Market: Some Implications." Discussion Paper DRD210, Development Research Department. Washington, D.C.: World Bank, October.

Curzon, G., and V. Curzon (1987) "Follies in European Trade Relations with Japan." *World Economy,* vol. 10, no. 2 (June), pp. 155-76.

Desai, P. (1984) "How Should the Role of Foreign Trade in the Soviet Economy be Measured?" Columbia University International Economic Research Center, Working Paper no. 244, April.

Dinopoulos, E. (1987) "Quid Pro Quo Foreign Investment." Paper presented at the World Bank conference, Political Economy: Theory and Policy Implications, 17-19 June.

Dinopoulos, E., and J. Bhagwati (1986) "Quid Pro Quo Foreign Investment and Market Structure." Paper presented at the 61st Annual Western Economic Association International Conference in San Francisco, July.

McCulloch, R. (1986) "U.S.-Japan Economic Relations." University of Wisconsin, Madison, photocopy.

Meade, J. (1956) "Japan and the General Agreement on Tariffs and Trade." Joseph Fisher Lecture in Commerce, University of Adelaide, Australia.

74   **Jagdish Bhagwati**

Shishido, T. (1986) "Capital Transfer from Japan to U.S. for Avoiding Trade
Friction." In *Beyond Trade Friction: Japan–U.S. Business and Economic
Cooperation,* Japan–U.S. Symposium of the Center for Japan–U.S. Busi-
ness and Economic Studies (New York University) and Center for Japan–
U.S. Relations (International University of Japan). Tokyo, 1–2 September.
Uyeda, T. (1936) *The Recent Development of Japanese Foreign Trade.* Institute
of Pacific Relations, Japanese Council, Paper no. 3.
Wong, K. (1987) "Optimal Threat of Trade Restriction and Quid Pro Quo For-
eign Investment." Paper presented at the World Bank conference, "Polit-
ical Economy: Theory and Policy Implications," 17–19 June.
World Bank (1987) *World Development Report.* Washington, D.C.

CHAPTER 6

What do VERs do?

KALA KRISHNA

1   Introduction

The post–World War II era is often hailed as a period of great trade liberalization, which led to gains for all parties through free trade. Owing
to a series of negotiations conducted under the auspices of GATT, tariffs have been negotiated steadily downward, and at present they are at
an average level of about 4 percent on manufactured goods.[1] However,
this figure does not necessarily indicate that protection has fallen over
time. Since 1970, a new kind of protectionism involving nontariff barriers
(NTBs) has arisen.

The leading instruments of this "new protectionism" have been the so-
called voluntary export restraint (VER) and its relative, the orderly marketing arrangement (OMA). Although the articles of GATT explicitly
forbid quotas since they are inherently discriminatory, the proportion of
total world trade that moves under some kind of quantitative restraint is
thought to be between 30 and 50 percent.[2]

The rise in the new protectionism coincided with the slow economic
growth and higher unemployment of the early 1970s, and is often linked
causally to the adverse economic environment faced by established industries in this period. The popularity of VERs stems from their legal, political, and economic advantages over more traditional protectionist measures. This is likely to make them even more popular in the future. VERs,
however, tend to be socially inefficient ways of providing protection, although they do have advantages for certain groups.

VERs are being increasingly used for two broad sets of reasons. The
first set relates to the legal and political environment, the second to the
economic environment.

They offer at least three legal and political advantages:

Research support from the Clark Fund and Center for International Affairs at Harvard is
gratefully acknowledged.

(1) GATT places several restrictions on the use of the more traditional forms of protection, tariffs, and quotas. Tariffs have been restricted through agreements on bindings (which are promises to bind tariffs) and through negotiated reductions in tariffs. Quotas are expressly forbidden by article XI of GATT. Thus, it is natural for substitution to occur toward other legal forms of protection, such as VERs.

(2) Compared with less discriminatory measures, VERs are set on particular industries and countries. Their inherently discriminatory nature allows producer and labor groups in the affected industry, who stand to gain from a VER, to easily coordinate their efforts in the hope of mutual advantage. On the other hand, consumer losses from higher prices are spread over all consumers, and this makes it harder to coordinate opposition to such measures from consumers, since an individual consumer has less to lose than the interest groups in the affected industry. As VERs on each industry are imposed in a piecemeal fashion, consumers and consumer groups are even less likely to strongly oppose an individual VER.

(3) More important, VERs tend to circumvent the public debate associated with policies that have to go through Congress. Since VERs are "negotiated" between the executive branch and foreign governments who agree to enforce them, industries can, in effect, obtain VERs without prolonged public debate.[3]

A major economic advantage of VERs is that they, unlike tariffs, offer a bribe to the foreign producers in the form of the implicit quota rents that accrue to foreigners. This, it is felt, makes them more amenable to such arrangements. This is particularly true since the carrot of additional revenues is accompanied by the threat of tariffs. However, Tumlir (1985), for example, argues that this threat is not necessarily credible, given that tariffs are hard to obtain from Congress. In addition, they are often illegal under GATT, so that a presidential veto would almost certainly have to follow congressional approval. This lack of credibility is not, however, an issue if producers are better off with a VER. This is quite probable since a VER in effect legally creates a cartel organized by the agency implementing it. This is another advantage of a VER for foreign and domestic producers, since such a cartel is likely to raise their profits.

In an imperfectly competitive market, a cartel is not required for foreign firms to benefit from a VER. This is due to the fact that the VER itself alters the "game" that domestic and foreign firms play by acting as a credible constraint on the output of the foreign firm. For one thing, a VER allows a foreign entrant in an established domestic industry to precommit to a small size. In the sequential game that follows, the entrant sets a low enough price so that the established domestic firm does not find it worthwhile to undercut the foreign firm and accommodate entry. This is an example of the "Judo economics" described by Gelman and Salop (1983).[4]

Second, the capacity constraint on the foreign firm acts as a facilitating device making it optimal for the domestic and foreign firms to raise their prices in equilibrium when they produce substitute goods. This gives them higher equilibrium profits. This argument is independent of the cartelization of foreign firms by the implementing authority previously mentioned (see Krishna, 1983).

This chapter examines alternative ways of modeling VERs in imperfectly competitive markets. This is an important exercise, since the effects of VERs are sensitive to the models used. The central argument here is that it is essential to be clear about the timing of players' moves and to model the effects of a VER carefully. To illustrate this point, I extend a model I described elsewhere (Krishna, 1983) to allow complementary goods to be produced by domestic and foreign firms. If goods are substitutes, VERs set at free-trade levels raise all profits, whereas if they are complements, the VERs have no effect. Thus, tariffs and quotas are fundamentally nonequivalent under Bertrand duopoly when substitute goods are produced, but are equivalent when complementary goods are produced. This is in contrast to the case of Stackelberg leadership. It is important to specify the effects of *any* restriction on the payoff functions of agents and use this to analyze its effects on equilibrium of the game. The next section briefly reviews some of the work in this area.

2   Approaches to the analysis of VERs

The analysis of voluntary export restrictions has attracted much attention since 1981, when they were imposed on the import of Japanese automobiles to the United States. A number of approaches have been taken to modeling their effects in imperfectly competitive markets, at both a theoretical and empirical level. The classic work of Bhagwati (1965) on the nonequivalence of tariffs and quotas in the presence of a domestic monopoly is the starting point of much of this work.

The approaches used to analyze the effects of VERs vary from static oligopoly models to dynamic repeated game models. Static models tend to give more clear-cut, empirically testable results than dynamic ones. This is both because of the normal multiplicity of equilibria that arise in dynamic models, and because the more varied effects that occur in such models can offset each other. Ultimately, the choice of modeling strategy should, of course, be guided by the empirical validity of its predictions. For this reason, it is worthwhile focusing on the empirically testable implications of a given modeling technique.

I focus on static models in this essay and argue that it is important to model *carefully* the effects of a VER upon the game played by the firms, particularly when neither the domestic nor the foreign firm is a Stackelberg leader. Recent work by Harris (1985) and Itoh and Ono (1984) does not adequately model this case. As a consequence, their results differ from those obtained when the effects of a VER on the profit function of the firms, and hence on the game itself, are more carefully analyzed, as in Krishna (1983). I first discuss how the work of Harris (1985) and Itoh and Ono (1984) relates to my work, and then briefly review other recent work in the area that is less closely related to this discussion.

Itoh and Ono (1984) analyze the effects of a VER in an oligopoly model with one foreign and one domestic firm. Firms are assumed to compete in price and to produce differentiated substitute products. Itoh and Ono argue that tariffs and quotas are equivalent in such a model. However, their results hold only when excess demand for the foreign good has no effect on the demand for the domestic good. Since the goods are substitutes, this is hard to justify. When the game is carefully modeled, as in Krishna (1983), it is clear that VERs have effects by their very existence and that this makes tariffs and quotas fundamentally nonequivalent when foreign and domestic goods are substitutes.

Harris (1985) argues that VERs are truly voluntary, since they raise profits of all firms. However, he does not model the effects of the VER on the profit functions of both firms and hence on the game itself in a careful way. Rather, he *assumes* that a VER makes the domestic firm into a Stackelberg leader. Krishna (1983) does not make this assumption, but *proves* that, in the unique mixed-strategy equilibrium, the domestic firm earns the same profits as a Stackelberg leader when a particular rationing rule is used. Both works deal only with the case in which the products of the two firms are substitutes. In this chapter, I show that when the products produced by the two firms are complementary, the VER has *no* effect on equilibrium and does not even give the domestic firm the profits of a Stackelberg leader.

The essence of the argument that the game itself changes owing to a VER can be understood by realizing that a VER produces three effects in oligopolistic markets. I call these the "competitive," "monopoly," and "interactive" effects.

The competitive, or C, effect is the only one that operates in competitive environments. In a competitive framework, a VER works by altering market demand and/or supply functions wherever the constraint is binding. If the VER is set at the free-trade level of imports, it will have no effect, since such policies affect equilibrium in competitive markets only by being set at restrictive levels.

With domestic monopoly and foreign competition, even VERs set at free-trade levels have effects. These arise because VERs alter demand and/or supply conditions at points other than the unconstrained equilibrium point and thus affect the decision of the domestic monopolist. In this manner, restrictions can have significant effects by their very presence. This point was made by Bhagwati (1965). I call this the monopoly, or M, effect and it operates in addition to any C effect that may occur.

In an oligopoly model, not only do the effects present under monopoly occur, but because each agent can be affected in the same manner as the monopolist and the actions of all agents are interdependent, an additional effect, which I call the interactive, or I, effect, arises.

In the analysis of VERs with differentiated products, when firms compete in price and produce substitute goods, the imposition of a VER on the foreign firm makes the domestic firm's demand function less elastic for price *increases*. This makes it profitable for the domestic firm to raise its price at what would be the free-trade equilibrium. This is the M effect. The increase in the domestic firm's price makes the constraint bind on the foreign firm and induces the foreign firm to also raise its price since it is effectively supply constrained. This is the essence of the I effect.

Both I and M effects raise domestic profits when the goods are substitutes. Moreover, as long as foreign supply is not constrained too far below the free-trade level, foreign profits also rise along with prices. This is basically how VERs facilitate collusion with substitute goods. In Krishna (1983), the equilibrium with a VER is shown to be a mixed strategy, which gives the domestic firm the profits of a Stackelberg leader when a particular rationing rule is used and raises profits both at home and abroad.

Since Harris (1985) assumes that a VER makes the domestic firm into a Stackelberg leader, his results on profits are similar to those of Krishna (1983) when goods are substitutes. However, when complementary products are considered, there are no M, and therefore no I, effects, as is shown in the following analysis. Thus, with complementary products, tariffs and quotas are equivalent even under Bertrand duopoly. This is not the result obtained by assuming that a VER makes the domestic firm into a Stackelberg leader.

A good deal of work has been done on the effects of VERs in other market structures and using other strategic variables. I briefly review some of this literature in order to relate the results to those of this study.[5] Previous work has focused on the effects of VERs in Stackelberg leadership models, Cournot models, repeated game models, and the quality change effects of quotas. Traditionally, duopoly or monopoly models are used since they are the simplest ones with which to address such issues.

Stackelberg leadership models show that quotas are not in general equivalent to a tariff in such a setting and that a VER may have effects even when set at free-trade levels. Moreover, these models show that the endogenous determination of a Stackelberg leader tends to work in favor of the home firm being the leader. The work of Itoh and Ono (1982, 1984) addresses such issues. However, it is not clear why one or the other firm should be expected to have a first-mover advantage, and it is desirable to consider models without this requirement.

The effect of a VER and the equivalence/nonequivalence of tariffs and quotas when neither firm is a Stackelberg leader and firms compete in quantity à la Cournot is elementary. When quantity is the strategic variable, tariffs and quotas are obviously equivalent, and a VER at the free-trade level has no effect.

Although both price and quantity competition models (and their variants) are widely used, it is somewhat unsatisfactory to use Cournot models in analyzing quantity constraints, since such constraints restrict the strategic variable itself and leave no room for firms to change their strategic behavior endogenously. This is the main reason in favor of using price-setting models in the analysis of VERs. The sensitivity of the results of trade restrictions in oligopoly models to the strategic variable used has been analyzed by Eaton and Grossman (1986).[6]

The effects of VERs have also been studied in the context of repeated games. Their effects in such models are harder to predict, since a VER reduces the profitability of deviations from a collusive outcome, but also curtails the ability to punish such deviations. In addition, the usual problems of having too many equilibria also arise in such games. Davidson (1984) deals with the effects of tariffs, and Rotemberg and Saloner (1986) deal with quotas. Lambson and Richardson (1986) deal with the effects of quotas in such models, from both a theoretical and an empirical point of view.

In the long run, firms could choose to modify product type as well as price in response to a VER. This has been studied for monopoly and competitive situations by Rodriguez (1979), Santoni and Van Cott (1980), Das and Donnenfeld (1984), Falvey (1979), and Krishna (1984, 1987). Das and Donnenfeld (1985) also analyze the effects of trade restrictions with a special duopoly model of vertical product differentiation. However, to the extent that product adjustment takes longer than price adjustment, models focusing on the short-run effects of trade restrictions can safely neglect such effects.

A good deal of empirical work has also been done in this area, particularly by Feenstra (1984, 1985, 1987), who documents the rise in quality of automobile imports following the VER, and by Aw and Roberts

(1986) on footwear. In addition, Dixit (1986) and Levinsohn (1987) offer a mix of theory, simulation, and empirical work in the automobile industry that seems particularly promising. Although none of the empirical work explicitly tests whether the VERs on automobiles made firms behave more collusively, there are indications that they may have done so. For example, although the VERs imposed in March 1981 for the period March 1981 to April 1984 were at 1.68 million cars per year, which was about 5 percent below the existing level of imports, the price of Japanese imports increased almost 20 percent in the first year of the VER.[7] Levinsohn (1987) estimates the own price elasticity of demand for Japanese imports to be around 1.57. This would seem to suggest that the VER may have had the kinds of effects suggested by the model of Krishna (1983) and that it is important to understand such models better.

In this chapter I concentrate on the effects of a VER with complementary goods in order to explain the difference between Harris's approach and mine. Its effects when goods are substitutes are more complex and are dealt with in Krishna (1983). The model is presented in Section 3, and a VER, along with a tariff, is analyzed in Section 4. Tariffs and quotas are shown to be equivalent when goods are complements, but are nonequivalent when goods are substitutes.

3   The model

There are two firms, domestic and foreign, producing differentiated goods in amounts x and x^*, respectively. Demand arises from utility maximization by an aggregate domestic consumer of $u(S) + n$, subject to a budget constraint. The scalar, $S = F(x, x^*)$, represents the services produced by the two goods. Services can be thought of as being produced by the aggregate consumer in which case $F(\cdot)$ is a household production function. Alternatively, S could be thought of as being produced by competitive suppliers of services who in turn require x and x^* to make S. F is assumed to be a constant return-to-scale production function; n is the amount of the numeraire good consumed. As usual, the budget constraint is given by

$$P_s S + n \leq I + T,$$

where P_s is the price of a unit of *services,* which of course depends on the prices of x and x^* and the production technology. I and T denote lump-sum income and any tariff revenue that arises. I and T are taken as given constants in the maximization of utility.

These assumptions give rise to a demand function for S, S^D, where

$$S^D = D(P_s).$$

Of course, $P_s = C(P, P^*)$, where $C(\cdot)$ is the unit cost of producing a service associated with the production function $F(\cdot)$, given that the prices of goods produced at home and abroad are P and P^*, respectively. This is because of either competition in the market for services or because of household production of S. The demand for the home firm is therefore given by

$$x(P, P^*) = a(P/P^*)D[C(P, P^*)],$$

where $a(P/P^*) = C_P(P, P^*)$ by Shephard's lemma and is the amount of x needed to produce a unit of S at minimum cost, given the prices of x and x^*. Similarly, the foreign firm's demand function is given by

$$x^*(P, P^*) = a^*(P/P^*)D[C(P, P^*)],$$

where $a^*(P/P^*) = C_{p^*}(P, P^*)$.

An increase in the price of the imported good, P^*, has two effects: It raises $x(\cdot)$ since it raises $a(P/P^*)$, but it also reduces $x(\cdot)$, as it raises $C(\cdot)$, and hence reduces $D[C(\cdot)]$. The intensity of the first effect depends positively on the elasticity of substitution between x and x^* in making S. The intensity of the second effect depends on ϵ, the price elasticity of demand for S. With a constant elasticity of substitution, σ, between x and x^*, goods are substitutes when $\sigma - \epsilon > 0$ and complements when $\sigma - \epsilon < 0$.[8]

Consider the case where $\sigma - \epsilon < 0$, so that the goods are complements in demand. Firms are assumed to compete in price.[9] In order to eliminate the possibility of multimarket interactions, I assume that marginal costs of production of the two firms are constant at r and r^*. The domestic firm chooses P to maximize its profits $\pi(\cdot)$, where

$$\pi(P, P^*) = (P - r)a(P/P^*)D[C(P, P^*)].$$

It takes P^* as given and chooses its optimal P for every P^*, which yields its best response function $B(P^*)$. Similarly, the foreign firm's maximization of $\pi^*(P, P^*)$ defined analogously yields $B^*(P)$. The intersection of $B(\cdot)$ and $B^*(\cdot)$ gives a Nash equilibrium point. I assume that $\pi(\cdot)$ and $\pi^*(\cdot)$ are concave in their own price for any given price of the other and that a unique stable Nash equilibrium exists. In order to focus on any possible effects of a VER, I assume for simplicity that in its absence firms are identical.

Both upward- and downward-sloping best-response functions are possible, so that no assumptions about the slopes of $B(\cdot)$ and $B^*(\cdot)$ are made aside from their both being of the same sign, and the system being stable. The stable equilibrium with downward-sloping best-response functions is depicted in Figure 6.1. Profits of each firm increase as the other's price decreases, as is shown by the direction of the arrows in Figure 6.1.

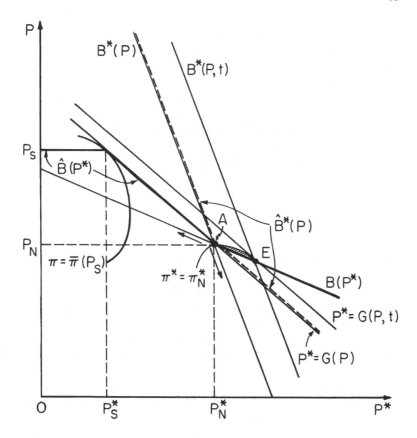

Figure 6.1

4   The effects of trade restriction

Having specified the operation of the model in the absence of trade restrictions, I turn to the effects of trade restrictions on the equilibrium of the game. I first consider the effects of VERs and then turn to the tariffs.

The first step is to identify the region of prices where the VER is binding. To do so, consider the set of prices such that the constraint on imports is exactly met. I assume that the VER is set *at* the free-trade level. The analysis generalizes for any level of the VER in a straightforward manner.

The line $P^* = G(P)$ depicts the set of P and P^* such that the demand for x^* equals its level under free trade. Hence, it passes through (P_N, P_N^*), the

Nash equilibrium point. As the goods are complements, $G(P)$ is downward sloping, and the constraint binds on the foreign firm at points below the line $G(P)$. For a given P, low values of P^* raise its demand and make the constraint bind. For a given P^*, low values of P raise the demand for x^*, making the constraint bind.

Consider the effect of the VER on the best-response function for the foreign firm in the case depicted in Figure 6.1 with downward-sloping best responses. It should be obvious that similar arguments can be used to analyze upward-sloping best responses. For $P < P_N$, the foreign firm would, in the absence of a VER, choose to charge a price such that its demand exceeds the level of the VER. This is evident from Figure 6.1 as $B^*(P)$ lies to the left of $G(P)$ for $P < P_N$. The VER, however, forces the foreign firm to sell less than it would desire, and its optimal strategy is to sell all that it is allowed at the price that clears the market – that is, at $G(P)$.[10] For prices above P_N, $B^*(P)$ lies to the right of $G(P)$ and the constraint does not affect the foreign firm's behavior. Thus, the foreign firm's best-response function in this region is given by $\hat{B}^*(P)$, which is depicted by the dashed line in Figure 6.1.

Next, consider the effect of the VER on the profits of the domestic firm. Define $\bar{\pi}(P) = \pi(P, G(P))$; $\bar{\pi}(\cdot)$ gives the profits for the domestic firm along the line $G(P)$. It is assumed that $\bar{\pi}(P)$ is concave and reaches a finite maximum at $P_S < \infty$, shown in Figures 6.1 and 6.2. Figure 6.2 depicts $\bar{\pi}(P)$.

Figure 6.2 also depicts $\pi(P, P^*)$ for a given value of P^*. Notice that $\pi(P, P^*) = \bar{\pi}(P)$ when P is such that $G(P) = P^*$ – that is, at $P = G^{-1}(P^*)$. At this point it is easy to see that $\pi_p(P, P^*) < \bar{\pi}_p(P)$. This is because an increase in P reduces P^* along G, which acts to raise $\bar{\pi}$, while no such effect operates on π.

Let $\hat{\pi}(P^*, P)$ be the profit function of the domestic firm when the VER is imposed on the foreign firm. For a given value of P^*, the domestic firm can charge a low price and make the constraint bind on the foreign firm, or charge a high price and leave the foreign firm unconstrained by the VER. If the domestic firm charges a relatively low price, that is, below $G^{-1}(P^*)$, the foreign firm is supply constrained at P^* since its supply is limited by the VER and its demand exceeds this level. In this case, I assume that the following rationing rule applies: Consumers fortunate enough to obtain the foreign good at P^* will resell it at a price that clears the market. Since the form of the domestic consumer utility function implies that there are no income effects, the effect on the domestic firm is exactly that of the foreign firm charging $G(P)$ itself. However, this is exactly what $\bar{\pi}(P)$ is defined to be. Hence, if $P < G^{-1}(P^*)$, $\hat{\pi}(P, P^*) = \bar{\pi}(P)$.

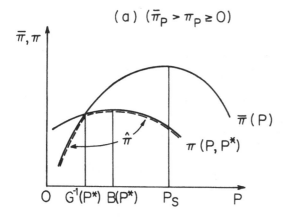

(a) $(\bar{\pi}_P > \pi_P \geq 0)$

$\bar{\pi}, \pi$

$\bar{\pi}(P)$

$\hat{\pi}$

$\pi(P, P^*)$

O $G^{-1}(P^*)$ $B(P^*)$ P_S P

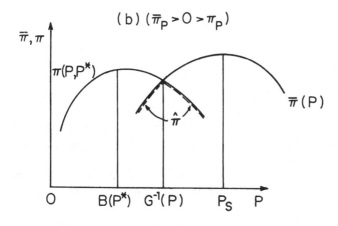

(b) $(\bar{\pi}_P > 0 > \pi_P)$

$\bar{\pi}, \pi$

$\pi(P, P^*)$

$\bar{\pi}(P)$

$\hat{\pi}$

O $B(P^*)$ $G^{-1}(P)$ P_S P

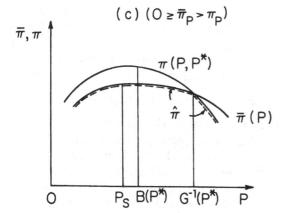

(c) $(0 \geq \bar{\pi}_P > \pi_P)$

$\bar{\pi}, \pi$

$\pi(P, P^*)$

$\hat{\pi}$

$\bar{\pi}(P)$

O P_S $B(P^*)$ $G^{-1}(P^*)$ P

Figure 6.2

If, on the other hand, the domestic firm charges a high price – that is, $P > G^{-1}(P^*)$ – the VER does not bind on the foreign firm when it charges P^* so that it is not supply constrained and the domestic firm's profits remain $\pi(P, P^*)$. Hence, if $P \geq G^{-1}(P^*)$, $\hat{\pi}(P, P^*) = \pi(P, P^*)$.

Figure 6.2 depicts $\hat{\pi}(\cdot)$. Notice that $\hat{\pi}(\cdot)$ is continuous in P by definition. Since $\bar{\pi}_p(P) > \pi_p(P, P^*)$ at $P = G^{-1}(P^*)$ and $\pi(\cdot)$ and $\bar{\pi}(\cdot)$ are concave in P, one of the three cases must hold. Either

$$\bar{\pi}_p(\cdot) > \pi_p(\cdot) \geq 0, \quad \text{Case (a)};$$

$$\bar{\pi}_p(\cdot) > 0 > \pi_p(\cdot), \quad \text{Case (b)};$$

or

$$0 \geq \bar{\pi}_p(\cdot) > \pi_p(\cdot), \quad \text{Case (c)}.$$

These three cases are depicted in Figure 6.2(a), (b), and (c).

Notice that even though $\hat{\pi}$ is made up of segments of π and $\bar{\pi}$, it remains concave. Thus, the best-response function of the domestic firm with a VER, $\hat{B}(P^*)$, is continuous. In fact, it is easy to see what $\hat{B}(P^*)$ is from Figure 6.2. In Case (a), $\hat{B}(P^*) = B(P^*)$; in Case (b), $\hat{B}(P^*) = G^{-1}(P^*)$; and in Case (c), $\hat{B}(P^*) = P_S$. Also, each case is completely characterized by the slopes of π_p and $\bar{\pi}_p$ along $G(P)$. Thus in Figure 6.1, when $P^* > P_N^*$, the relevant case is (a). When $P_S^* < P^* < P_N^*$, it is (b); and when $P^* < P_S^*$, it is (c). This gives rise to the $\hat{B}(P^*)$ function depicted by the solid line in Figure 6.1.

Notice that a VER at the free-trade levels has no effect on the equilibrium when goods x and x^* are complements. Intuitively, this result can be explained as follows. Consider the effect of the VER on the demand for x at (P_N, P_N^*); $x(P, P_N^*)$ is depicted in Figure 6.3(a). Let $\bar{x}(P)$ be the demand for the domestic product on the *assumption* that the foreign firm sells the exact amount of the VER that requires that $P^* = G(P)$. Hence, $\bar{x}(P) \equiv x(P, G(P))$. Note that $\bar{x}(P)$ is also depicted in Figure 6.3(a). It intersects $x(P, P_N^*)$ at $P = P_N$. It is also steeper than $x(P, P_N^*)$ at $P = P_N$, as depicted in Figure 6.3(a). This is because

$$\bar{x}_p(P_N) = x_p(P_N, G(P_N)) + x_{p^*}(P_N, G(P_N) G'(P_N)),$$

which exceeds $x_p(P_N, P_N)$ as $x_{p^*}(\cdot) < 0$ and $G'(\cdot) < 0$.

The demand function facing the domestic firm in the presence of a VER is given by the curve *AEC* since the VER binds on the foreign firm only when $P < P_N^*$ because the goods are complements. Although the demand function for the domestic firm on the *assumption* that the foreign firm sells the amount of the VER is less elastic than the demand curve facing the domestic firm when the foreign firm's *price* is given, the VER restricts the foreign firm only when P is low. Thus, the VER makes the

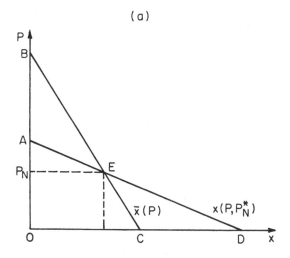

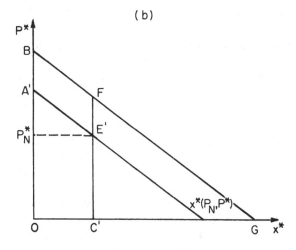

Figure 6.3

demand facing the domestic firm less elastic, but only for price levels below the competitive equilibrium price. This does not create any incentive
to raise or lower price on the part of the domestic firm – that is, no M
effect occurs.

Figure 6.3(b) depicts for $x^*(P_N, P^*)$: $\bar{x}^*$ is the demand facing the foreign firm on the assumption that the VER is binding; and $\bar{x}^*$ is just the
vertical line at the level of the VER. It intersects $x^*(P_N, P^*)$ at $P^* = P_N^*$.

The VER is binding only when $P^* < P_N^*$. Thus, the VER makes the demand curve facing the foreign firm into $A'E'C'$. Hence, the foreign firm also has no reason to change its price given P_N, and the free-trade equilibrium remains an equilibrium. Moreover, the VER does not give the domestic firm the profits of a Stackelberg leader.

This is in contrast to the effects of a VER with substitute goods. It is easy to see that if $\pi_{p^*}(\cdot) > 0$, as it is with substitute goods, $G(P^*)$ is upward sloping. However, even in this case, $\bar{\pi}_p$ remains greater than $\pi\hat{p}$ at $P = G^{-1}(P^*)$. Therefore, the three cases previously mentioned remain the only ones. However, the constraint binds for *high* values of P and not low ones. This is what creates a nonconcavity in $\hat{\pi}(\cdot)$ when goods are substitutes. This nonconcavity causes a discontinuity in the best-response function and makes the unique equilibrium a mixed-strategy one. However, since the peak of $\bar{\pi}(p)$, the profits of a Stackelberg leader, can be attained by the domestic firm by charging a high enough price, the domestic firm's profits must be at least those of a Stackelberg leader, and in equilibrium can be shown to be equal to those of a Stackelberg leader.

The details of this analysis can be found in Krishna (1983). In equilibrium, all prices and profits are shown to rise when a VER at or close to the free-trade level of imports is imposed. Some intuition for this comes from noticing that the relationship between $x(P_N, P_N^*)$ and $\bar{x}(P_N)$ with substitute goods remains the same as with complementary goods. This is because $G'(P) > 0$ and $x_{p^*}(\cdot) > 0$ so that $x_p(P_N, P_N^*) < \bar{x}_p(P_N)$, as before. However, the constraint now binds for high values of P, given P^*. Hence, the demand curve facing the domestic producer is given by BED in Figure 6.3(a) and becomes more inelastic for prices above P_N. This creates an incentive for the domestic firm to raise its price. This in turn shifts the foreign firms' demand function outward to BG in Figure 6.3(b), and makes it optimal for the foreign firm to also raise its prices to that corresponding to the point F in Figure 6.3(b). This is why all prices tend to rise, which tends to raise profits as well.

Returning to the effects of a VER with complementary goods, it is easy to verify that if best-response functions are upward sloping, exactly analogous arguments show that there is no effect of a VER at free-trade levels. In this case, $\hat{B}^*(P)$ always lies to the right of $P^* = P_N^*$, so the Nash equilibrium profits also equal the profits when the domestic firm is a Stackelberg leader.

Now consider the effects of a tariff. A tariff on imports shifts the foreign firm's best-response function outward to one such as $B^*(P, t)$ in Figure 6.1. This leads to an equilibrium at E. The line $P^* = G(P, t)$ depicts the set of prices that lead to the demand for imports being equal to their level under the tariff t. As $G(P, t)$ lies above $G(P)$, the level of imports falls. It is easy to verify, by using arguments analogous to those previously made, that if this level of imports is set as a VER, the equilibrium of the game remains at E. Thus, tariffs and VERs are equivalent with complementary goods. The only difference between them lies in the fact that no revenues are collected by the domestic government under a VER. However, tariffs and VERs are not equivalent when the goods are substitutes for one another. In this case, VERs have effects by their very presence, even when they are not set at restrictive levels.

Given that tariffs and quotas have different effects depending on whether goods are substitutes or complements, the natural question to ask is when one might expect to see lobbying in favor of VERs and by whom.

If goods are complements, a restrictive VER reduces foreign output, which reduces domestic profits. (This can be seen in Figure 6.1 as profits rise in the direction of the arrow so that domestic profits at E are lower than at A.) Intuitively, the reason is that a reduction in the availability of the foreign good reduces the willingness to pay for the domestic one because of their complementary nature. Therefore, it is unlikely that domestic firms would lobby for VERs. For the same reason, the domestic firm would not lobby for a tariff on imports. The foreign firm is also unlikely to desire VERs that are even moderately restrictive. It will not desire them if best-response functions are upward sloping. However, if best-response functions are downward sloping, *slightly* restrictive VERs would raise its profits. This is because the isoprofit contours are horizontal at A and a slight VER would move the equilibrium into the shaded area in Figure 6.1, where the foreign firm's profits rise. However, the increase in profits is likely to be marginal.

The incentives to lobby when goods are substitutes are completely different. In this case, a VER serves as a precommitment device that facilitates collusion, and all profits rise in a discrete manner when a VER at or close to free trade is imposed. Lobbying for VERs by both foreign and domestic firms is to be expected in this case. Tariffs, on the other hand, improve the competitive position of domestic firms and raise their profits, but reduce those of the foreign firm. This is because the tariff tends to raise the foreign price when goods are substitutes. This acts to raise domestic profits along the domestic best-response function – and reduce foreign profits. Here, a domestic firm will lobby for a tariff and a foreign one will oppose it – which is the usual presumption.

5 Conclusion

The results of the preceding analysis suggest that we should see efforts to lobby for VERs when substitution possibilities between products in making the services are large compared to the elasticity of demand for services – that is, when goods are substitutes in demand. We should not see such efforts when they are complements. Thus, if domestic producers made only speakers and foreign ones made only amplifiers, one would not expect to see lobbies for VERs on amplifiers. However, if both made complete systems and sold them only as a unit, one would expect to see such lobbies. Moreover, the results imply that tariffs and quotas are equivalent when goods are complements – even with oligopoly. However, they are fundamentally nonequivalent when goods are substitutes.

This analysis suggests that large price increases should be associated with the imposition of a VER with substitute goods, but not with complementary goods. This is so even when the VER is set at a level close to the free-trade one. Although a VER does give the domestic firm the profits of a Stackelberg leader when goods are substitutes, and a particular rationing rule is employed, it does not necessarily do so when they are complements. Thus, it is inappropriate to assume that a VER makes the domestic firm into a Stackelberg leader.

Finally, the profusion of models used to study the effects of VERs and the variety of results yielded by them make further work on the empirical side highly desirable.

Notes

1 See Cline (1983), p. 4.
2 See Tumlir (1985), p. 2.
3 See Tumlir (1985), p. 42.
4 In Gelman and Salop (1983), capacity choice plays the same role that a VER plays here. However, it can be prohibitively expensive for the foreign firm to constrain capacity if it sells in other markets as well. A VER then operates as a selective capacity constraint.
5 This is necessarily a brief review of the work in the area. More detailed references can be found in the papers cited.
6 Recent work by Kreps and Scheinkman (1983) also relates price and quantity competition models by showing that the Cournot outcome arises as the equilibrium of a two-stage game, where firms first choose capacities and then compete in price, given capacities.
7 See Feenstra (1984).
8 See Krishna and Itoh (1988) for a proof.
9 See Sonnenschein (1968) and Singh and Vives (1984) on the relation between Bertrand and Cournot Nash equilibrium with substitutes and complements being produced.
10 The unconvinced reader should draw a concave $\pi^*(P, P^*)$ for a given P and verify that the VER alters $\pi^*(P, P^*)$ by creating a linear segment for low P^*. The resulting kink in π^* is what makes it optimal to price at $G(P)$.

References

Aw, B. Y., and M. J. Roberts (1986) "Measuring Quality Change in Quota - Constrained Import Markets: The Case of U.S. Footwear." *Journal of International Economics,* vol. 21, no. 1/2 (August), pp. 45–60.

Bhagwati, J. N. (1965) "On the Equivalence of Tariffs and Quotas." In R. E. Baldwin et al., eds., *Trade, Growth and the Balance of Payments. Essays in Honor of Gottfried Habeler.* Chicago: Rand McNally.

Cline, W. R. (1983) "Introduction and Summary." Chap 1 in W. R. Cline, ed., *Trade Policy in the 1980s.* Washington, D.C.: Institute for International Economics; distributed by MIT Press, Cambridge, Mass., and London.

Das, S. P., and Donnenfeld, S. (1984) "Rent and Quality Seeking: The Role of Trade Policies." Photocopy.

(1985) "Trade Policy and Its Impact on Quality of Imports." Photocopy.

Davidson, C. (1984) "Cartel Stability and Tariff Policy." *Journal of International Economics,* vol. 17, pp. 219–37.

Dixit, A. (1986) "Optimal Trade and Industrial Policies for the U.S. Automobile Industry." Photocopy.

Eaton, J., and G. Grossman (1986) "Optimal Trade and Industrial Policy under Oligopoly." *Quarterly Journal of Economics,* vol. 101, issue 2 (May), pp. 383–406.

Falvey, R. (1979) "The Composition of Trade within Import Restricted Categories." *Journal of Political Economy,* vol. 87, no. 5, pp. 1105–14.

Feenstra, R. (1984) "Voluntary Export Restraint in U.S. Autos, 1980–81: Quality, Employment and Welfare Effects." In Robert Baldwin and Ann Krueger, eds., *The Structure and Evolution of Recent U.S. Trade Policy.* Chicago: University of Chicago Press.

(1985). "Quality Change under Trade Restraints: Theory and Evidence from Japanese Autos." Discussion Paper No. 298, Columbia University.

(1987) "Automobile Prices and Protection: The U.S.-Japan Trade Restraint." Chap. 15 in Dominick Salvatore, ed., *The New Protectionist Threat to World Welfare.* New York-London-Amsterdam: North Holland.

Gelman, J., and S. Salop (1983) "Judo Economics: Capacity Limitation and Coupon Competition." *Bell Journal of Economics,* vol. 14, no. 2, pp. 315–25.

Harris, R. (1985) "Why Voluntary Export Restraints Are Voluntary." *Canadian Journal of Economics,* vol. 18, no. 4 (November), pp. 799–809.

Itoh, M., and Y. Ono (1982) "Tariffs, Quotas, and Market Structure." *Quarterly Journal of Economics,* vol. 97 (May), pp. 295–305.

(1984) "Tariffs vs. Quotas under Duopoly of Heterogeneous Goods." *Journal of International Economics,* vol. 17, no. 3/4 (November), pp. 359–74.

Kreps, D., and J. Scheinkman (1983), "Quantity Precommitment and Bertrand Competition Yield Cournot Outcomes." *Bell Journal of Economics,* vol. 14 (Autumn), pp. 326–37.

Krishna, K. (1983) "Trade Restrictions as Facilitating Practices." Woodrow Wilson School, Princeton University, Discussion Paper no. 55. Also, National Bureau of Economic Research Working Paper no. 1546.

(1984) "Protection and the Product Line." National Bureau of Economic Research Working Paper no. 1537.

(1987) "Tariffs vs. Quotas with Endogenous Quality," *Journal of International Economics,* vol. 23, pp. 97–122.

Krishna, K., and M. Itoh (1988) "Content Production and Oligopolistic Interaction." *Review of Economic Studies,* vol. 55(1), no. 181 (January), pp. 107–25.

Lambson, V., and J. D. Richardson (1986) "Tacit Collusion and Voluntary Restraint Agreements in the U.S. Auto Market." Paper presented at National Bureau of Economic Research Conference on Empirical Studies of Strategic Trade Policy.

Levinsohn, J. (1987) "Empirics of Taxes on Differentiated Products: The Case of Tariffs in the U.S. Automobile Industry." University of Michigan, Discussion Paper no. 208.

Rodriguez, C. A. (1979) "The Quality of Imports and the Differential Welfare Effects of Tariffs, Quotas, and Quality Controls as Protective Devices." *Canadian Journal of Economics,* vol. 12, no. 3, pp. 439–49.

Rotemberg, J., and G. Saloner (1986) "Quotas and the Stability of Implicit Collusion." National Bureau of Economic Research Working Paper no. 1948.

Santoni, G. J., and T. N. Van Cott (1980) "Import Quotas: The Quality Adjustment Problem." *Southern Economic Journal,* vol. 46, no. 4, pp. 1206–11.

Singh, N., and X. Vives (1984) "Price and Quantity in a Differentiated Duopoly." *Rand Journal of Economics,* vol. 15, no. 4 (Winter), pp. 546–54.

Sonnenschein, H. (1968) "The Dual of Duopoly Is Complementary Monopoly or Two of Cournot's Theories Are One." *Journal of Political Economy,* vol. 76, pp. 316–18.

Tumlir, J. (1985) "Protectionism: Trade Policy in Democratic Societies." American Enterprise Institute for Public Policy Research. Washington, D.C.

CHAPTER 7

Domestic and international mergers: competition or cooperation?

RYUZO SATO and RICHARD ZECKHAUSER

1   Introduction

The recent boom in merger and acquisition activity in the United States has become a sensitive issue in the ongoing dialogue among consumers, labor, business, and government.[1] According to a recent survey, 3,064 merger transactions involving U.S. firms were completed in 1984, with a total value of more than $125 billion.[2] In 1985 there were 3,165 merger transactions with a total value of over $139 billion; interim figures for the first three quarters of 1986 suggest annualized rates of 3,337 mergers and $158 billion.[3] Some recent developments suggest that the movement may decelerate in 1987 and 1988: (1) the insider trading scandal associated with arbitrage activities surrounding mergers, (2) the increase in the tax rate on capital gains, and (3) the vast surge in stock market valuations of existing assets. As a long-run phenomenon, however, merger activity is likely to continue at a substantial pace in the future. Quite simply, as long as there are incentives to change ownership structures for corporations, mergers will be a fact of life. In addition, industry-specific developments will foster mergers in particular areas.

Ryuzo Sato is C. V. Starr Professor of Economics and director of the Center for Japan–U.S. Business and Economic Studies, Graduate School of Business Administration, New York University, and research associate of the National Bureau of Economic Research.

Richard Zeckhauser is Frank P. Ramsey Professor of Political Economy, John F. Kennedy School of Government, Harvard University, and research associate of the National Bureau of Economic Research.

Paper presented at the NYU–IUJ International Conference, "Beyond Trade Friction: U.S.–Japan Business and Economic Cooperation," September 1 and 2, 1986, Tokyo, Japan.

A major portion of this chapter is taken from the authors' joint work, "Toward a Positive Theory of Mergers," a research project supported by the Toyota Motor Company. The authors wish to express their sincere thanks to the Toyota Motor Company, especially to Mr. Tokio Horigome and Mr. Joichi Suzuki of the Research Department. The authors would also like to thank John A. Rizzo, Howard L. Frant, John D. Donahue, Jay Patel, Einkul Kim, and Robert Printz for their cooperation and participation in this project. We appreciate, in particular, the contributions of Brian Sullivan, who has permitted us to reproduce some of the empirical results in his earlier study (1984).

94   **Ryuzo Sato and Richard Zeckhauser**

Deregulation. The deregulation in banking, started by the passage of the Depository Institutions Deregulation and Monetary Control Act of 1980 and continuing under the Depository Institutions Act of 1982, will entail new consolidations (mergers). Moreover, a variety of banks that are in difficulty – notably savings and loans and banks in Texas – are likely to merge to survive. The airline industry is having a similar experience.

Maturation shakeouts. The computer industry is widely believed to be ripe for mergers.[4] After the first draft of this chapter was written, Burroughs and Sperry merged to form the computer giant Unisys. In this important industry, which is always in flux, product life spans are unprecedentedly short. Now the industry shakeout is accelerating in response to Japanese and European competition. Other emerging industries, such as biotechnology, are also likely to experience mergers as they mature and consolidate.

Rapidly changing environments. The structure of the health care industry is changing in response to major changes in the structure of payments for Medicare and Medicaid, now to be based on diagnosis related groups. As a result, merger and acquisition activity is likely to increase in this traditionally conservative field. Recently, for example, a merger was proposed between the American Hospital Supply Corporation and Hospital Corporation of America, two large players in the health care industry. (In the end, American Hospital Supply Corporation merged with Baxter Travenol Laboratories, Inc.) Besides such industry-specific mergers, other giant corporate consolidations continue apace, like General Motors' $7.6 billion purchases of Electronic Data Systems in 1984 and Hughes Aircraft in 1985. The atmosphere today is reminiscent of the merger wave of the 1960s.

The rash of recent merger activity has been closely scrutinized by the press, the Congress, labor unions, and business leaders who may be potential targets or potential bidders. The ripple effects are also felt in foreign countries, which worry about the role of newly merged American companies in the international marketplace. But what are the determinants of merger waves, if they exist? Is there a good economic rationale for this cyclical activity, or is it simply a case of "speculative mania"?[5] We propose to analyze evidence on these and other issues. We also examine the motives behind the recent flurry of international merger and acquisition activity, with specific emphasis on U.S.-Japanese mergers, acquisitions, joint ventures, and related cooperative efforts.

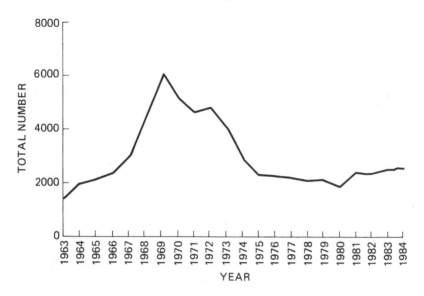

Figure 7.1

The merger wave of the 1960s prompted the development of two classes of explanations for mergers: (1) those emphasizing immediate financial gain achieved through tax code manipulation or accounting legerdemain or by remedying (or capitalizing on) market inefficiencies; and (2) "managerialist" theories positing managerial pursuit of goals other than profit maximization. Strategies consistent with the first class of theories include tax code manipulation, P/E "magic," reduction of earnings variance, and market valuation discrepancy. Examples of strategies consistent with managerialist theories are aggrandizement and risk reduction.

The current merger wave differs from its predecessors in several respects. In the typical merger of the 1960s, a small firm was acquired by a large conglomerate, whereas recent mergers – particularly those that have been the focus of attention – have occurred predominantly between large companies. Many have been hostile. Although the annual number of mergers consummated was higher in the 1960s than in recent years, the *dollar value* of recent mergers is much higher (Figures 7.1 and 7.2).

2   Two explanations of merger gains

Several studies have shown that acquirers must pay (often hefty) premiums over market prices to acquire shares in a publicly traded target firm. But how can aspiring bidders afford to pay substantial premiums if

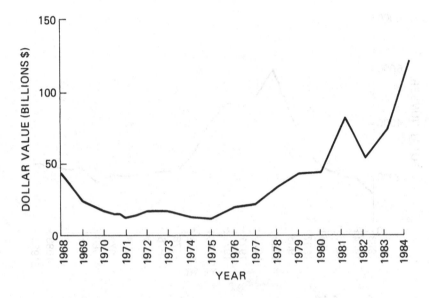

Figure 7.2

we start with the assumption that market prices reflect value? In his comprehensive survey of the scientific evidence on mergers, Jensen (1984) concludes, "knowledge of the sources of the takeover gains still eludes us."

Perhaps the new managers can simply run the firm better. Some acquirers doubtless are more diligent, more experienced, or just plain smarter than previous management. But this explanation probably does not apply to many hostile takeovers, and we need to look elsewhere for the sources of the premium prices.

We present two possible explanations for some over-the-market-price takeover bids. These explanations merely illustrate what we consider to be some important factors driving acquisitions that have not received enough attention in the past. We make no claim that these are the only possible explanations or the most important ones. Such lofty conclusions must await the availability of substantially better industry-level data. Indeed, in our empirical discussion below, we examine case studies that illustrate the great variety of motives driving acquisitions.

2.1   *Abrogating contracts*

Our first proposition is that acquirers can offer premiums because, once installed as managers, they expect to expropriate the claims of other members of the enterprise in a way that current managers could not or would not.[6] The premium represents value to be extracted from workers, suppliers, or creditors for the acquirer's own financial aggrandizement or an expectation that the acquirer will be able to manage the target's assets better.

We hypothesize that in some cases acquirers extract value from an acquired firm by breaking implicit contracts made by previous managers. The firm's traditional suppliers – who may have sunk money into capacity for serving the newly acquired firm – may be forced to accept new terms that will not cover their investment costs. Workers' tenure may be rendered less secure, or the pension fund may be subjected to more risk, thus reducing the welfare of past and prospective retirees. Prime assets may be sold, jeopardizing the future of all those associated with the firm. Clever financial maneuvers may let the new managers issue new debt, weakening the security of existing creditors in unanticipated ways. Such a pattern of expropriation could pay for the premium over market price associated with the takeover.

Most managers would balk at this kind of strategy, whether because of personal integrity or a prudent concern for reputation.[7] Moreover, once known to have pursued such a strategy, a manager would have a hard time building or maintaining an organization. But we posit that some people have not invested as much in reputation. They may be willing to break implicit contracts, particularly those made by other managers. Indeed, some of them may deliberately cultivate a reputation for toughness. We speculate that some hostile acquirers should be thought of as specialists in breaking implicit contracts. The premium they pay comes from expropriated value that is transferred to shareholders from other groups associated with the business.[8]

If such a class of organization-busting businesspeople exists – and anecdotal evidence suggests it does – what are the implications for the economy as a whole? Is it a good thing, a terrible thing, or somewhere in between? It may be useful to distinguish between "housecleaners" and "homewreckers." The distinction turns on the difference between business alliances and valid claims. An alliance exists when parties conventionally do business together but neither has any enduring stake in the other's behavior beyond habit and familiarity. Breaking the alliance may be inconvenient or uncomfortable or even costly to one of the parties, but the parties separate with all accounts squared, and neither loses unfairly from the separation. The disbanding of a rock group might be an example. A claim, on the other hand, is an account due from earlier dealings: One party is in another's debt. Breaking the relationship leaves the ledger unbalanced. (If all contracts can be formally articulated and enforced externally, of course, this is a simple matter. We are concerned about cases in which important elements of contracts must remain implicit.) An example might be the executive who allows an employer to pay his moving expenses to a new locale, where he shortly takes a position with another firm.

Some organizations surely need shaking up. Alliances may be outdated or exploitative. If current managers will not or cannot sever pernicious business ties – whether because a concern for personal reputation overrides the firm's interests, or because they prefer the comfortable status quo – an outsider can do the firm and the economy good by taking over and reconfiguring the organization's goals and commitments. This is what we mean by a "housecleaner." Housecleaners reconfigure business relationships.

On the other hand, the organization may constitute a well-working network of implicit contracts. Corporate commitments that look disadvantageous at present may merely represent the firm's side of reciprocal deals on which creditors, workers, and suppliers have already delivered. If outsiders – "homewreckers" – take control and disavow pledges made by previous managers, they can cut the firm's obligations and realize a one-time increase in value for stockholders, at the expense of other participants. Homewreckers disown valid claims.

2.2   *Firm factor disequilibrium theory*

Our second explanation for acquisition prices in excess of market prices is related to disequilibria that may arise over the course of the normal business cycle. Brian Sullivan (1984) undertook the original empirical work in support of this theory. We thank him for permission to reproduce his results here.

Traditional theories of economics assume that factors flow costlessly among firms, thereby equating marginal productivities of factors across firms. There is ample evidence that this view is oversimplified. For example, many firms finance all their expansion from internal funds, year after year. Quite obviously, they are not equilibrating their rates of return with the market rate of return on capital.

Our major hypothesis is that there are a number of impediments to the flow of factors among firms and that mergers are a valuable second-best mechanism for ameliorating the disequilibria that arise. In particular, mergers enable firms to restore an appropriate factor balance at least in part. Three classes of impediments may be identified: (1) those that result from government-imposed distortions, primarily taxes,[9] (2) those characteristic of the factors themselves, and (3) the consequences of impacted information flow. Mergers may thus be a reaction to conditions that develop from these classes of market inefficiencies; these conditions act as a spark and create the impetus to merge. Indeed, mergers can be viewed as a long-term mechanism to deal with otherwise persistent disequilibria. They speed the flow of factors to new equilibria. Although our hypothesis is couched primarily in terms of disequilibria in the allocation of capital endowments, the effect applies as well to disequilibria in labor factors, warehousing capacity, and so on – even corporate reputation. The firm factor disequilibrium theory of mergers is free-standing, and is listed as one of our five principal theories of mergers in Section 3.2. We now report some preliminary evidence for this hypothesis.

If conglomerate mergers are sought as a means of alleviating such factor imbalances, one would expect small, fast-growing firms to account for a significant amount of merger activity. Since such firms will typically be seeking factors they lack, they will be acquired by others. Thus, if the firm factor disequilibrium hypothesis of merger activity is valid, the acquired firms should be small, fast-growing entities. If mergers are prompted by other motivations or occur as a random event in the manager's decision making, one would not expect the acquired firms to be of any particular character.

A firm is defined as rapidly growing if its sales are growing faster than those of its main industry. Measuring a firm's growth against the equilibrium growth rate of its industry, instead of the economy as a whole, seemed a more accurate method of detecting conditions of disequilibrium. For example, a firm growing faster than the economy as a whole, but merely keeping up with its industry's relatively rapid growth, would appear to be obtaining an equilibrium level of capital for the industry. The base figures used in calculating these growth rates were the sales of the firm and industry three years before the merger was consummated. The change in sales over that three-year period was then divided by three to get an average growth rate of the firm and industry during the period before the merger.

The difference between these growth rates was then calculated. The null hypothesis, that the difference in the growth rate between the acquired firms and their main industries is zero, was tested against the alternative hypothesis, that the acquired firms were faster growing. In the sample of 158 conglomerate mergers,[10] the mean difference in growth rates was 0.049; that is, *on average,* the acquired firm grew 4.9 percent faster than its industry in the period preceding the mergers. This higher growth rate is statistically significant for the sample size (see Table 7.1a). (See Sullivan, 1984, for an elaboration of the sample, statistical methods, and implications of the findings in Tables 7.1.)

A second implication of the factor disequilibrium theory of mergers, under profit-maximizing assumptions, is that the acquired firm is likely

Table 7.1a. *Difference between acquired firm's growth rate and growth rate of its main industry*[a]

$X_1 = 0.049$
Standard deviation $= 0.294$
t statistic $= 2.11$
$X_1 =$ Average difference between acquired firm's growth rate and growth rate of its main industry

---

[a] $n = 158$.

Table 7.1b. *Difference between acquiring and acquired firm profitability*[a]

$X_2 = 0.004$
Standard deviation $= 0.176$
t statistic $= 0.411$
$X_2 =$ Difference between return/net equity of acquired firm and its acquirer

---

[a] $n = 158$.

Table 7.1c. *Acquired firm's change in market share three years after merger*[a]

$X_3 = 0.67$
Standard deviation $= 1.48$
t statistic $= 2.062$
$X_3 =$ Percentage change in market share of acquired firm first three years after merger

---

[a] $n = 21$.

to be more profitable than the acquiring firm. Evidence of high profitability in acquired firms would suggest that acquirers use mergers to shift their assets to higher-yielding uses, which would support our hypothesis.

To examine this issue, we employed net income and shareholders' equity figures from *Moody's Industrials* for the two years before the merger. Each year's return on shareholder's equity was calculated, and these figures were then averaged. Our factor disequilibrium hypothesis suggests that the acquiring firm should undertake a merger when it believes it can reap a higher return at the margin by investing its capital in the acquired firm than in its own traditional activities. Unfortunately, information on marginal returns is not normally tabulated. As a proxy, we employed the average rates of return on stockholder equity for the two years before the merger. The difference between acquired and acquirer rates of return was then examined. The observed mean difference between the rates of return was 0.4 percent; although not statistically significant, this difference runs in the predicted direction (see Table 7.1b). This is consistent with the findings of several studies completed in the early 1970s (Mueller, 1977). Unlike those studies, this analysis did not isolate its sample according to the type of acquiring firm; furthermore, it is examining a different hypothesis.

Given the inability of past empirical tests to identify substantial inefficiencies or efficiencies as a result of mergers, we cannot expect indirect profit measures to provide strong evidence about factor reallocations within the merged firm. A more revealing test would be to look directly at the intrafirm behavior of the merged companies to see whether, in fact, they reallocated factors between themselves.

Pure conglomerate mergers present a unique opportunity, however, because the markets of the two merging firms do not overlap. One can trace the sales performance of the acquired firm after the merger simply by observing the acquirer's level of sales in its newly entered market. This provides a proxy for the overall performance (or at least the scale) of the acquired firm after the merger. The acquired firm's sales performance is thus a useful available indicator of whether it experienced an influx of factors after the merger. If the acquired firm continues to grow rapidly, one can infer that it is functioning as a capital sink for its acquirer, which is presumably expanding its operations, and hence using capital. Had the small firm been able to generate enough funds internally for expansion, it would have been less likely to sell in the first place. An equivalent argument would apply for other surplus factors in the acquirer as a motivation for merger.

To test whether the acquired firms continued to grow rapidly (i.e., faster than the industry, according to our previous definition), one needs data on the sales of the acquiring firm in the newly entered market. Such information is usually compiled in the form of market share statistics, indicating each firm's contribution to total industry output. Few industries release such information, however. Fortunately, a private firm that collects market share information and sells it to interested parties was willing to provide some data for this study to Sullivan over the period of 1972–7.

The investigation showed that the average market share of the acquired firms was 4.59 percent before the merger and increased to 5.26 percent three years after the merger, a mean change of 0.67 percentage points.

On average, that is, the acquired firm increased its market share two-thirds of one percent, consistent with our hypothesis. The fact that the acquired firms were small initially, and hence had small market shares in their main industry, explains the small absolute share change that was detected. As a fraction of initial market share, the increase was more than one-seventh, which is fairly dramatic for a three-year period. Although one cannot attach too much significance to the finding because of the small size of the sample, it does lend some support to the hypothesis that the acquired and acquiring firms use each other to balance their factor endowments (see Table 7.1c).

3   Empirical evidence

3.1   *Current merger trends*

The current merger wave, the fourth since the late 1890s, began in 1974. The previous merger waves occurred from 1896 to 1904, when monopolies like U.S. Steel and Standard Oil were formed in reaction to the Sherman Act, which outlawed trusts but not monopolies; from 1919 to 1929, when companies like General Motors, Swift, and Pullman bought up suppliers and expanded horizontally; and from 1960 to 1969, when conglomerates used their overpriced stock to buy other companies and manipulate their earnings.

Two large mergers effected in 1974 were portents of things to come. Mobil made what was essentially a $1.6 billion hostile takeover of Montgomery Ward, and the International Nickel Company, with the aid of the investment banking firm of Morgan Stanley, won a bitter takeover battle for ESB, Inc.

From this time on, established companies would use the surprise takeover tactics of the conglomerate upstarts and the advantage of greater resources to outbid other firms. The day of gentlemanly, friendly mergers for America's business establishments and cooperative investment banking activity had passed.

Larger and larger firms have been involved in contested takeovers (Table 7.2). The number of megamergers has risen from a handful in 1974 and 1975 to 40 in 1976, 80 in 1978, and 200 in 1984. Similarly, the total assets acquired have increased dramatically during these years.

Table 7.3 shows the increasing value of assets acquired through these mergers, using W. T. Grimm & Co.'s $100 million merger series as a guide.

The steady rise in the number of large mergers came at a time of vacillating stock market averages. Indeed, the depressed stock market seems to have abetted the large takeovers. Grimm's figures show that these firms

Table 7.2. *Largest contested takeover*

Year	Buyer	Seller	$ Value
1975	United Technologies	Otis Elevator	398 million
1977	McDermott	Bobcock & Wilcox	748 million
1981	Elf Aquitaine	Texasgulf	4.3 billion
1981	Du Pont	Conoco	8.0 billion
1984	Texaco	Getty Oil	10.1 billion
1984	Chevron	Gulf Oil	13.2 billion

Table 7.3. *Total dollar value of mergers, 1974–84*

Year	Assets acquired (in billion of dollars)
1974	12.5
1975	11.8
1976	20.0
1977	21.9
1978	34.2
1979	43.5
1980	44.3
1981	82.6
1982	53.8
1983	73.1
1984	122.0

Source: W. T. Grimm & Co., *Mergerstat Review* (1984).

used their ample reserves of cash, whereas conglomerateurs (Gulf and Western, ITT, Textron) had to depend on stock swaps.

3.2   *A taxonomy of mergers by motives*

In addition to the merger theories advanced in the 1960s (i.e., immediate financial gains theories, managerialist theories) and the more recent theories (i.e., abrogating contracts and firm factor disequilibrium theory), two other explanations for mergers have often been advanced: Mergers may be intended (1) to avoid competition or (2) to take advantage of scale

Table 7.4. *Management motives for merger: relationship to theories*

Immediate financial gains
 1. Diversify to reduce the risks of business
 2. Use tax loopholes not available without merging
 3. Reap promotional or speculative gains attendant on new security issues or changed price-earnings ratios
 4. Exploit a potential capital gain by acquiring an undervalued company and liquidating it

Managerialist
 5. Displace an existing management
 6. Create a personal image as an aggressive manager
 7. Manage a larger empire of subordinates
 8. Thwart a (possible) takeover attempt

Firm factor disequilibrium
 9. Overcome critical lacks in acquiring company by buying the necessary complementary resources
10. Make better use of particular resources or personnel controlled by the firm, especially managerial skills
11. Achieve sufficient size to have efficient access to capital markets
12. Q-ratio theory, i.e., purchasing desired assets for less than what they would cost if purchased apart from the firm

Market power
13. Limit competition or achieve monopoly profits
14. Exploit unused market power

Growth and scale economy
15. Grow through acquisition
16. Achieve a large enough size to realize an economical scale of production and/or advertising

economies. We may refer to these explanations as the market power and scale economy theories of mergers.

To assess the relative merit of these theories, we examined companies' public statements about merger activity between 1983 and 1985. Our primary sources of data were the *Wall Street Journal,* the *New York Times,* the *Boston Globe, Business Week, Fortune,* and *Forbes.*

Management has provided a plethora of specific motives for mergers, as shown in Table 7.4. To the extent possible, these specific motives have each been assigned to one of the merger theories discussed above. We have not included abrogating contracts in this categorization for two reasons: It is often difficult to determine how extensive contract breaking may be (particularly since managements rarely specify this goal), and it usually accompanies other merger motives. Thus we have five categories of merger theories.

It is a regrettable fact of empirical research that actual data seldom correspond perfectly to our hypotheses. Yet, of the 16 merger motives specified by management, only one, the desire to "grow through acquisition," is too broad to ascribe to any one of the five theories. The desire for growth could be driven either by a desire to realize scale economies, or to increase market power, or to lower earnings variance, and so on. (For tidiness, we have lumped growth and scale economies together.)

We studied 79 cases of large mergers ($400 million or more) consummated in the United States during this period. Seven of those cases were leveraged buyouts by investment banking firms like Kohlberg, Kravis, Roberts & Co. Their motives were well described by the *Wall Street Journal* (August 12, 1985):

> More often, the motive is the same as that of the takeover raiders, such as T. Boone Pickens Jr. and Carl Icahn: seeking to capitalize on companies whose stock prices are far below the value of their assets. By going private, companies frequently have more flexibility to realize fuller values by selling assets or by redeploying them more profitably.

Our findings about the other 72 cases are summarized in Table 7.5. First, although no one specific motive dominates the scene, two are clearly quite important – the search for economies of scale and the search for growth. Given the relaxed interpretation of antitrust policy under the Reagan administration, this finding comes as no surprise. Market extension (or product extension) mergers have rarely been opposed by the Federal Trade Commission in recent years. These types of mergers may make newly created companies more efficient through economies of scale and/or complementarities in the organizations' capabilities. Moreover, vertical integration, which is expected to be approved easily, may achieve more efficient coordination of the different levels and consequently improve competitiveness.

These kinds of efficiencies may be very attractive to managers, particularly when their markets are overcrowded and/or demand for their products has matured. In addition, a company that foresees sluggish growth in its own industry may try to grow through acquisition. That route to growth is seen as particularly attractive in managers' conventional wisdom, which holds that acquisitions achieve growth "more rapidly" and that mergers avoid risks associated with internal expansion.

Recent developments in several industries may have reinforced these beliefs:

> "Ten years ago, $5 million to $20 million could establish a brand. Today you are talking about a $50 million to $100 million annual investment.

> Only about 3 of every 10 new products achieve even minimal success. The number that become household names is minuscule. That's why buying a well-known

Table 7.5. *Occurrence of recent mergers by motives*

Motivation	Number of cases	Percentage of total
Immediate financial gains		
1. Diversify	6.5	9.0
2. Tax loopholes	1.0	1.4
3. P/E magic	0.0	0.0
4. Capital gain	3.0	4.2
	10.5	14.6
Managerialist		
5. Displace management	0.0	0.0
6. Personal image	2.0	2.9
7. Empire building	3.5	4.8
8. Thwart takeover	3.5	4.8
	9.0	12.5
Factor disequilibrium		
9. Acquire complements	5.5	7.6
10. Redeploy resources	4.0	5.6
11. Access to capital	0.0	0.0
12. Q ratio	6.5	9.0
	16.0	22.2
Market competition		
13. Limit competition	0.5	0.7
14. Exploit market power	0.0	0.0
	0.5	0.7
Growth and scale economy		
15. Growth	19.5	27.1
16. Achieve economic scale	16.5	22.9
	36.0	50.0

brand can be a shortcut to above-average profitability," asserts Marc C. Parti-
celli, vice-president at Booz, Allen & Hamilton Inc. (*Business Week,* October 21,
1985)

Growth through acquisition also offers a means of increasing market
power. Fewer than 1 percent of the firms in our sample explicitly cited a
desire to increase market power as the reason for their merger, but even
in this age of relaxed antitrust policy, they have substantial reason to dis-
guise such a motivation. Many of the firms citing growth as the major

reason for their merger (27.1 percent of our sample) may have been interested primarily in growth in market power.

Another factor that makes it hard to judge the importance of the market power motivation is that our data set lumps together conglomerate mergers with intraindustry mergers. Market power cannot be a factor driving a conglomerate merger (except perhaps vertical mergers).[11] The presence of such mergers in our data set diminishes the relative importance of market power. As a practical matter, our sample includes too few intraindustry mergers to draw even tentative conclusions from those cases alone.

Factor market disequilibrium theory explains a substantial portion of the mergers in our data set (22.2 percent). Since our study deals with only large mergers, it excludes some of the most typical situations in which this theory applies (namely, acquisition of a small firm by a large firm). Hence factor market disequilibrium theory may explain a larger proportion of overall merger activity than our data suggest.

Our study indicates that corporate raiders play an important role in the current merger wave. In fact, 2.9 percent of the managers cited a desire to create a good image of themselves as aggressive managers as a determining factor behind the merger. This may be considered the direct effect of corporate raiders on mergers. But there are often indirect effects, as in the case of a firm merging with a third party to avoid a takeover by corporate raiders. This factor accounts for 4.8 percent of the mergers in our sample. Thus, corporate raiders were directly or indirectly responsible for 7.7 percent of the mergers in our sample.

4   International mergers and joint ventures

In the years 1983 to 1985, according to *Mergers and Acquisitions,* over 300 foreign firms made acquisitions in the United States and over 250 U.S. companies made acquisitions abroad. U.S. companies involved in foreign acquisitions typically were dealing with firms from Canada and the United Kingdom. Historically, trading relationships between these nations and the United States have been strong, because of geographic proximity, a common language, and similar business practices. In recent years, however, activity between the United States and Japan has increased substantially (see Appendixes 7.1 and 7.2).

We analyze this flurry of international merger and acquisition activity with specific emphasis on joint U.S.–Japan mergers, acquisitions, and ventures. In evaluating the theory of international mergers, we focus on the previously described theories of merger activity, but pay due attention to important differences in the culture and business practices of Japan and the United States as these affect mergers between the two countries.

4.1   *Openness of markets*

The U.S. market has fewer barriers to entry for foreign investors than do most other countries in the world. The free-market policies of President Reagan have facilitated entry by foreign firms, and the leniency of U.S. antitrust policies has enabled foreign multinationals to enter in increasingly large numbers without fear of regulatory intervention.

Similarly, in Japan basic standards for assessing mergers are expressed in simple legislative terms and are subject to parallel judicial and administrative review. The primary concern in Japan, as in the United States, is continued competitiveness and the possible impact of the merger on market power (by affecting market structure and the performance of an industry). From a strict legal perspective, both countries provide liberal access to their markets. However, cultural barriers and the lack of a sound understanding of Japanese business practices have, without doubt, strongly inhibited many American companies seeking to make acquisitions in Japan.

4.2   *Access to markets*

The United States, with its population of over 240 million, and Japan, with its population of over 130 million, constitute the two largest markets in the noncommunist world. Thus the strategic rationale behind foreign direct investment in either country, whether through an acquisition, joint venture, or wholly owned subsidiary, centers on access to these lucrative markets. Behind every corporation's announcement of a venture in the United States or Japan is the thought of increased sales and revenues of a magnitude that it could not realize in any other single nation.

Japanese companies coming to America have received a great deal of publicity, but American firms have also gained access to the Japanese market. For instance, in April 1986 Lotus Development Corporation opened a wholly owned subsidiary in Tokyo in order to capitalize on the vast Japanese market. (Its 1-2-3 program is the leading business software product in Japan.) Stratus Computer Inc. is forging a link with C. Itoh Data Systems in an effort to market its products more effectively in Japan. With the recent liberalization of the Japanese financial markets, Manufacturers Hanover Trust has established a wholly owned investment advisory subsidiary in Japan. It is the first foreign bank to enter Japan's trust market and to incorporate a wholly owned investment advisory company. *Japan Economic Journal* (March 16, 1986) quoted the chairman of Citicorp as saying that his institution was "very interested in acquiring a medium-sized Japanese bank in order to strengthen its consumer business in Japan. The second biggest market in the noncommunist world is Citibank's number one strategic goal." Most recently, a number of Japanese localities have even been courting American institutions of higher learning to open up branch campuses in Japan.

Although access to markets is the primary motive for foreign investment, there are also reinforcing factors. The rapid increase of major Japanese corporations' direct investment in the United States stems in part from the lighter tax burden there, a factor likely to be reinforced by the U.S. tax reform and its lower corporate rates. In essence, tax benefits supplement the decision to seek access to a new market, as companies considering investment abroad are influenced by tax incentives in their decision on location.

Sharp Corp. and RCA recently located a joint venture in microelectronics in Washington to benefit from that state's special tax treatment legislation. In addition, Meiji Seika set up a joint venture with D. E. Stauffer Biscuit Co. Inc. in Pennsylvania because they got preferential tax treatment and a well-established brand name. (Meiji is the first Japanese confectioner to come to America.)

4.3   *Strategic motives*

Protectionism: The threat of protectionism plays an integral role not only in determining foreign direct investment, but also in motivating international mergers and acquisitions. Protectionism is a short-run measure to prevent the restructuring and product cycle development that would be induced by free trade. In the United States, the recent support for protectionism in uncompetitive industries has been substantial, most notably in the automotive industry. For years now, Japan has voluntarily restrained its automobile exports to the United States, and the result has been higher automobile prices and increased profits to all sellers in the U.S. market.

Technological development: Another motivation for international cooperation derives from complementary technological capabilities in two nations. In hundreds of cases, Japanese and American companies have established long-term ties for the purpose of mutual technological development: "Globalization by Japanese firms means that they are departing from Japan-based internationalization to a more diversified, multi-faceted international corporate strategy. Efforts are designed to build up research and development links with foreign research organizations" (*Japan Economic Journal,* March 1, 1986).

Table 7.6. *Cases of U.S.–Japan industrial cooperation (1984)*

	Joint development, technology exchange	Direct investment	Total
High-tech	113	43	156
Semiconductors and IC related	(17)	(13)	(30)
Computer related	(21)	(9)	(30)
Biotechnology and chemical related	(20)	(3)	(23)
Communications and information related	(15)	(4)	(19)
New materials	(3)	(3)	(6)
Industrial robots	(6)	(1)	(7)
Miscellaneous	(31)	(10)	(41)
	7	5	12
Machinery	19	9	28
	16	23	39
Iron and steel	12	3	15
Chemicals	13	8	21
Textile	6	2	8
Food	5	7	12
Other manufacturing	7	6	13
Finance	13	6	19
Real estate	6	8	14
Miscellaneous	26	27	53
Total	243	147	390

International cooperation is becoming indispensable for Japanese and American firms in the high-tech age. These relationships typically do not involve an acquisition of one firm by another. Rather, they may be viewed as a joining together of the firms' marketing and technological skills to pursue goals in a particular area.

The joint venture between Toyota and General Motors is a good example. A complementary factor input disequilibrium allows GM to capitalize on Toyota's superiority in small car production, and Toyota benefits from GM's vast marketing network in the United States. (See Appendix 7.3 for a summary of automotive industry cooperation in 1984.)

There were at least 390 cases of U.S.–Japan industrial cooperation in 1984 (Table 7.6). Most of the cooperative activity was in the high-tech area. At present, companies in both countries are pursuing a goal of mutual benefit and knowledge building, recognizing that they can progress more quickly by exchanging ideas, personnel, information, and capabilities than by working alone. Cooperative efforts involving companies with vast and sophisticated resources, including Toyota–GM, Mitsubishi–AT&T, and NEC–Honeywell, exemplify commitments to innovate together.

Follow the leader: As major Japanese manufacturers have entered the U.S. market to avoid protection and to develop new technologies, their competitors and smaller companies have followed. Competitors among Japanese firms seem to be governed by a sort of "follow-the-leader" principle. If a major producer in a particular industry enters a foreign market, rival firms follow suit to maintain the competitive status quo. Failure to contest the leader's access to a foreign market might give this producer an outlet for growth that would make it a more formidable opponent in domestic markets. Thus foreign investment by industry tends to occur in clusters. The major Japanese automotive producers all established footholds in America within months of the first instance of foreign investment. Similarly, once a major electronics manufacturer entered the U.S. market directly, the other majors were quick to follow.

Other companies have essentially followed their customers overseas. When a large multinational enters foreign markets without an established supplier base, its smaller parts suppliers have a rare opportunity to expand internationally with little business risk.

4.4 *Some motivations for domestic merger are not applicable to international mergers*

Conglomerate mergers and the price-earnings game are not significant factors in the international setting for mergers. Companies expanding abroad are often reacting to shrinking opportunities for growth and/or profit in their own country, or at least to relatively greater opportunities abroad. They are usually more interested in diversifying geographically rather than by product. Within Japan and the United States, the number of conglomerate mergers rose throughout the 1970s. In Japan, conglomerate mergers represented 44.1 percent of the total in 1970 and 49.4 percent in 1979. In the United States, comparable statistics show an increase from 78.1 percent (1967–78) to 89.7 percent (1979) (Organization for Economic Co-operation and Development, various publications). None of the *intercountry* mergers studied, however, was motivated by a desire for product diversification or other activities to help broaden a conglomerate.

Neither is there any evidence that international takeovers were attempts to take advantage of price-earnings discrepancies. The average price-earnings ratio for foreign/U.S. acquisitions was almost identical to that of domestic acquisitions from 1976 to 1984. Thus, foreign purchasers appear to be paying prices comparable to domestic price levels.

Similarly, the recent emergence of corporate raiders has had apparently little effect on international merger activity, at least not between Japan and the United States.[12] Entering a foreign market with the full cooperation of a merger partner is difficult enough without having to deal with the complexities of a hostile takeover bid. Furthermore, corporate raiders find it difficult to gain information on foreign companies and establish an atmosphere conducive to an international takeover.

Japanese society regards hostile takeovers as unacceptable, although the first glimmerings of such activity are now being seen there. In fact, the merger of Japanese firms with foreign companies is socially acceptable only when the Japanese firm is in deep financial trouble. Faced with strong competition at home from larger Japanese companies, many troubled small and medium-sized companies simply cannot maintain their market share or profits and are forced either to merge with a larger Japanese company or to unite with a foreign firm. Frequently such firms choose the latter alternative, as did Isuzu when it teamed up with General Motors.

In America, because there are many receptive merger prospects and because many Japanese firms can offer an advantage in management, technology, or access to capital, Japanese companies have not had to resort to the hostile takeover tactic, which in any case would be contrary to Japanese tradition. As more Japanese companies become accustomed to the U.S. market, this pattern could change.

4.5   Predictions

The role of corporate raiders, the price-earnings game, and the formation of diversified conglomerates are likely to become important factors in future international merger activity within the United States. Ivan Boesky, one of the foremost practitioners of risk arbitrage in the United States as it relates to mergers, before he was indicted for insider trading activities, discussed the role of corporate raiders in international transactions.

With all the corporate restructurings and all the mergers and acquisitions, which I predict will come at a much faster and greater rate than ever before over the next five years, there will be little pieces of paper [stock] floating around with differentials. And so we believe that we will have more to do than ever before as arbitrageurs, trying to take advantage of these humble $2 bills [opportunities]. (*Mergers and Acquisitions*, March/April 1986)

As inefficiencies within the domestic market become more difficult to find, these arbitrageurs will try to take advantage of international market inefficiencies; as a result, playing the price-earnings game and initiating hostile takeover bids will become more important.

Concurrently, it appears that international conglomerate diversification will inevitably become a relevant force. On February 15, 1986, it was announced that Hitachi and General Motors will set up joint research and development production projects in five high-tech areas: automobile parts, electronics parts and semiconductors, computers, optical fibers, and factory automation. Efforts such as this one may be facilitated by joint ventures, the creation of new jointly owned companies, or other cooperative agreements that need not entail mergers.

Diversification efforts by the automotive industry reflect U.S. automakers' realization that their competitiveness and market share are in decline. In recent years, cost advantage in automobile production has shifted from the United States to Japan and now perhaps to Korea. This kind of progression can be observed in industries from textiles to semiconductors. Technologically sophisticated countries (the United States, Japan, West Germany, etc.) will continue to concentrate on capital-intensive, high-tech, innovative products. Countries such as Korea and Taiwan will move from light manufacturing toward heavy manufacturing. Less developed nations will concentrate on labor-intensive activities and light manufacturing. Although this evolution has not yet eliminated midtechnology U.S. production (as classical Ricardian theory and product cycle theory would dictate), it has provided the impetus for U.S. manufacturers to work with the Japanese, and now the Koreans, cooperatively. The automobile industry illustrates the need for major U.S. firms to diversify into other growth areas.

Diversification, accessibility to markets, technological advancement, and minimization of corporate tax burdens will all be important motivations for international mergers and acquisitions. The impact of protectionism on merger and acquisition decisions, although critically important today, should decline if Japan opens its markets sufficiently. As Japanese markets open, we hope U.S. protectionist threats will subside, and a step will be taken toward a freer market environment.

International mergers and other cooperative relationships between U.S. and Japanese firms seem inevitable, given the often complementary capabilities of firms in the two countries. Indeed, if access to and understanding of the markets and production methods are viewed as factor endowments within the firm, this prediction follows from our firm factor disequilibrium theory of mergers. This theory suggests that major industrial companies in Japan and the United States will take the lead in initiating the globalization approach to production and marketing. This form of internationalization can strengthen Japanese–American relations and provide each nation with continued economic growth and success.

Appendix 7.1. *Foreign sellers, dollar total by country, 1980–4*

Country of seller	Total dollar value (base[a])				
	1980	1981	1982	1983	1984
Canada	2,493.0 (5)	155.2 (2)	89.3 (9)	398.6 (11)	1,191.0 (14)
Great Britain	1,224.4 (15)	552.2 (15)	367.6 (11)	656.5 (16)	554.8 (16)
Australia	3.8 (1)	–	–	–	339.6 (3)
Hong Kong	–	–	8.3 (1)	–	180.8 (3)
West Germany	–	61.7 (4)	13.2 (3)	6.7 (1)	120.4 (2)
France	35.0 (1)	9.3 (3)	43.0 (1)	–	110.1 (4)
Brazil	–	–	–	–	20.0 (1)
Switzerland	–	–	178.0 (3)	565.4 (3)	18.7 (2)
Japan	–	–	–	313.5 (1)	7.0 (1)
Sweden	–	2.5 (1)	–	–	4.9 (1)
Denmark	–	–	–	–	2.7 (1)
Argentina	–	145.0 (1)	–	–	–
Finland	–	–	–	3.0 (1)	–
Italy	–	17.5 (2)	55.0 (1)	288.2 (2)	–
Mexico	11.5 (1)	95.0 (2)	–	6.5 (1)	–
Netherlands	–	26.0 (2)	–	180.2 (3)	–
New Zealand	–	5.6 (1)	–	–	–
Nigeria	3.5 (1)	–	–	–	–
Peru	4.5 (1)	–	–	–	–
Puerto Rico	–	3.0 (1)	2.2 (1)	55.0 (1)	–
Spain	4.0 (1)	–	–	17.2 (1)	–
Zimbabwe	–	–	13.5 (1)	–	–
Total	3,779.7 (26)	1,073.0 (34)	770.1 (31)	2,490.8 (41)	2,550.0 (48)

[a] Base: The number of transactions disclosing a purchase price.
Source: W. T. Grimm & Co.

Appendix 7.2. *Foreign buyers, dollar total by country, 1980–4*

Country of buyer	Total dollar value (base[a])									
	1980		1981		1982		1983		1984	
Netherlands	197.9	(4)	230.3	(3)	90.1	(3)	48.8	(3)	5,605.4	(2)
Switzerland	254.7	(3)	113.3	(3)	557.9	(3)	107.7	(3)	2,904.6	(3)
Great Britain	2,618.6	(40)	1,458.5	(51)	1,780.3	(33)	1,119.5	(23)	2,754.1	(31)
Canada	2,356.8	(31)	8,193.1	(34)	1,299.2	(19)	1,309.9	(16)	1,266.6	(19)
Australia	34.3	(2)	615.3	(3)		–	2,468.4	(3)	626.3	(4)
Japan	311.5	(6)	122.2	(7)	237.0	(2)	688.7	(4)	430.4	(3)
Kuwait	40.0	(1)	2,486.1	(1)	150.0	(1)		–	340.0	(1)
France	519.2	(9)	4,804.5	(7)	224.5	(3)	15.0	(1)	236.8	(4)
West Germany	240.8	(5)	400.6	(6)	9.3	(2)	44.0	(1)	214.5	(2)
Trinidad		–		–		–		–	175.0	(1)
Sweden	17.4	(2)	138.9	(3)	118.8	(3)	8.3	(1)	137.6	(4)
Denmark		–		–		–		–	113.0	(1)
Malaysia		–		–		–		–	71.0	(1)
Bahrain		–		–		–		–	70.0	(1)
Belgium		–		–		–		–	46.0	(2)
Norway	260.0	(1)		–		–		–	45.0	(1)
New Zealand		–		–	242.0	(1)		–	36.0	(1)
Bahamas		–		–		–		–	24.8	(1)
Greece		–		–		–		–	23.0	(1)
Israel		–	50.0	(1)		–	10.0	(1)	8.0	(1)
Finland	4.7	(1)		–		–		–	3.7	(1)
Argentina		–	11.2	(1)		–		–		–
Bermuda		–		–		–	39.7	(1)		–
Brazil		–		–	5.6	(1)		–		–
Colombia		–		–	50.0	(1)		–		–
Hong Kong	21.8	(2)		–	160.6	(3)		–		–
Italy		–	103.1	(2)	4.5	(1)	56.1	(1)		–
Mexico		–		–	11.8	(1)		–		–
Philippines		–	14.7	(1)		–		–		–
Puerto Rico		–		–		–	11.4	(1)		–
Saudi Arabia		–	12.4	(2)		–		–		–
South Korea		–		–	60.0	(1)		–		–
Spain	5.5	(1)		–	64.3	(2)		–		–
Undisclosed	204.1	(2)	24.0	(1)	40.0	(1)		–		–
Total	7,087.3	(110)	18,778.2	(126)	5,105.9	(81)	5,927.5	(59)	15,131.8	(85)

[a] Base: The number of transactions disclosing a purchase price.
Source: W. T. Grimm & Co.

Appendix 7.3. *Joint development and technology exchange with respect to automobiles*

Japanese company	American company	Line of business	Date	Outline
Mitsubishi	Chrysler	Compact cars	January 1984	Joint venture: Presently under study for manufacture from about 1986 in the United States (January 28, A et al.).
Jidosha Kiki	Bendix	Brake doubling device for compact cars	January 1984	Technology transfer: Agreement on supply of manufacturing technology was announced on the 23d, based on which Bendix is to apply the technology for producing toggle systems primarily for "Japanese cars made in the United States" (January 24, A).
Toyota	General Motors (GM)	Compact passenger cars	February 1984	Joint venture: Both companies announced that they established a joint venture, "New United Motor Manufacturing Inc." on February 23. FTC permission has already been obtained. Final approval in April. (March 3, A et al.)
Yamaha	Ford Motor	Automobiles in general	March 1984	Business affiliation: Agreement extending over a wide range from supply of engine parts to joint development of compact cars. Provisional agreement was reached but difficulties were subsequently encountered. (March 1, A evening)
Nippon Denso	New United Motor Manufacturers	Parts for compact cars	April 1984	Technical cooperation: In view of the Toyota–GM joint venture setup, this technical agreement clarifies Nippon Denso's policy to comply wherever possible with technical cooperation requests placed by GM-line local parts manufacturers. (April 18, A.)

Notes

1 We use the term "merger" to encompass several types of takeovers of publicly traded firms. These include mergers (where the top management and board of directors have approved the bid), tender offers (where the bidder directly approaches the shareholders), proxy contests, and leveraged buyouts by private investment groups.

2 Only mergers in which more than $1 million is paid are counted. Obviously many mergers at the bottom end of this range are missed. Source: *Mergers and Acquisitions,* 1986, 1987.

3 Source: *Mergers and Acquisitions,* 1986, 1987.

4 "Computer Industry Called Ripe for Mergers," *Wall Street Journal,* June 19, 1985.

5 Keynes believed that the major gyrations in the stock market were driven by waves of pessimism and optimism, and had little to do with market asset fundamentals. In this view, a reasonable case can be made for government interference to dampen such cycles.

6 We thank Jack Donahue for his helpful contributions to this discussion.

7 Fama (1980) offers an extensive discussion of the role of reputation in managerial labor markets. Reputation considerations are important in alleviating the agency problem that arises with absentee ownership in modern corporations. Also see Pratt and Zeckhauser (1985).

8 An immediate candidate group for expropriation is the bondholders. However, preliminary studies reported by Schipper and Thompson (1983) do not find any evidence of bondholder expropriation in mergers.

9 There has been much discussion of tax incentives to merge – for example, to use tax loss carry-forwards or investment tax credits of another firm. Proposals have been made to limit the tax deductibility of interest paid on "junk" (high-risk) bonds used to finance purchases of firms. Today there is a great deal of speculation as to how the new tax bill, with higher capital gains taxes and lower corporate tax rates, will substantially affect merger activity.

10 Conglomerate mergers were used to test the firm factor disequilibrium theory because intraindustry mergers might be motivated by distinctive considerations (e.g., a large acquirer might merge with a small upstart to maintain a monopoly position). Financial information was available for only 158 of the 337 pure conglomerate mergers that took place in the 1967–77 period. Information was usually available for the acquiring firms, since they tended to be much larger and hence publicly traded. Many more of the acquired firms were privately held, and so information was available for fewer of them. Note that this was a different data set from the one used in the case study analyses discussed here.

11 Some radical critics suggest that large companies garner disproportionate political power, which ultimately results in market power. We know of no studies that document this assertion.

12 International mergers associated with Rupert Murdoch (Australia) and Sir James Goldsmith (England) do illustrate raiding on the international level.

118   Ryuzo Sato and Richard Zeckhauser

References

Amihud, Yakov, and Baruch Lev (1981) "Risk Reduction as a Managerial Motive for Conglomerate Mergers." *Bell Journal of Economics,* vol. 1 (Autumn), pp. 605–16.

Archer, S. H., and L. G. Faerber (1966) "Firm Size and the Cost of Externally Serviced Capital." *Journal of Finance,* vol. 21 (March), pp. 69–83.

Asquith, P. (1983) "Merger Bids, Uncertainty, and Stockholder Returns." *Journal of Financial Economics,* vol. 11, pp. 51–83.

Asquith, P., and H. Kim (1981) "The Impact of Merger Bids on the Welfare of the Participating Firm's Securityholders." Working Paper, Harvard Business School.

Asquith, P., R. Bruner, and D. Mullins, Jr. (1983) "The Gains to Bidding Firms from Merger." *Journal of Financial Economics,* vol. 11, pp. 121–39.

Azzi, Corry (1978) "Conglomerate Mergers, Default Risk and Homemade Mutual Funds." *American Economic Review* (March), pp. 161–72.

Dodd, P. (1980) "Merger Proposals, Management Discretion and Stockholder Wealth." *Journal of Financial Economics,* 8, pp. 105–38.

Fama, E. (1980) "Agency Problems and the Theory of the Firm." *Journal of Political Economy,* 88, pp. 288–307.

Gort, Michael (1969) "An Economic Disturbance Theory of Mergers." *Quarterly Journal of Economics,* 83, pp. 624–42.

Grabowski, Henry, and Dennis Mueller (1972) "Managerial and Stockholder Welfare Models of Firm Expenditures." *Review of Economics and Statistics,* 53 (February), pp. 9–24.

Grimm, W. T., & Co. (1984) *Mergerstat Review.*

Jensen, M. (1984) "Takeovers: Folklore and Science." *Harvard Business Review* (November–December), pp. 109–21.

Langetieg, T. (1978) "An Application of the Three-Factor Performance Index to Measure Stockholders' Gains from Mergers." *Journal of Financial Economics,* 6, pp. 365–84.

Levy, Haim, and Marshall Sarnat (1970) "Diversification, Portfolio Analysis and the Uneasy Case for Conglomerate Mergers." *Journal of Finance,* 25, pp. 795–802.

Lintner, John (1971) "Expectations, Mergers and Equilibrium in Purely Competitive Securities Markets." *American Economic Review,* 61 (May), pp. 101–11.

McConnell, J., and T. Nantell (1985) "Corporate Combinations and Common Stock Returns: The Case of Joint Ventures." *Journal of Finance,* 40 (June), pp. 519–36.

Malatesta, P. (1983) "The Wealth Effect of Merger Activity and the Objective Functions of Merging Firms." *Journal of Financial Economics,* 11, pp. 155–81.

Mandelker, G. (1965) "Mergers and the Market for Corporate Control." *Journal of Political Economy,* 73, pp. 110–20.

Mergers and Acquisitions (1986) Vol. 20 (May/June, 1985 Almanac), p. 45.
     (1987) Vol. 21 (January/February), p. 71.

Mueller, Dennis (1977) "The Effects of Conglomerate Mergers." *Journal of Banking and Finance,* 1, pp. 315–47.

(1969) "A Theory of Conglomerate Mergers." *Quarterly Journal of Economics,* 83 (November), pp. 643–59.

Poterba, James M., and Lawrence R. Summers (1984) "The Economic Effects of Dividend Taxation." National Bureau of Economic Research, Inc., Working Paper no. 1353 (May).

Pratt, John W., and Richard Zeckhauser, eds. (1985) *Principals and Agents: The Structure of Business.* Boston: Harvard Business School Press.

Schipper, K., and R. Thompson (1983) "Evidence on the Capitalized Value of Merger Activity of Acquiring Firms." *Journal of Financial Economics,* 11, pp. 85–119.

Sherman, Roger (1972) "How Tax Policy Induces Conglomerate Mergers." *National Tax Journal,* 25 (December), pp. 521–9.

Steiner, Peter (1975) *Mergers: Motives, Effects, Policies.* Ann Arbor: University of Michigan Press.

Stiglitz, J. (1985) "Credit Markets and the Control of Capital." *Journal of Money, Credit and Banking,* 17, pp. 133–52.

Sullivan, Brian Francis (1984) "Conglomerate Mergers as a Second Best Solution to Firm Disequilibrium Amidst Factor Market Inefficiencies." Honors Thesis, Harvard College.

Weston, J. Fred, Keith Smith, and Ronald Shrieves (1972) "Conglomerate Performance Using the Capital Asset Pricing Model." *Review of Economics and Statistics,* 54 (November), pp. 357–63.

On international mergers

Abbeglen, James C., and George Stalk (1985) *Kaisha: The Japanese Corporation.* New York: Basic Books, Inc.

Block, Zenas (1983) "Joint Venturing in Japan." New York University.

Boesky, Ivan F. (1985) *Mergermania.* New York: Holt Rinehart and Winston.

Bowman, James S. (1985) "The Rising Sun in America: Japanese Management in the United States." Florida State University.

Davidson, Kenneth M. (1985) *Mega-mergers.* Cambridge, Mass.: Ballinger.

Eiteman, David K., and Arthur I. Stonehill (1983) *Multinational Business Finance.* Reading, Mass.: Addison-Wesley.

Ommae, Kenichi (1985) *Triad Power.* New York: Free Press.

Reich, Robert, and Eric Maskin (1986) "Joint Ventures in Japan Give Away Our Future." *Harvard Business Review* (March/April), pp. 78–86.

Salvatore, Dominick (1983) *International Economics.* New York: Macmillan.

Shapiro, Alan C. (1982) *Multinational Financial Management.* Boston: Allyn and Bacon.

Cooperations between American and Japanese Firms (1985) Japan External Trade Organization.

Merger Policies and Recent Trends in Mergers (1984) Organisation for Economic Co-operation and Development.

120   **Ryuzo Sato and Richard Zeckhauser**

Mergerstat 1984 (1985) W. T. Grimm and Co.
"Do Mergers Really Work?" (1985) *Business Week,* June 3, pp. 88–100.
"Why Is No One Safe?" (1985) *Forbes,* March 11, pp. 134–40.
"Is Any Company Safe from Takeover?" (1984) *Fortune,* April 2, pp. 18–23.

PART III

Financial integration issues

CHAPTER 8

Competitive performance and strategic positioning in international financial services

INGO WALTER

1   Introduction

A dominant feature of the international financial services industry today is the changing intensity of competition. Among the important environmental forces driving this change are continued exchange rate and interest rate volatility, persistent financial disintermediation and securitization, progressive financial deregulation and market interpenetration, and rapid technological evolution in financial processes and products.

It is an environment that is increasingly forcing a radical reassessment of strategic positioning on the part of firms in the industry. In addition, structural change in the industry has encouraged regulators to rethink the trade-offs between financial efficiency and creativity on the one hand, and safety and stability of the financial system on the other. Theirs is an effort to strike an optimum balance for regulatory treatment of the financial sector in its central role as an agent for national economic growth and development.

The purpose of this chapter is to develop, in a coherent analytical framework, the principal variables that appear to explain differential competitive performance among players in the international financial services industry. This framework is then used to evaluate the sources of market power and the strategic behavior of individual institutions. For example, the acquisitions in 1986 and 1987 of significant shares in Goldman Sachs and Shearson Lehman Brothers by Sumitomo Bank and Nippon Life, respectively, can be interpreted in a coherent manner. Similarly, penetration of the U.S. and European securities markets by Nomura, Daiwa, Nikko, and Yamaichi – as well as penetration of Japanese securities markets by U.S. and European firms – can be assessed.

The research assistance of Fergal Byrne is gratefully acknowledged. Part of the text is adapted from Walter (1987).

123

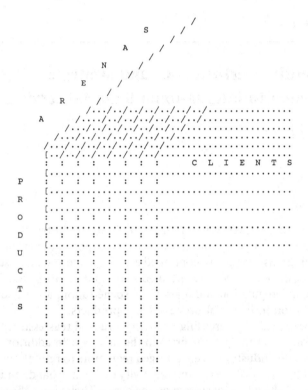

Figure 8.1 International financial services activity matrix (C-A-P model).

2   The C-A-P model

The global market for financial services has three principal dimensions:

1. Client   (C-dimension)
2. Arena   (A-dimension)
3. Product   (P-dimension).

Firms in the financial services industry have an unusually broad range of choice with respect to each of these dimensions, and different combinations yield different strategic and competitive profiles. Figure 8.1 depicts these dimensions in the form of a three-dimensional matrix. Each cell in the matrix has a distinctive competitive structure based on fundamental economic as well as public-policy considerations.

Note that the C-A-P matrix is quite different from the payoff matrix in a formal game, such as the "prisoner's dilemma." The cells in the C-A-P matrix represent distinct markets and contain much more information than the cells in an ordinary payoff matrix. Nor are they independent of one another, as would be the case in a payoff matrix (see the discussion in Section 4).

Largely as a result of technological change and deregulation, financial institutions face increasing potential access to each of the dimensions in the C-A-P opportunity set. Financial deregulation, in particular, has had an important influence in terms of (a) accessibility of geographical arenas, (b) accessibility of individual client groups by players originating in different parts of the financial services business, and (c) substitutability among financial products in meeting personal, corporate, or public sector financial needs.

2.1 Clients

The conventional distinction between wholesale and retail financial services is not particularly helpful in the context of the C-A-P model, and the following categorization of the major client groups may be more appropriate:

A. *Sovereign:* Sovereign states and their instrumentalities
B. *Corporate:* Nonfinancial corporations regardless of industry classification, ranging from multinational corporations (MNCs) and parastatals to middle-market and small, privately owned companies
C. *Correspondent:* Other financial institutions in the same industry subcategory (e.g., correspondent banks)
D. *Private:* Individuals with high net worth and high net income
E. *Retail:* Other individual clients, generally in significant volume.

The clients in groups A–E can be broken down into narrower segments, each differing with respect to product-related attributes such as currency requirements, liquidity and maturity needs, risk levels, industry categories, overall service-level requirements, price sensitivity, and timing aspects. Effective market definition and segmentation involves identifying coherent client groups that embody relative uniformity with respect to each of these variables. Note that, in the C-A-P matrix, each client group is further distinguished on the basis of geographic location (arena). This ensures that the identity of individual client groups will not vary across arenas and products.

2.2 Arenas

The international market for financial services can be divided into on-shore and offshore arenas with respect to geographic location. The arenas in question are those in which the financial services involved (or bundles of those services) are actually sold to clients, not those in which the financial institutions providing those services are home based. Each arena is characterized by different risk/return profiles, levels of financial efficiency, regulatory conditions, client needs, and other variables.

Geographic interpenetration of financial institutions with respect to various domestic and offshore markets has become very significant indeed. For example, in 1950 only 7 American banks, with 95 branches, had activities abroad. By 1970 there were 79 banks with 536 branches, and by 1984 there were about 150 banks with over 1,000 branches that booked assets in excess of $337 billion. This actually understates the degree of internationalization by U.S. banks, since forms of involvement other than branches are not captured in the data. Nor do they capture the growing involvement abroad by U.S. investment banks, brokerage houses, and other types of financial services firms. Institutions based in countries other than the United States have witnessed equally dramatic increases in their overseas presence, especially in recent years.

Meanwhile, according to a study by Morgan Guaranty (1986) foreign banks in the United States in 1986 had 577 branches, agencies, and subsidiaries booking $411 billion in deposits (13 percent of the U.S. total) and $110 billion in business loans (22 percent of the total U.S. market and 50 percent of the New York City market). In dollar-denominated acceptance financing, they took 33 percent of the U.S. market. Japanese banks alone captured a 40 percent share of foreign bank assets in the United States and an 80 percent share of the dollar-denominated acceptances of foreign banks.

The rapid growth in the activities of financial institutions in various onshore and offshore arenas can be largely attributed to the nature of the services provided. It is often imperative to be physically close to the client in order to do business effectively. Although a certain amount of business can certainly be done through correspondent relationships and travel, the increasingly complex nature of financial services and client needs has made reliable "direct connect" relationships all the more important.

The A-dimension in Figure 8.1 can be taken into the analysis at the global, regional, national, subregional, and location-specific levels.

2.3   *Products*

Financial services offered in the international market have proliferated in recent years. With a clear requirement for product differentiation in the marketplace, firms in the industry have created new instruments and techniques tailored to the needs of their clients.

It is useful to categorize the activities of financial institutions into (a) liability-based activities, (b) asset-based activities, and (c) off-balance-sheet activities provided for clients. There is also a fourth category containing activities in which the financial institution is acting on its own behalf on either the asset or the liability side of its balance sheet. This involves arbitrage and positioning, and to a large extent makes possible the other two types of activities.

In essence, financial institutions sell four more or less distinct primary products to clients. All products that appear in the market, including the most complex innovations, can be broken down into one or more of these categories (see the appendix for a detailed product breakdown).

(1) *Credit products:* Although credit products have become a less significant source of returns for many international institutions, they remain the core of much of the business. Credit activities range from straightforward general-purpose term lending to sophisticated and specialized forms such as project finance.

(2) *Financial engineering products:* These constitute the design and delivery of financial services specifically structured to satisfy often complex client objectives at minimum cost. In a world where borrowers, issuers, savers, and investors often have distinctive and complex objectives, financial engineering is perhaps the ultimate form of product differentiation and accounts for a great deal of the value-added creation observed in the international capital markets. It can be either "disembodied" or "embodied," depending on whether the engineering components are part of specific financial transactions. Purely disembodied financial engineering may take the form of advisory functions that an American investment bank might undertake, on the basis of client-specific information, for a Japan-based multinational manufacturing firm seeking an acquisition in the same industry in the United States. Embodied financial engineering combines this with one or more financial transactions sold to the same client as part of a financing package. Other examples include the structuring of project financings, leveraged buy-outs, complex multicurrency financings, advice on appropriate capital structure, and the like.

(3) *Risk management products:* Risk bearing has long been recognized as one of the key functions of financial institutions, and one of the reasons they tend to be heavily regulated. The main forms of exposure include credit risk, interest rate risk, liquidity risk, foreign exchange risk, country risk, project risk, commodity risk, and technical risk in areas such as cash transmission. Risk management activities can be broken down into (a) those in which financial institutions themselves assume all or part of the exposure, and (b) those in which the institutions provide the technology needed to shift the risk or to take on the exposure themselves only

on a contingent basis – that is, an off-balance sheet commitment to buy or sell, borrow or lend. Effective risk reduction through diversification clearly depends on the independence of the various risks represented in the portfolio. Financial institutions provide risk management services that range from simple standby credit lines and forward interest rate agreements to explicit, tightly defined products addressed to a broad range of contingencies.

(4) *Market access products:* Financial institutions can provide value-added services to clients by using their internal networks to transfer information, funds, or securities from one client or arena to another. Accomplishing this requires both tangible and intangible networks. The former consist of physical assets such as branches or other outlets covering various clients and arenas. The latter can be looked upon as the institution's access to actual or potential customers in arenas in which it may or may not have a physical presence. To a significant extent, state-of-the-art internal operations and systems capabilities drive the competitive positioning of individual players in supplying market-access services internationally.

(5) *Arbitrage and positioning:* Activities that financial institutions engage in on their own behalf facilitate and in many cases make possible the supply of the first four types of financial services to clients internationally.

Arbitrage opportunities occur when the same asset is priced differently in different markets (or market segments), often because of information asymmetries. "Pure" arbitrage takes place when an asset is simultaneously bought and sold. By this definition, financial institutions rarely engage in pure arbitrage. Rather, they engage in "risk arbitrage" – they buy an asset in a particular market, hold it for a time (however short), and re-sell it in the same or different market. The institution is thus exposed to "differential risk," owing to the possibility that the underlying price differential may evaporate or be reversed during the time needed to complete the transaction. Exposure to differential risk depends jointly on the time needed to complete the transaction and the underlying volatility in the price of the specific asset and the markets in which it is traded.

Positioning is a form of risk arbitrage that has become an integral part of managing international financial institutions during a time of significant exchange rate and interest rate volatility. Positioning linked to the interest rate and to foreign exchange drives securities, options, and futures trading and dealing.

This classification of international financial services into more or less distinct categories can be broken down still further into the specific services made available to individual client segments in various market arenas. As noted earlier, this breakdown is presented in the appendix.

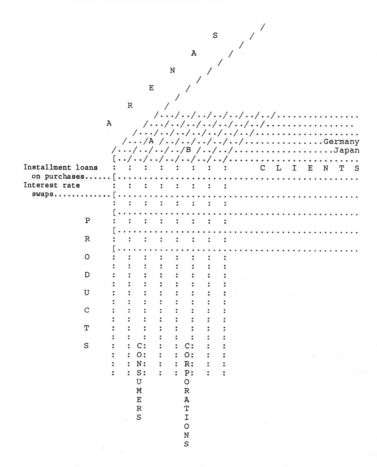

Figure 8.2 Examples of cell identification in the C-A-P model.

In summary, we can now put the three dimensions together once again in Figure 8.2, which uses two cells in the matrix to illustrate the respective markets for consumer installment lending in Germany (A), and the market for interest rate swaps corporations in Japan (B).

3   Cell characteristics

The inherent attractiveness of each of the cells in Figure 8.2 will depend on the *size and durability* of prospective returns that can be extracted from that cell, adjusted for the perceived risks involved. Each cell has embedded within it a certain value quotient potentially available to the set of players. The aggregate level of the cell-specific returns depends on the level of demand for a particular financial service, its price and cost, and the price elasticity of demand, which in turn is affected primarily by the existence of product substitutes. The actual returns captured by each institution will depend on its competitive positioning. Their durability will be based in part on the ability of new players to enter the cell and the development of substitute products over time. Cell characteristics can be analyzed in terms of conventional competitive-structure criteria. Examples include the Japanese markets for pension fund management and mutual funds sold to individual investors, the U.S. market for commercial paper backstop facilities and middle-market lending, and the German market for new securities issues and leveraged buy-outs.

3.1   Market power of suppliers

Suppliers of the principal inputs for the production of financial services – capital and labor – can absorb some of the available rents in a particular C-A-P cell. Their ability to do so will depend on their market power, which can be expected to vary substantially from one arena to another, somewhat from one product to another, and sometimes from one client to another.

First, depositors and purchasers of securities issued by financial institutions demand returns commensurate with the perceived level of risk. This depends heavily on the credit rating of the individual financial institution. To the extent that an institution is perceived as being less creditworthy owing to the quality of its assets or its exposure to other types of risk, its market power is eroded as bondholders and depositors demand higher yields for the funds they supply. In this context, the removal of regulations on interest payable with respect to various types of deposit accounts clearly raises the market power of capital suppliers and the cost of liabilities for financial institutions. Moreover, the more financially sophisticated the suppliers of funds become, the more aware they are of alternative opportunities.

To a large extent, the leverage of savers derives from the growing availability of alternative outlets for funds, rather than from individual strategic exercise of market power with respect to financial institutions. Under deregulation, funds are shifted to markets with higher yields, which may then be matched by the affected financial institutions that raise their deposit rates. Certainly, this pattern tends to be the case at the retail level. In the Japanese context, deregulation of interest rates since 1980 has given suppliers of funds to financial institutions considerably greater leverage.

Second, the labor market that financial institutions face has also changed in some of the C-A-P cells in which they operate. The increased market power experienced by suppliers of highly skilled labor to financial institutions has occasionally led to dramatic increases in compensation levels, enabling labor to capture some of the returns derived from the cell. Again in the Japanese example, there has clearly been a conflict between the need to develop considerable institutionalized financial expertise in the new competitive environment and the traditions of promotions based on seniority and loyalty to a single employer. There are signs, however, that both of these are gradually breaking down.

3.2   Market power of clients

Buyers of financial services naturally seek the highest value-added at the lowest cost. The more successful they are, the narrower the margins and the lower the rents available to the financial institution in a specific C-A-P cell. Especially in international wholesale markets, buyers of financial services are sought after by a large number of institutions competing fiercely for their business. Client groups such as multinational corporations and individuals with a high net worth have significantly more monopsony power than other client groups for whom competition is markedly less intense. The market power of buyers of financial services can be expected to differ in all three dimensions of the C-A-P matrix – from one client group to another, from one product category to another, and across different arenas.

3.3   Availability of product substitutes

Product substitutes available to clients in a given cell clearly increase the price elasticity of demand, which in turn determines the price-volume vectors that are accessible to the financial institution and consequently the overall level of returns. The closer the substitutability among financial services, the higher the price elasticity of demand and the lower the level of returns that are available within a given C-A-P cell. One would expect the degree of product substitutability to differ from one client group to the next and across different arenas.

The most important factor relating to product substitutes in financial services is information and technology content, so that the creation of product substitutes has become one of the most important and pervasive effects of financial innovation. Successful innovations that an institution introduces into a given cell are those embodying a low degree of product substitutability over a relatively long period of time.

3.4   *Competitive structure and strategic groups*

Clearly, the competitive structure of each C-A-P cell is a major determinant of the excess returns that an institution may be able to obtain. To the extent that competition takes place on the pricing variable, prospective returns are transferred to clients. Competitive structure is conventionally measured using concentration ratios based on the number of firms, distribution of market share among firms, and similar criteria.

Normally, the addition of players to a particular C-A-P cell would be expected to reduce market concentration, increase the degree of competition, erode the margins, and lead to a more rapid pace of financial innovation. If the new players are from the same basic strategic groups as existing players (e.g., one more investment bank joining a number of other investment banks competing in a given cell), then the expected outcome would be along conventional lines of intensified competition. But if the new player comes from a completely different strategic perspective (e.g., the finance affiliate of a major oil company penetrating the same market cell for investment banking services), the competitive outcome may be quite different. Cell penetration by a player from a different strategic group may lead to a greater increase in competition than penetration by an incremental player from the same strategic group, owing to the potential diversification benefits, scope for cross-subsidization and staying power, and incremental horizontal or vertical integration gains that the player from a "foreign" strategic group may be able to capture.

The 1980s have seen enormous geographic market interpenetration between Japan, Europe, and the United States. Banks and securities firms based in all three areas have developed impressive footholds in the other's markets, with the result that 24-hour trading now takes place in various financial instruments and also global competition for all kinds of financial services has intensified. This has eroded margins in many types of financial services, particularly because of the activities of competitors emanating from different strategic groups. The Bank of Tokyo finances international trade in New York, Ford Motor Credit finances car buyers in the United Kingdom, Morgan Guaranty and Swiss Bank Corporation are active in the Tokyo capital market, and Yamaichi Securities operates in the emerging Euro-equity market, to cite just a few examples.

3.5   *Natural barriers to entry and contestable markets*

The higher the barriers to entry, the lower the chances that new entrants will reduce the level of rents available in each C-A-P cell. Natural barriers to entry include capital adequacy, human resources, financial technologies, and economies of scale. Another barrier is created by the contracting costs avoided by a close relationship between a financial institution and its client, which in turn is related to the avoidance of opportunistic behavior by either party. Not least, the competitive structure of each cell depends on the degree of *potential* competition. This represents an application of the "contestable markets" concept, which suggests that the existence of potential entrants cause existing players to act *as if* those entrants were already active in the market. Hence margins, product quality, and the degree of innovation in a given cell may exhibit characteristics of intense competition, even though the degree of market concentration is in fact quite high. Regulatory barriers to entry are discussed in Section 3.6.

3.6   *Price discrimination and predation*

In penetrating a particular cell or set of cells, a particular player may find it advantageous to "buy into" the market by cross-subsidizing financial services supplied in that cell from returns derived in other cells. This may make sense if the assessed horizontal, vertical, or lateral linkages (see Section 3.7) are sufficiently positive to justify such pricing, either now or in the future. It may also make sense if the cell characteristics are expected to change in future periods, so that an unprofitable presence today is expected to lead to a profitable presence tomorrow. And it may make sense if a player's behavior in buying market share has the potential to drive out competitors and fundamentally alter the structure of the cell in his or her favor. The latter can be termed predatory behavior, as it is no different from predation in the markets for goods. The institution "dumps" (or threatens to dump) financial services into the cell, forcing out competitors either as a result of the direct effects of the dumping in the face of more limited staying power or because of the indirect effects, working through expectations. Once competitors have been driven from the market, the institution takes advantage of the reduced degree of competition to widen margins and achieve excess returns.

Conversely, it may also be possible for an institution with significant market power to keep potential competitors out of attractive cells through explicit or implicit threats of predatory behavior. A well-established firm can make it clear to new entrants that it will respond very aggressively to incursions, and that they face a long and difficult road to profitability. In this way, new competitors may be discouraged and the cell characteristics kept more monopolistic than would otherwise be the case.

Note that the predatory behavior described here is not consistent with the view of market contestability presented in Section 3.5. The greater contestability and the credibility of prospective market entry, the less will be the scope for price discrimination and predation.

3.7   *Artificial barriers to competition and protectionism*

Firms in the international financial services industry are obviously sensitive to incremental competition in C-A-P cells in which natural barriers to entry are limited. Market penetration by foreign-based competitors – especially in the wholesale and capital markets end of the business – can erode indigenous players' returns and raise protectionist motivations. Given the economic interests involved, banks and other financial institutions are in an excellent position to convert them into political power in order to achieve protection. They are often exceedingly well connected politically, and their lobbying power can be awesome.

The U.S. Treasury (1979), the Organization for Economic Co-operation and Development (1983), and Walter (1985a) have undertaken extensive surveys of restrictions that are imposed on foreign-based banks and other firms in the financial services industry. There are basically two types of barriers to market penetration in the financial services sector: entry barriers and operating barriers. To a large extent, both operate by limiting access to all or certain segments of the market, although some act by making market access more costly than it would otherwise be.

Barriers to entry: Entry barriers inhibit foreign-based firms in the financial services industry in servicing the needs of domestic clients across an entire arena tranche of the C-A-P matrix. As Walter (1985a) has noted, the barriers in the banking industry range from complete embargoes (including visa denial to foreign bankers) and limiting foreign presence to a representative office only (with no banking powers), to restrictions on the forms that foreign presence can take and limits on foreign equity positions in local financial institutions. These may apply equally to all foreign-based institutions, or selectively, depending on the specific foreign institution involved or on its home country. Factors such as reciprocity and assessed contribution to the domestic financial system often influence the structure of these barriers to entry.

If reciprocity is an issue, protected domestic institutions must strike a balance in lobbying for protection between their interest in accessing foreign markets for financial services and their desire to keep foreign-based players out of domestic markets. On the other hand, foreign-based institutions that are already in a particular national market – either because they were grandfathered at the time entry barriers were imposed or because they have achieved entry in some other manner – will tend to resist further opening of the market to foreign players. They have no reciprocity incentive with respect to their home country or third countries, and unless they perceive significant external benefits from additional entrants, they have every reason to oppose additional, potentially powerful competition.

Entry barriers restrict the movement of financial services firms across the lateral arena dimension of the matrix. A firm that is blocked out of a particular national market faces a restricted lateral opportunity set that excludes the relevant tranches of client cells and product cells. To the extent that they are the outcome of protectionist political activity, the entry barriers will themselves create excess returns in some or all of the cells in the tranche. Windows of opportunity, created by countries relaxing entry barriers, tend to be taken advantage of by institutions envisioning potential supernormal returns in some of the previously inaccessible cells.

Firms that are allowed into a particular market only through travel or representative offices may nevertheless be able to access particular client or product cells in that tranche, securing returns by transferring the actual transaction to a different arena – for example, one of the Euromarket functional or booking centers or the institution's home country. This option applies primarily to the wholesale and private banking (financial services provided to high-net-worth and high-income individuals) components of the client and product dimensions.

Correspondent relationships with local banks are another alternative for sharing in the returns associated with the blocked cells having to do with international trade, foreign exchange, syndications, and other wholesale transactions. And the value of a physical presence of any sort in an otherwise restricted market may support competitive positioning elsewhere in the institution's international structure. For example, even a limited scope for transactions with the local affiliate of a multinational enterprise may generate business with that company elsewhere in the world.

Distortions of operating conditions: Once in a particular market, foreign-based financial institutions generally become fully subject to domestic monetary policy and to supervisory and regulatory controls. At this point, there are three possibilities: (a) domestic controls, in law or in administrative practice, fall less seriously on foreign players than on their domestic competitors; (b) the nominal incidence of regulation is identical for both; or (c) foreign players are subjected to more restrictive regulation than their local competitors. In the last case, operating barriers are explicitly used to restrict competitive positioning of foreign-based institutions after they have achieved market access. The measures range from restrictions on expatriate employment, number and location of offices, client groups that may be served, types of businesses that may be handled (including trust business, lead management in securities underwriting, and retail deposit taking), mandatory linkage of allowable business to international transactions, permissible sources of funding, and the like. The firm now has access, in one form or another, to the arena tranche, but is constrained either in the depth of service it can supply to a particular cell or in the feasible set of cells within the tranche. This can severely reduce profitability associated with the arena concerned.

Tolerance of anticompetitive behavior: Besides applying entry and operating restrictions to foreign-based players, regulators may tolerate a certain amount of anticompetitive, cartel-like behavior on the part of domestic institutions. In attempting to gain a significant market share with "sensitive" client groups, obtain funding in the local currency market, place securities with domestic investors, and obtain underwriting mandates, foreign firms intruding into the national marketplace may be stepped on by indigenous players, with the authorities turning a blind eye to the implications for competitive performance.

Equality of competitive opportunity: Given the structure of competitive barriers in the financial services industry, "national treatment" would seem to be the substantive equivalent of liberal international trade in a highly regulated industry such as financial services. This means that foreign-based players are subject to precisely the same regulatory controls as domestic players. Yet even this can have differential effects on domestic and foreign-based institutions because of different starting positions and operating characteristics, as can stringent home country capital requirements for banks doing business in international and foreign markets, where they may compete with players treated much more leniently. What is really required is "equality of competitive opportunity," in the sense of a level playing field – an extraordinarily difficult concept to define, much less to deliver, in the case of an industry as complex as financial services.

Regulatory structures thus clearly affect the competitive environment in the international financial services industry. They underlie noncompetitive market structures and excess returns attributable to these structures, make possible price discrimination and predation, and erode market contestability. They also weaken static efficiency and dynamic gains in financial markets, and therefore are being reexamined by governments around the world in a host of moves toward financial deregulation – including initiatives taken in Japan and the United States.

4   Cell linkages

Financial institutions will want to allocate available resources to those
C-A-P cells in Figure 8.1 promising to throw off the highest risk-adjusted
returns. In order to do this, they will have to appropriately allocate costs,
returns, and risks across cells. But beyond this, the economics of supplying financial services internationally is subject to economies of scale
and economies of scope. The existence of both types of economies has
strategic implications for players in the industry. Economies of scale suggest an emphasis on *deepening* the activities of individual firms within
a cell, or across cells in the product dimension. Economies of scope suggest an emphasis on *broadening* activities across cells – that is, a player can
produce a given level of output in a given cell more cheaply or effectively
than institutions that are less active across multiple cells. This depends
greatly on the benefits and costs of linking cells together in a coherent web.

The gains from linkages among C-A-P cells depend on the possibility
that an institution competing in one cell can move into another cell and
can perform in that second cell more effectively than a competitor lacking a presence in the first cell. The existence of economies of scope and
scale is a determining factor of institutional strategy. Where scale economies dominate, a firm will strike to maximize throughput of the product
within a given C-A-P cell configuration, driving for market penetration.
Where scope economies dominate, a firm will work toward aggressive
cell proliferation.

4.1   *Client-driven linkages*

Client linkages exist when a financial institution serving a particular client
or client group can, as a result, supply financial services either to the same
client or to another client in the same group more efficiently in the same
or different arenas. With respect to a particular client, this linkage is part
of the value of the relationship. With respect to a particular client segment, it will clearly be easier for an institution to engage in business with
a new client in the same segment than to move to another client segment.
It is possible that client linkages will decline as market segmentation in
financial services becomes more intense.

4.2   *Arena-driven linkages*

Arena-driven linkages are important when an institution can service a
particular client or supply a particular service more efficiently in one arena

as a result of having an active presence in another arena. The presence of nonfinancial MNC clients in the same set of arenas as their financial institutions is one important form such linkages can take. By competing across a large number of arenas, a financial institution also has an opportunity to decrease the overall level of risk to which it is exposed and thereby increase its overall risk-adjusted rate of return.

4.3   *Product-driven linkages*

Product-driven linkages exist when an institution can supply a particular financial service in a more competitive manner because it is already producing the same or a similar financial service in different client or arena dimensions. Product specializations would appear to depend upon the degree of uniformity of the resource inputs required, as well as information and technology commonalities. Thus, certain types of skills embodied in human resources may be applied across different clients and arenas at relatively low marginal cost within a given product category, as may certain types of information about the environment, markets, or client needs.

4.4   *Competitive and cooperative behavior*

Whether within cells or across cells, one complication in analyzing the competitive behavior of firms in the financial services industry that does not arise as often in other industries is the need to cooperate closely with rivals on individual transactions while competing intensively with them. Examples include securities underwriting and distribution, loan syndication, project finance, and credit card networks. When does it make sense for an institution to compete and when to cooperate in order to extract maximum returns from the individual cells in the C-A-P matrix? Following Gladwin and Walter (1980), the diagram in Figure 8.3 can be used to model an institution's behavior with respect to a particular cell or a transaction within that cell.

The vertical axis measures the degree of assertiveness that the institution will tend to bring to bear vis-à-vis the competition. This is a joint product of the perceived stakes the organization has in the game and its competitive power. The higher the stakes and the greater its power to override the competition, the more assertive the institution will want to be. Both stakes *and* power have to be high in order for the assertive mode to make sense. Both relative stakes and relative power are defined here in ordinal rather than cardinal terms in view of the difficulties involved in

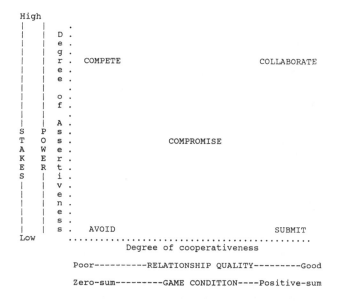

Figure 8.3 A behavioral model of competition and cooperation in international financial services.

measuring these variables – although the existence of differences in relative stakes and power between protagonists in conflict situations is beyond doubt.

The horizontal axis measures the extent to which the relationship is perceived as a zero-sum (what one gains the other loses) or positive-sum (both can gain) game, and it measures the quality of the relationship with other players – usually a cumulative product of past experience. The more the relationship is viewed as a positive-sum game and the better the relationship, the more likely it is that the institution will want to cooperate with others.

The grid in Figure 8.3 can be divided into five zones based on how these four underlying variables appear in a particular case – compete, collaborate, comply, avoid, and compromise. It is thus likely that one institution will be seen to work closely together with another in a given project in a particular cell even though it is competing vigorously elsewhere, submitting to the dominance of the other institution or avoiding involvement on the same kind of project in a different cell or a different project in the same cell. A large number of combinations are clearly possible in imposing this behavioral grid onto the underlying market matrix in Figure 8.1.

The compete zone means that management should attempt to achieve its own objective, even if in the process the objective of the protagonist is thwarted. The collaborate zone means that management should work actively with the protagonist to achieve an outcome in which both sides clearly stand to gain. The submit zone means either that the stakes are insufficiently high or that the institution has insufficient power, so that management has little choice but to accept an outcome dictated by the other side. Finally, the avoid zone means that management will want to withdraw from a zero-sum game in which relationships with the other side are poor and stakes and/or power are minimal.

Normally, large institutions are likely to have a greater degree of market power than smaller institutions, so that even with moderate stakes they can often be expected to "call the shots" in conflict situations. They may thus be able to capture a disproportionate share of the gains from financial projects in which both larger and smaller institutions are involved, for example. On the other hand, small institutions may find that very high stakes ride on the outcome of a particular conflict, and may take a very assertive stance even in the absence of a great deal of power.

The evolution of international correspondent banking relationships provides an interesting example of cooperative behavior in a fundamentally competitive market structure. Correspondent banking includes a number of activities, such as managing local currency accounts, effecting payments, providing access to the local clearing system, opening and confirming documentary credits arising from international trade transactions, participating in loans and syndicated credits, and providing custody services in securities business – traditionally paid for largely through correspondent balances. Banks that do not pose a direct threat to their correspondents in their own home markets, either because of their strategic positioning or because of government restrictions, have been in an ideal position to develop correspondent relationships – this is a classic case of collaboration, in terms of the diagram in Figure 8.3.

Things have changed, however. Improvements in communications and automation have provided banks with direct access to services previously accessible only through correspondents. Disintermediation – which means that issues and investors can circumvent banks altogether or in large part – has altered the value of correspondent banking on the lending side, and high real interest rates have raised the cost of correspondent balances. The result has been a significant "unbundling" of the previously stable correspondent relationship into a less stable and more price-sensitive one centered around a specific set of services that one bank sells to another. Like international finance in general, the drift has been from a relationship-driven to a transactions-driven business. In terms of Figure 8.3, the cor-

	GLOBAL	EUR/ME/AF	LATIN AMERICA	ASIA
CITICORP	48	32	87	56
CHASE MANHATTAN	46	32	73	55
MORGAN GUARANTY	69	82	95	73
MANUFACTURERS	44	43	50	39
BANK OF AMERICA	42	41	32	70
CONTINENTAL	45	52	51	20

Data from Bank of America.

Figure 8.4 Three-year return on average assets of major U.S. international banks, 1980–2 (hundredths of 1 percent).

respondent banking business has drifted laterally from "collaboration" in the direction of "competition."

It is important to remember that the conflict management grid in Figure 8.3 applies only to a single institution evaluating its own situation against a protagonist, and using it to derive a normative conflict management strategy. One can argue that a number of joint banking ventures such as Sumitomo–Goldman Sachs, Shearson Lehman Brothers–Nippon Life, and Credit Suisse–First Boston are products of management assessments yielding outcomes in the "collaborate" zone of Figure 8.3. Whether these relationships are stable over time, or whether the outcome will drift into the tension-filled compete zone or the avoid zone (with a joint venture being taken over by one of the partners) or the submit zone (with one partner being taken over by the other) remains to be seen.

5   Sources of competitive advantage

One of the striking aspects of the international financial services industry is the high degree of variation in competitive performance among institutions, as measured by earnings. Financial institutions faced with the identical feasibility as represented by the C-A-P matrix come away with entirely different results. A limited example of this is depicted in Figure 8.4, which gives the return on average assets figures for major U.S. commercial banks during a relatively "normal" period, 1980–2, that is, before the accounting problems associated with the developing country debt crisis.

All six players are subject to U.S. financial deregulation and exposed to the full rigors of the offshore markets. None are protected by the kinds of home country regulation and barriers to competition that make these numbers look weak in comparison with banks from other countries with relatively sheltered home markets. Yet the differences are remarkable.

The ability of financial institutions to exploit profit opportunities within the C-A-P framework depends on a number of key firm-specific attributes. These include the adequacy of the institution's capital base and its institutional risk base, its human resources, its access to information and markets, its technology base and managerial culture, and the entrepreneurial qualities of its people.

5.1   Adequacy of the capital base

In recent years, financial institutions and their regulators have started to pay increasing attention to the issue of capital as a source of competitive power as well as prudential control. This has always been true with respect to activities appearing on the balance sheet. But with the increasing concentration of domestic and international finance in the securities markets, the role of capital has become important as the principal determinant of risk-bearing ability in securities underwriting and dealing, as well as in insurance-related off-balance sheet activities such as standby letters of credit or facilities backstopping the issuance of notes or commercial paper. One step removed, a large capital base that allows an institution to be a successful player in securities underwriting and dealing also may enable it to undertake mergers and acquisitions activities, private placements, and other value-added services for its clients.

Capital adequacy thus conveys a decided competitive advantage (a) in bringing specific products to specific international markets, (b) in maximizing firepower and reducing costs in funding operations, (c) in being able to stick with particular clients in good times and bad – thus being considered a reliable financial partner, and (d) in achieving compliance with capital requirements mandated by the regulators. At the same time, of course, institutions are, in general, reluctant to increase equity capital, for reasons having to do with leverage.

5.2   The institutional risk base

Financial institutions fund themselves by creating financial assets held by others. In a deregulated environment where financial institutions are forced to bid for funds, the perceived quality of an institution is an important determinant of its ability to fund itself at the lowest possible cost. The international debt problems of the 1980s, as well as sectoral problems in real estate, energy, agriculture, and other troubled industries have called into question the credit standing of certain financial institutions in terms of the fundamental soundness of their asset structures. This in turn has accelerated the pace of disintermediation, with many large corporations and other institutions going straight to the capital markets on the basis of their own credit standing.

The level of institutional risk has become particularly significant in the interbank market and has led to a substantial spread in funding costs between institutions from time to time, particularly in crisis situations. Institutions of lesser perceived quality can be caught in a difficult position if they are forced to pay a premium over the other banks in order to fund themselves in the interbank market. This premium may also be taken by other institutions as a sign of an impairment of their credit standing. A premier credit rating thus assures a financial institution substantial advantages on the funding side. This is also true in dealings with corporate and other institutional clients that are often highly sensitive to the perceived quality of suppliers of financial services.

5.3   Quality of human resources

Although it has long been recognized that financial services are basically a "people business," the importance of having truly superior human resources has only recently become apparent to all of the major players. As Guth (1986) has noted, human capital can be viewed as a financial institution's most important asset, and many of the critical opportunities to exploit individual or clusters of C-A-P cells depend directly upon the quality of human resources encompassed within the organization.

In particular, both credit and risk evaluation depend upon the intellectual caliber, experience, and training of the decision maker – qualities that are no less important in the securities business than they are in the more traditional dimensions of banking. Owing to the increase in transactions-driven financial services, individuals are having to make more and more highly complex decisions very quickly or lose deals. The need for rapid and accurate decision making is particularly evident in the trading function, where traders have to react almost instantly to exploit risk arbitrage opportunities and where incorrect decisions can mean substantial and unambiguous losses for the firm. Yet they are no less important in maintaining relationships with clients, specifically to anticipate client financial requirements and respond to them in ways that add value. Growing competition and increased complexity have placed a premium on human resources, as reflected in the keen rivalry to attract top-quality people in the labor markets of various financial centers, with compensation levels bid up at an extraordinary rate.

Beyond devoting significant time and resources to attracting and retaining superior people, firms in the industry are investing heavily in training at increasingly high levels of sophistication. This represents nothing more than investment in human capital, which is as critical in this industry as provisions for depreciation and physical capital investment are in other industries.

Human resources profiles of U.S. and Japanese financial institutions appear to differ significantly. U.S. institutions have traditionally been open to foreigners and are increasingly open to women as a source of talent. This has facilitated their penetration of global markets and provided the base for high internal mobility in a business that has increasingly become a meritocracy. Global U.S. financial institutions will find growing numbers of foreign nationals among the ranks of senior management, which is entirely in the American tradition. Japanese institutions face a challenge in this area, coming from a closed society that has traditionally been suspicious of foreigners and less than fully open to women in management. Yet even if alleviating these bottlenecks proves to be slow, it simply means that Japanese houses will have to rely more heavily on capital, for example, as a source of competitive power in global markets.

5.4   Information asymmetries

If money is "information on the move," then financial services constitute the most information-intensive industry in the international economy. The drive by financial institutions to move beyond commodity-type activities into higher value-added services is making information-intensive products all the more important, both quantitatively and qualitatively. Indeed, *asymmetries* of information among various competitors and their clients contribute a great deal toward explaining differentials in competitive performance. Information is embedded in specific financial services sold in various arenas to various clients, and all forms of lending and credit-related activities depend upon the collection, processing, and evaluation of large amounts of information. Similarly, the assimilation of information about the needs of clients is critical in the development of services addressed to their needs.

Information affects competitive performance in three ways. First, information is the only resource that can be used simultaneously in the production of any number of services, and this gives it some unique characteristics. For example, information generated to build an international cash management system for a multinational corporate client can also be used to develop a long-term financial strategy for the same company, or perhaps to develop a slightly different international cash management system for another multinational firm.

Second, the half-life of information as a source of competitive advantage may be decreasing. Owing to a great deal of market volatility, important types of financial information decay at a rapid rate, and actions that may have been warranted at one moment in time may no longer be appropriate shortly thereafter. It is an environment consisting of many small windows of opportunity.

Third, the growing complexity of the international financial environment and the wide variety of services on offer have made it increasingly difficult for companies and individuals to plan in a straightforward manner. In effect, what clients often need is a means to evaluate the information that is available, and some way of distinguishing relevant information from irrelevant. Financial institutions can provide information-related services that help accomplish this.

Client insight: Information asymmetries are of particular concern when an institution is attempting to maximize client-driven linkage effects. Client insight exists when a financial institution has developed a certain base of client-specific knowledge over time, in the course of satisfying that client's financial needs. A transition from relationship-driven banking to transaction-driven banking would imply (a) that the amount of client insight needed to satisfy its needs is decreasing over time or (b) that more institutions have the core stock of client-specific information necessary to satisfy their requirements. However, client insight seems to persist as a key to providing differential value added in financial services.

Arena insight: Just as a financial institution will, over time, generate an important degree of client-specific knowledge, it will also generate potentially valuable arena-specific information. The nature of this information will depend on the aggregation level of the arena definition. It is at the national level that many arena-specific information characteristics are most relevant, but supranational (regional) and subnational (local) expertise may be important as well. One might argue, for example, that Japanese firms have arena-specific insight in the Pacific Rim that could give them an advantage over other players in that particular arena. With suitable adaptation, information and analytical skills derived from dealing in particular arenas can be transmitted through the organization and used in other arenas as well.

Placing power: With continued securitization in the financial markets, the ability of underwriters to place securities with individual and institutional investors has become an increasingly important competitive variable – perhaps most clearly exemplified in the Eurobond market. The modern securities industry, in essence, is about distribution, and firms must focus on the number of securities they will be able to allocate to each investor and the range of investors over whom they may be able to allocate them. Both depend on the institution's information base regarding portfolio preferences of institutional and individual investors, as well as its own control over portfolios as a result of discretionary trust and investment business. Placing power as a product of information is also important in loan selling and syndication.

5.5   *Financial technology and innovation*

Financial innovation depends heavily on information incorporated into value-added services sold to clients. The parts of the international financial services industry that have seen the most far-reaching structural changes are those that appear to be the most knowledge intensive. Information technologies allow financial institutions to have at their disposal increasing amounts of data and reduce the time necessary to transfer data across arenas, client segments, and product applications. With more information hitting institutions at a rapid pace, internal decision and filter systems have come under pressure and new ones have had to be built, as have transaction-driven "back office" systems. Along with management and marketing know-how, these systems are principally *process*-related.

There is an equally important set of *product*-related financial technologies, which to a significant degree are made possible by such advances in financial processes. Technology-intensive financial services may be either embodied or disembodied. The former incorporate technology in a financial transaction, and differentiate that transaction from others available in the market. Disembodied technology is provided to clients independent of a specific financial transaction (e.g., in the form of financial advice), although it may subsequently lead to transactions. Returns on financial technology may come through fees or, more commonly, enhanced returns associated with product differentiation.

Whether process- or product-related, financial technology permits the innovating firm to open up an "intertemporal gap" between itself and its competitors, reflected either in the cost of delivering financial services or in product differentiation. That gap has both *size* and *duration* implications. It may also be more or less cell specific within the C-A-P model, in accordance with the following taxonomy: (a) client specific, (b) arena specific, (c) product specific, (d) client/arena specific, (e) arena/product specific, (f) client/product specific, and (g) client/product/arena specific. Duration describes the time-path (decay) of excess returns that can be extracted from financial innovation in this context, and their discounted present value can be compared with the cost of innovation or technology transfer across clients, arenas, and products.

In general, there appears to be a strong positive relationship between innovation and client specificity in the international financial services industry. There also seems to be a positive relationship between the complexity of the innovation and the imitation lag, which is perhaps partly offset by a negative relationship between product complexity and success of the innovation – with some innovations being too complex to be put to effective use. In the absence of anything like patent or copyright protection, the imitation lag for financial innovations tends to be relatively short and may be decreasing over time. It is therefore important for an institution to maintain a continuous stream of innovations. In this sense, an institution's most important innovation is its *next* one.

Innovation in this industry can thus be looked upon as the introduction of a new process or technique – new in terms of a particular cell – that provides durable returns and adds significant value to the client. The spread of an innovation through the matrix allows the firm to take advantage of its inherent profit potential across the cells. Innovation is particularly important to those players with a substantial presence in the offshore markets, where there are few barriers to competitive behavior and where the relative absence of regulation allows each of the players to have far more freedom in terms of innovative behavior than is true in many onshore markets.

Innovative capabilities – the continuous application of new product and process technologies – are a function of the quality of human capital and of investments in the financial equivalent of research and development, which is usually much more market driven, informal, and inductive than industrial research and development. Innovative capabilities are also highly sensitive to the "culture" of an organization, its management, the incentives associated with successful innovations versus the penalties of unsuccessful innovation, and the amount of horizontal communication and information transfer that takes place within the organization. Financial institutions compete in the same capital and labor markets, and people move from one institution to another with growing frequency, yet some institutions appear to be consistently more innovative than others.

5.6   *Franchise*

An institution's "franchise" is its most intangible asset, yet one that clearly distinguishes ex post the most successful competitors in the international financial services industry from the rest. It is generally linked to a specific type of competence and expertise that the market values and that the institution has developed over time. One can argue that Morgan Guaranty or Citicorp have developed strong franchises in various areas

COMPETITIVE RESOURCES

FINANCIAL SERVICES	A	B	C	D	E	F	G
Funding	1					3	1
Lending	3	3	2				
Financing	3	3	2				2
Credit activities	1	2	2		2	2	
Trading	3	3	3		2		
Brokering	2	2	3	2		1	
Advisory services		3	3		1	2	3
Asset management services		3	3		1	3	1
Underwriting	3	2	2		2	3	3
Distribution			1	3			
Payments activities			3		3		
Insurance services	3	2	2				
International trade services		2	2		2	1	

3 Principal factor
2 Important factor
1 Contributing factor

Key:

A. Adequacy of capital base   E. Technology
B. Quality of human capital   F. Innovative capability
C. Information   G. Franchise
D. Placing power

Figure 8.5 Alignment of competitive and product dimensions in international financial services.

of international finance over the years, franchises that are of great value when seeking new business.

The franchise concept has been used to explain a variety of competitive phenomena, and appears to be related to an institution's standing in the market as a result of a synergistic combination of all the above attributes – where the whole is greater than the sum of the parts. The franchise embedded in the value of the firm is thus a product of its past performance, projected into the future.

An initial attempt to match the principal competitive resource of international financial institutions with the principal product groups is presented in Figure 8.5.

6   Institutional strategy

A firm in the financial services industry faces a given C-A-P cell configuration and linkages at a point in time, alongside a particular institutional capability profile. Some of the cells have already been accessed, and some form a feasibility set for possible further development. The firm's expansion path – and the desired cell configuration of its business – depends on the level of perceived risk-adjusted economic rents associated with the feasibility set of cells, resistance lines impeding access to those cells, and the assessed value of intercell linkages. Successful players must therefore identify (a) the specific sources of their competitive advantage; (b) those cells where this competitive advantage can be applied, adds value, and is sustainable; and (c) the competitive potential inherent in the cell linkages. Application of a competitive framework, such as the one presented here, will help identify the cells and cell clusters in which significant returns based on market power are likely to exist, and (equally important) in which they are likely to be durable.

Given the size of the matrix presented in Figure 8.1 and the complexity of the linkages that exist among the individual cells, it becomes clear how wide the range of strategic options is that faces a financial institution in the global environment. Consequently, it is not surprising that the international structures of individual organizations and their development through time often appear somewhat haphazard, lacking in consistency or coherence. This is the result of management actions under conditions of *bounded rationality* when faced with the task of determining expansion paths – in effect, management confronts an enormous opportunity set, but it is usually familiar with only a small part of the set. Therefore, much of the time it appears to operate by a process of trial and error – trying various options under the best available information, assessing results to the extent this is possible, and trying again. It is not surprising that many institutions appear ex post to have a relatively ambiguous strategic positioning in the global market for financial services.

Nevertheless, some sort of coherent competitive positioning is needed in the strategic process. As illustrated in Figure 8.6, at least 27 options fall out of a taxonomy of possible strategies for international financial institutions. At the product level, the strategy can be defined as niche, diversified, or supermarket; at the arena level it can be defined as national, international, or global; and at the client level it can be defined as focused, segmented, or uniform. Across this taxonomy, an institution's strategic positioning and strategic clarity is invariably projected to clients, regulators, and competitors alike, and becomes a significant competitive advantage or disadvantage in the marketplace.

The strategic implications of barriers to competition in financial services likewise seem clear. They reduce the feasibility set within the C-A-P matrix. They place a premium on "windows of opportunity." They increase the importance of horizontal linkages that remain available. And

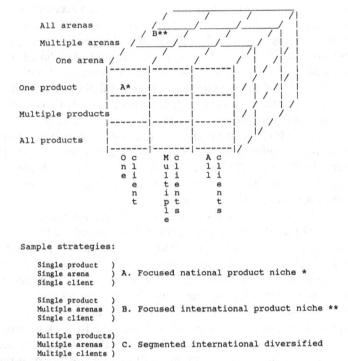

Figure 8.6 Strategic positioning options in international financial services.

they raise the importance of lobbying activity to open up markets in which cells having potentially attractive returns are blocked or restricted, and to keep them that way when barriers to competition are the source of such returns.

In order to perform well as they work through the strategic process, institutions must first develop the ability to scan the environment and to identify potential changes in that environment, including strategic moves by competitors and changes in the regulatory setting. Some institutions will be able to react more quickly than others to changes in the competitive environment and therefore may have a key advantage over their rivals.

7   Summary

The analysis in this chapter suggests that an institution's competitive performance in the international financial services industry is a function of (a) the competitive power of the organization, based on its institutional resource profile, (b) the structural characteristics of the various cells in which it chooses to compete, (c) the lateral, horizontal and vertical integration gains associated with cell linkages, and (d) scale economies available from transactions volume within cells or across cells. That is,

$$\text{Performance} = f \text{ (organizational resources, cell characteristics,}$$
$$\text{scope vector, scale vector).}$$

These dimensions jointly determine the returns that can be extracted from each cell and from the market as a whole. The goals of strategic positioning in this industry are to correctly assess each of these dimensions, including the institution's relative strengths and weaknesses, and then to create and project an unambiguous strategic profile.

Appendix

Subclassification of international financial services

	Primary classification			
Product	Credit products	Financial engineering products	Risk management products	Market access products
Deposit taking				
Time deposits	L			
Demand deposits	L			
Other	L			
Interbank dealing	X/L			
Sale of bank securities				
Certificates of deposit	L			
Ordinary shares	L			
Preferred shares	L			
Floating rate notes	L			
Short- and long-term debt	L			
Asset-based activities:				
Lending (local or foreign currency)				
Sovereign	X	X		
Corporate				
Indigenous majors	X	X		
MNC affiliates	X	X		

Product	Primary classification			
	Credit products	Financial engineering products	Risk management products	Market access products
Parastatals	X	X		
Indigenous middle market	X	X		
Foreign middle market	X	X		
Correspondent				
Indigenous banks	X	X		
Foreign banks	X	X		
Private				
High net worth	X	X		
High net income	X	X		
Retail	X	X		
Financing activities				
Asset-based financing	X	X		
Equity financing	X	X		
Export financing	X	X		
Project financing	X	X		
Venture capital financing	X	X		
Real estate financing	X	X		
M & A financing	X	X		
Leveraged buyout financing	X	X		
Underwriting				
Sovereign debt			X	
State debt, revenue, and agency bonds			X	
Mortgage-backed securities			X	
Insurance			X	
Equities			X	
Other			X	
Distribution			X	
Domestic			X	
Fixed income			X	
Equities			X	
Other			X	
International			X	
Fixed income			X	
Equities			X	
Other			X	
Advisory services				
Corporate cash management		X	X	X
Corporate fiscal planning		X	X	
General corporate financial services		X	X	X
Real estate advisory		X	X	X
Mergers and acquisitions		X	X	
Domestic		X	X	
International		X	X	

	Primary classification			
Product	Credit products	Financial engineering products	Risk management products	Market access products
Risk management services		X	X	
Interest rate risk (incl swaps)		X	X	
Foreign exchange risk (incl swaps)		X	X	
Country risk		X	X	
Other		X	X	
International trade advisory services		X	X	X
Trust and estate planning		X	X	
Legal and investment advisory services		X	X	
Tax advisory services		X	X	
General financial advice		X	X	
Consumer services				
Credit cards	X			X
Travelers checks			X	X
Other consumer services	X		X	X
Asset management services				
Private/retail		X	X	
Fiduciary activities		X	X	
Safekeeping/lock box services		X	X	
Mutual funds		X	X	
Corporate/correspondent		X	X	
Safekeeping/lock box services		X	X	
Pension fund management		X	X	
Mutual fund management		X	X	
Brokerage				
Money market				X
Eurocurrencies/Foreign exchange				X
Fixed income (government and corporate)				X
Equities				X
Financial futures				X
Options				X
Commodities				X
Gold				X
Insurance				X
Payments mechanism				
Domestic funds transfer				X
International funds transfer				X
Insurance-related services				
Standby letters of credit			X	
NIFs/RUFs			X	
Revolving credits	X		X	
Standby lines of credit	X		X	
Life insurance	X		X	
Property and casualty	X		X	

Primary classification

Product	Credit products	Financial engineering products	Risk management products	Market access products
International trade services				
International collections			X	X
Letter of credit business		X	X	X
Bankers acceptances	X		X	X
Countertrade		X		X
Market intelligence				X

Note: Middle market = local small and medium-sized corporations. L = credit extension by counterparties.

References

Aliber, Robert Z. (1984) "International Banking: A Survey." *Journal of Money, Credit and Banking,* November.

Bailey, Elizabeth E., and Ann F. Friedlander (1982) "Market Structure and Multiproduct Industries." *Journal of Economic Literature,* September.

Bank for International Settlements (1986) *Recent Innovations in International Banking.* Basel: Bank for International Settlements.

Baumol, William, J. Panzar, and R. Willig (1982) *Contestable Markets and the Theory of Industry Structure.* New York: Harcourt Brace Jovanovich.

Caves, Richard (1984) "Economic Analysis and the Quest for Competitive Advantage." *American Economic Review,* May.

Caves, Richard, and Michael Porter (1977) "From Entry Barriers to Mobility Barriers: Conjectural Decisions and Contrived Deterrence to New Competition." *Quarterly Journal of Economics,* May.

Channon, Derek F. (1986) *Bank Strategic Management and Marketing.* New York: John Wiley & Sons.

Cohen, Michael, and Thomas Morante (1981) "Elimination of Nontariff Barriers to Trade in Services: Recommendations for Future Negotiations." *International Law Journal,* Georgetown University Law Center.

Cooper, Kerry, and Donald R. Fraser (1986) *Bank Deregulation and the New Competition in Financial Services.* Cambridge, Mass.: Ballinger.

Corbet, Hugh (1977) "Prospect of Negotiations on Barriers to International Trade in Services." *Pacific Community,* April.

Cowhey, Peter F. (1986) *Trade in Services: A Case for Open Markets.* Washington, D.C.: American Enterprise Institute.

Crane, Dwight B., and Samuel L. Hayes, III (1982) "The New Competition in World Banking." *Harvard Business Review,* July–August.

Davis, Stephen I. (1985) *Excellence in Banking,* London: Macmillan.

Diebold, William, and Helena Stalson (1983) "Negotiating Issues in International Service Transactions." In William R. Cline (ed.), *Trade Policy in the 1980s.* Washington, D.C.: Institute for International Economics.

Dunning, John H. (1981) *International Production and the Multinational Enterprise*. London: Allen & Unwin.

Fieleke, Norman S. (1977) "The Growth of U.S. Banking Abroad: An Analytical Survey." In *Key Issues in International Banking*. Boston: Federal Reserve Bank of Boston.

Galbraith, Craig S., and Neil M. Kay (1986). "Towards a Theory of the Multinational Firm." *Journal of Economic Behavior and Organization,* March.

General Agreement on Tariffs and Trade (1984) *Articles of Agreement*. Geneva.

(1985) *The Scope, Limits and Function of the GATT Legal System*. Geneva.

Gladwin, Thomas N., and Ingo Walter (1980) *Multinationals under Fire*. New York: John Wiley & Sons.

Goldberg, Ellen S., et al. (1983) *Off-Balance-Sheet Activities of Banks: Managing the Risk-Reward Tradeoffs*. Philadelphia: Robert Morris Associates.

Gray, H. Peter, and Jean M. Gray (1982) "The Multinational Bank: A Financial MNC?" *Journal of Banking and Finance,* March.

Grubel, Herbert G. (1977) "A Theory of Multinational Banking." *Banca Nazionale del Lavoro Quarterly Review,* December.

Guth, Wilfried (1986) "Bank Strategy in the 1990s." *The Banker,* April.

Hayes, Samuel III, A. M. Spence and D. V. P. Marks (1983) *Competition in the Investment Banking Industry*. Cambridge, Mass.: Harvard University Press.

Hindley, Brian, and Alasdair Smith (1984) "Comparative Advantage and Trade in Services." *World Economy,* June.

Kallberg, Jarl S., and Anthony Saunders (1986) *Direct Sources of Competitiveness in Banking Services*. New York: Salomon Brothers Center for the Study of Financial Institutions (photocopy).

Ladreit de Larrechere, Guy (1984) *The Legal Framework for International Trade*. Geneva: General Agreement on Tariffs and Trade.

Letiche, J. M. (1974) "Dependent Monetary Systems and Economic Development." In W. Sellekaerts (ed.), *Economic Development and Planning*. London: Macmillan.

Leutwiler, Fritz et al. (1985) *Trade Policies for a Better Future*. Geneva: General Agreement on Tariffs and Trade.

Morgan Guarantee Trust Company (1986) "America's Banking Market Goes International." *Morgan Economic Quarterly,* June.

Neu, C. R. (1986) "International Trade in Banking Services." Paper presented at NBER/CEPS Conference on European–U.S. Trade Relations, Brussels, June.

Newman, H. (1978) "Strategic Groups and the Structure-Performance Relationships." *Review of Economics and Statistics,* August.

Organization for Economic Co-operation and Development (1983) *Trade in Services in Banking*. Paris.

Oster, S. (1982) "Intraindustry Structure and the Ease of Strategic Change." *Review of Economics and Statistics,* August.

Panzar, John C., and Robert D. Willig (1981) "Economies of Scope." *American Economic Review,* May.

Pastre, Olivier (1981) *Multinationals: Banking and Firm Relationships,* Greenwich, Conn.: JAI Press.
   (1981) "International Bank–Industry Relations: An Empirical Assessment." *Journal of Banking and Finance,* March.
Pecchioli, R. M. (1983) *Internationalization of Banking.* Paris: OECD.
Porter, Michael E. (1980) *Competitive Strategy.* New York: Free Press.
Sagari, Sylvia B. (1986) *The Financial Service Industry: An International Perspective.* Ph.D. dissertation, Graduate School of Business Administration, New York University.
Schwamm, Henri, and Patrizio Merciai (1986) *Multinationals and the Services.* Chichester: John Wiley & Sons.
Teece, David J. (1985) "Economies of Scope and the Enterprise." *Journal of Economic Behavior and Organization,* March.
Tschoegl, Adrian E. (1981) *The Regulation of Foreign Banks: Policy Formation outside the United States.* New York: Salomon Brothers Center for the Study of Financial Institutions, New York University.
   (1982) "Foreign Bank Entry into Japan and California." In Allen M. Rugman (ed.), *New Theories of the Multinational Enterprise.* London: Croom Helm.
   (1983) "Size, Growth and Transnationality among the World's Largest Banks." *Journal of Business,* vol. 56., no. 2.
Tugendhat, Christopher (1985) "Opening-up Europe's Financial Sector." *Banker,* January.
U.S. Congress, Office of Technology Assessment (1986) *International Competition in Banking and Financial Services.* Washington, D.C.: OTA, July (photocopy).
U.S. Department of the Treasury (1979) *Report to the Congress on Foreign Government Treatment of U.S. Banking Organizations.* Washington, D.C.: Department of the Treasury. Updated in 1984.
U.S. Office of the Comptroller of the Currency (1982) *Foreign Acquisitions of U.S. Banks.* Washington, D.C.: U.S. Government Printing Office.
Walter, Ingo (1985a) *Barriers to Trade in Banking and Financial Services.* London: Trade Policy Research Centre.
   (1985) *Secret Money.* London: George Allen & Unwin.
   (ed.) (1985) *Deregulating Wall Street.* New York: John Wiley & Sons.
   (1987) *Global Competition in Financial Services.* Cambridge, Mass.: Ballinger.
Walter, Ingo, and H. Peter Gray (1983) "Protectionism in International Banking." *Journal of Banking and Finance,* December.
Yannopoulos, George N. (1983) "The Growth of Transnational Banking." In Mark Casson (ed.), *The Growth of International Business.* London: George Allen & Unwin.

CHAPTER 9

Capital transfers from Japan to the United States: a means of avoiding trade friction

TOSHIO SHISHIDO

1 Introduction

This chapter examines rationales for capital transfer abroad by Japanese institutional investors and multinational enterprises. Both groups have invested heavily in the United States, running the risk of losses caused by the appreciation of the yen. In many instances, this money has been invested in the United States with little concern for the profitability of local production. Instead, the investments represent an effort to avoid trade friction.

The true meaning of Japanese corporate behavior, which is considerably different from that observed in other industrial nations, stems primarily from political and institutional factors rather than economic ones. In recent years, economic issues involving the United States and Japan have been much politicized. Japan has also had to confront many obstacles at home, such as business regulations and traditions, which have hindered its efforts to become a dominant capital exporting country.

In the future, Japan needs to promote direct investment in the United States through Japanese multinational enterprises, rather than portfolio investment channeled through Japanese financial institutions. This will serve not only to reduce trade friction, but also to revitalize the American manufacturing sector and to restructure the Japanese economy.

2 Japan's role as a major capital exporting country

In its 1984 economic white paper, the Japanese government announced that the structure of the Japanese economy had led Japan to become a net capital exporter.[1] In particular, the government predicted that Japan was likely to generate a current account surplus of more than 1 percent of GNP for the foreseeable future. The white paper concluded that Japanese economic policy must therefore be designed to maintain an international balance by encouraging the investment of excess of savings overseas.

The question of whether the Japanese economy does in fact generate excess savings has been the subject of considerable debate. However, given the current level of savings and the limited investment opportunities in Japan, due in part to the low growth rate of the economy and the passiveness of the government's financial policy, it seems that Japan's current account could continue to show a considerable surplus for at least the next decade. Its financial resources must therefore be transferred abroad.

Japan's transfer of capital abroad has already increased since 1980, with most of it going into portfolio investment. This is in sharp contrast to the capital transfers undertaken by other developed countries, such as England, Germany, and the United States, which have concentrated mainly on direct investments.[2]

After the price of oil jumped in 1973 and the so-called petrodollars began to accumulate, international capital markets became more liquid. These petrodollars have been held in liquid assets rather than used to finance direct investments. It was due in part to this fact that Japan was able to appear in the international capital market rapidly and rather easily, taking over the OPEC countries' role as a major exporter of capital. However, few Japanese bank executives and high-level managers have had experience in international business activities. Since Japan is a newcomer in international business, foreign direct investment and the current volume of international capital market transactions will remain a problem for the foreseeable future if Japan continues to be a major capital-exporting country. Having become a dominant capital-exporting country, Japan has to make the best use of the capital transferred abroad to promote the prosperity and stability of the world economy.

3   Characteristics of Japan's portfolio investment

The influence of Japanese institutional investors in world capital markets has grown along with the volume of Japanese capital exports. Prior to 1973, the merchant banks in London and the investment banks in New York essentially controlled the world capital market. After the 1973 OPEC oil embargo brought about a sharp increase in the price of oil, the dominant actors in these financial markets were still the institutional bankers of England and America. For example, the majority of the OPEC countries' foreign currency holdings were managed by the money market experts of England and America. Despite the magnitude of petrodollar holdings, there was little change in the behavior of the institutional and private investors in the West.

Table 9.1. *International banking assets*[a]

Country	Assets net of interoffice holdings	Percentage of total
Japan	471.0	24.5
United States	344.5	17.9
France	194.3	10.1
United Kingdom	160.0	8.3
Germany	152.5	7.9
Switzerland	82.4	4.3
Others	520.9	27.0
Total	1,925.6	100.0

[a] September 1985, $US billions.
Note: The interoffice position of U.S. banks is high for statistical reasons: The international assets of other banks are reported as being held in their overseas offices.
Source: Bank for International Settlements.

The theory of international portfolio investment consists of four elements: safety, profitability, liquidity, and convertibility. As the international diversification of portfolio investment advances and the instability of exchange rates increases, more attention will be paid to country-specific currency risk. Thus the convertibility and variability of a particular currency will be major criteria for portfolio investment.

With the growth in sources of international capital market instability, Japan's traditional investors have adopted behavior that is seemingly different from that of Western investors. From 1981 to 1985, Japan accumulated a current account surplus exceeding $US160 billion, of which less than $US10 billion has been added to Japanese official reserves. The remaining $US150 billion was recycled through Japanese banks and securities firms to the world capital market. In addition, Japan's financial institutions and enterprises have borrowed dollars in part to hedge the risk of exchange rate changes. By subsequently investing this money in the capital market, the investors have increased their earnings by borrowing Eurodollars on a short-term basis and investing them in the U.S. long-term capital market. As a result, Japan owned a 25 percent share of the total in international banking financial assets at the end of 1985. Japan thereby forced American banks into second place, with the latter accounting for 18 percent (see Table 9.1).[3]

Table 9.2. *Japan's balance of payments in 1984–6[a]*

Year	Current account	Long-term capital account	Short-term capital account	Errors and omissions	Balance of monetary movements	
					Foreign reserves	Others[b]
1984	35.0	−49.7	−4.3	3.8	1.8	−17.0
1985	49.3	−64.8	−0.7	3.9	0.2	−12.5
1986	85.8	−131.5	−1.3	2.4	15.7	−60.5

[a] $US billions.
[b] (−) shows deterioration in the external monetary position (increase in liability).
Source: Bank of Japan, "Balance of Payments Monthly."

3.1   *Japanese capital transfers and the interest rate*

Although Japan's share in the world capital market has recently increased rapidly, there is still some doubt as to whether its portfolio investment strategies actually follow the aforementioned four principles.

The net capital transfer from Japan for the past three years was higher than its current account surplus. This has been attributed to the high interest rates available in the U.S. capital market (see Table 9.2).

In fact, the correlation between Japan's capital account deficit and the long-term interest differential between Japan and the United States was very high only for the period from 1978 to 1984. Since the appreciation of the yen in September 1985, this correlation has not been noted (see Figure 9.1).

Despite the reduction in the interest rate gap between Japan and the United States and the capital losses due to the devaluation of the dollar, the large capital outflow from Japan to the United States has continued.

Many aspects of the behavior of Japanese financial institutions since the appreciation of the yen are difficult to understand. For example, the majority of the bonds that are held by insurance companies and trust banks could be cashed at any time. Although bond prices have been increasing because of the downward trend of nominal interest rates, little effort has been made to improve the combination of domestic and foreign equity in Japanese portfolios. In general, the capital outflows were still very large in 1985 and 1986.

Looking at Japanese long-term capital accounts, we find that the capital outflows in 1985 reached $US81 billion, of which $US53.7 billion was used to purchase bonds. Thus 66 percent of the total capital outflows turned out to be a highly liquid form of portfolio investment (see Table 9.3). In spite of the recent reduction in the interest rate gap between Japan and the United States, the investment in bonds continues. Japanese investors in 1985 and 1986 were more interested in the differential between the short-term interest rate and the returns from the short-term possession of bonds, than in converting yen to dollars to buy dollar-denominated bonds. They borrowed dollars to invest in dollars, thereby avoiding the exchange risk. This pattern of "borrow short, lend long" in the fund management of financial institutions is very risky. It is also putting downward pressure on the profits of Japanese financial institutions.

A recent report[4] observed that, given the nature of Japanese capital outflows and foreign investment, the main motivating force appears to be capital security, and not the market rate of return! This does not mean that Japanese financial institutions in general, or institutional investors in particular, are ignoring profits, but rather that the decision to engage in portfolio investment has undoubtedly been made for other reasons:

(1) For one thing, only the dollar market can absorb the high level of portfolio investment that Japan desires. In spite of exchange rate shifts, Japan's current account surpluses have persisted through 1986, when the surplus is expected to be $US85 billion. Excess savings (i.e., savings that exceed domestic investment) of this magnitude in one country are a problem. They can be absorbed only in America's capital market or in the Eurodollar market. America may have a heavy debt burden after accepting Japan's saving, but the confidence in the dollar cannot easily be jeopardized. Since the dollar is different from other currencies, Japanese institutional investors cannot avoid the dollar when they invest abroad, and must therefore accept, to some extent, the risk of the dollar's depreciation.

(2) The behavior of Japanese investors is in part a response to the changing regulations of the banking system. In the past, Japanese financial institutions, especially pension funds, operated under binding ceilings on overseas investments that were imposed by the Ministry of Finance. However, overseas bond investments were almost completely deregulated in the 1980s through the revision of the foreign exchange laws. As the scope of deregulation broadened, financial institutions, one by one, started to buy dollar-denominated bonds.[5]

Since international diversification is the basis for portfolio investment, some Japanese financial institutions that were not permitted to invest in foreign bonds in the past have begun investing in dollar bonds now that the restriction is gone, regardless of the interest rate or the exchange risk. With the increasing international diversification of Japanese financial portfolios, the investment strategies of international investors have

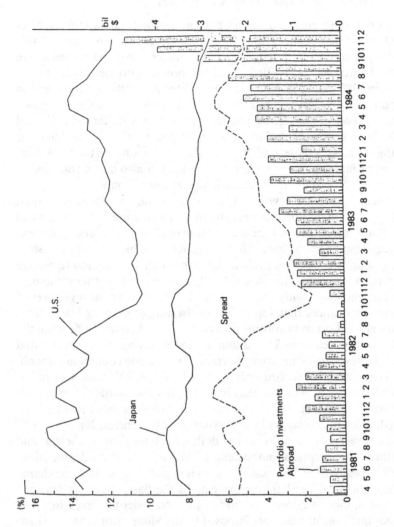

Figure 9.1 Overseas bond investments and the spread of interest rates between Japan and the United States.

Figure 9.1 (cont'd.) Overseas bond investments and the spread of interest rates between Japan and the United States.

Table 9.3. *Japanese long-term capital accounts*[a]

Year	Total	Direct investment[b]	Portfolio investment[b]	Bond investment[b]
1975	3,392	1,768 (52.1)	24 (0.7)	−41 (−)
1976	4,559	1,991 (43.7)	146 (3.2)	−64 (−)
1977	5,247	1,645 (31.4)	1,718 (32.7)	735 (14.0)
1978	14,872	2,371 (15.9)	5,300 (35.6)	1,897 (12.7)
1979	16,294	2,898 (17.7)	5,865 (36.0)	3,385 (20.7)
1980	10,817	2,385 (22.1)	3,753 (34.6)	2,996 (27.7)
1981	22,809	4,894 (21.4)	8,777 (38.5)	5,810 (25.5)
1982	27,418	4,540 (16.6)	9,743 (35.5)	6,076 (22.2)
1983	32,459	3,612 (11.1)	16,024 (49.4)	12,505 (38.5)
1984	56,775	5,965 (10.5)	30,795 (54.2)	26,773 (47.1)
1985	81,815	6,452 (7.9)	59,773 (73.1)	53,749 (65.7)

[a] Current $US millions.
[b] Numbers in parentheses represent percentage of total.
Note: Bond investment included in portfolio investment.
Source: Ministry of Finance, "Statistics of International Balance of Payments, 1986."

become more sensitive to interest rate and exchange rate fluctuations. The relatively late step-by-step deregulation of Japan's financial policy has made the behavior of institutional investors abnormally dollar oriented.

(3) Japanese investors are also strongly affected by accounting procedures. In the balance sheets of Japanese financial institutions, financial (and real) assets have been reported by purchase price (book value). To cope with the recent fluctuations in the exchange rate, the Ministry of Finance has asked banks to report assets at their current value. Since in many cases these equities had been reported at low book values, it has become routine procedure to reduce the impact on reported profits by selling some of the stocks at current market prices and realizing the capital gains.

This method of evaluating financial assets also requires banks to show a capital loss when the value of foreign currency bonds falls owing to an appreciation of the yen. When the yen appreciated from 240 to 150 yen to the dollar in 1985 and 1986, Japanese institutional investors who had purchased dollar-denominated bonds suffered huge losses. However, since Japanese institutional investors had held low-priced domestic equities they could close the books for the period without reporting losses by selling stocks at high current prices and realizing the capital gains in the booming domestic stock market. Their behavior – which originates from accounting procedures that make it easy to write off capital losses – is said to be insensitive to the interest rate or the rate of return on capital.

Table 9.4. *Japan's foreign securities holdings, by financial institution*[a]

	Foreign securities			Increase from 1982 to 1986	
	1982[b]	1986[c]	Percent	Amount	Percent
City banks	1.14	3.55	10.5	2.41	8.6
Local banks	0.35	2.53	7.5	2.18	7.9
Trust banks	0.73	7.96	23.5	7.23	26.1
Long-term credit banks	0.46	1.68	4.9	1.22	4.4
Mutual funds	0.17	3.91	11.5	3.74	13.5
Agricultural banks	0.50	1.93	5.9	1.43	5.2
Life insurance	1.90	7.31	21.5	5.41	19.5
Others	0.95	5.07	14.9	4.12	14.9
Total	6.20	33.94	100	27.74	100

[a] Trillions of yen.
[b] Figures represent balance at end of the year.
[c] 1986 figures have been adjusted for exchange rate fluctuation. They differ from Japan's holdings in dollar terms.
Source: Bank of Japan, "Economic Statistics Monthly."

(4) The mass psychology of the Japanese people also plays a role in investment behavior. As financial deregulation continued, Japanese financial institutions were released from the government's protection and were forced to bear the risks themselves. However, the general tendency in Japan is to follow tradition and avoid independent policies (see Table 9.4).[6] This mass psychology, or "bandwagon syndrome," is in part responsible for the aforementioned capital losses. In general, losses are perceived to be less troublesome if inflicted on all members of the group. Although this "groupism" does contribute to business efficiency when it appears in the form of company loyalty, in financial institutions it may create serious problems in an environment of increasing internationalization and liberalization of financing. Independence is already more important to those Japanese financial institutions active in markets where deregulation is well advanced.

Like the highly unbalanced trade accounts between Japan and the United States, these four conditions may continue for some time. As a result, Japan can expect to sustain great damage from reduced domestic investment, and the United States will have to carry an increasing debt burden. Since the financial capital transferred from Japan to America in large part covers the U.S. savings deficiency, the transferred capital cannot be said to have been used in more productive fields. It is also very risky for the U.S. Federal Reserve to cover an international trade deficit with liquid short-term capital. As long as the current rate of savings in Japan persists, there should be a shift from portfolio investment to direct investment, which lasts longer, is more stable, and helps increase productivity.

4   Japan's direct investment in the United States

In the early 1960s, Japanese enterprises began to expand their rate of direct investment in the United States. However, most of this investment has been used to promote the sale of goods exported by Japan. Japanese manufacturing firms have also sought investment opportunities in the developing countries, in view of labor costs and the natural resources required in Japanese industries.

Figure 9.2 shows the trends of Japanese direct investment abroad in manufacturing industries. Starting with the 1970s, there have been different trends in the level of direct investment in developed and developing countries. In fiscal 1981, Japanese manufacturing investment in the industrialized world accounted for 54.9 percent of the total direct investment abroad by Japanese firms, exceeding the level of direct investment in developing countries for the first time.

Three factors lie behind the rapid increase in manufacturing investments in the United States. The most important one is the growing need for overseas production to prevent increased trade friction between the United States and Japan, in other words, to prevent the further development of American protectionist trade policies. Congress has blamed Japanese exports of manufactured products for high unemployment in the United States. The numerous requests from state governors for the construction of new production facilities by Japanese firms further stimulates overseas investment. The second factor is a dramatic increase in the productivity of Japanese business, which has made an increasing number of Japanese companies internationally competitive. The third factor is the narrowing of the gap between labor costs in Japan and the United States.

Leading the surge in direct investment in the United States are the following industries: electric machinery and electronics, motor vehicles, and general machinery – that is, the major export industries in Japan. In those industries that are thought to be more internationally competitive in Japan than in America (e.g., the steel industry), investment takes the form of technical cooperation and capital participation. This policy does not mean acquisition but rather minority participation in joint ventures. Japanese entrepreneurs seem to think that they will be able to revitalize the American steel industry by introducing Japanese production control systems.

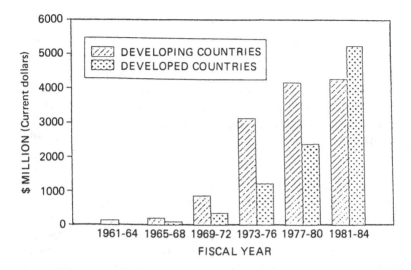

Figure 9.2 Japanese direct foreign investment in manufacturing industries. Figures based on investments reported to the Japanese government. Source: MITI, "Japan Direct Foreign Investment: A New Multidimensional Approach," Report by the Committee for Direct Investment Abroad, July 1985 (photocopy).

Given these three factors and the sharp depreciation of the dollar in 1986, direct investment in the United States by Japanese enterprises will no doubt continue to grow at a considerable rate. The forecast of Japanese foreign investment abroad made by the Ministry of International Trade and Industries (MITI) in 1985 shows that in the next decade, Japan might become the world's second largest owner of direct foreign investment. Furthermore, overseas production may reach 10 percent of domestic manufacturing production in 1995, rising from only 3 percent in 1985.[7]

5   Incentives for overseas direct investment

MITI, the Japan External Trade Organization (JETRO) and the Japanese Overseas Investment Research Institute of the Export & Import Bank have studied the factors motivating Japanese enterprises to invest abroad. In general, these enterprises have sought to invest abroad to secure (1) overseas markets, (2) raw materials, and (3) low wages.

Since the latter part of the 1970s, when the protectionist policies of Japan's trading partners began to limit its access to export markets, political factors have become more important in the shaping of policy. The main motive for overseas expansion has been the desire to avoid import restrictions. This motive represents a departure from the textbook theory of direct investment: Contrary to the theory proposed by Professor K. Kojima,[8] recent direct investment by Japan has not been of the export-increasing type.

Investments by Japanese enterprises in America have been "survival operations," not major profit centers. Again, the importance of mass psychology cannot be neglected. If one company steps forward for expansion, the other companies in the same business will definitely try to expand as well.

The color television market provides a good example of this friction. Prior to 1977, 3.5 million television sets were exported annually to America by Japan's major electronics manufacturers. In 1977, these manufacturers were accused of dumping, and their exports were essentially prohibited (Figure 9.3). Before import restrictions were adopted by the Federal Trade Commission, only Sony and Matsushita were manufacturing color television sets in the United States. After the import restriction, five other makers built or acquired local production facilities there (see Table 9.5). The combined volume of production at these facilities exceeded 3.2 million in 1980, which was almost the same amount as the historic peak export volume. According to some estimates, this local production led to a $500 million reduction in the U.S. bilateral current account deficit with Japan, as well as the creation of some 50,000 jobs in the United States.[9]

In an interview in 1973, the president of the U.S. subsidiary of the Sony Corporation, Masao Iwama, noted that the feasibility study for a factory then under construction in San Diego indicated that the local assembly of color television sets in the United States would not generate a profit at that time. However, Akio Morita, the chairman of Sony Corporation, felt strongly that Sony should begin local production despite the anticipated losses, since appreciation of the yen from 306 to 200 yen to the dollar would reverse the implication of the feasibility study. He did not necessarily expect a shift in the exchange rate to 200 yen to the dollar. His decision was not made from the profit-and-loss point of view of top management, but with the strained trade relationship between Japan and the United States in mind.

The automobile industry provides a second example. The imbalance in automobile trade has almost become a symbol of Japan–U.S. trade friction. In 1980, the United States imposed a quota in the form of a voluntary export restraint. Those Japanese automobile makers whose exports to the United States were limited by a quota decided to produce Japanese automobiles in America. This decision reduced market efficiency since it was less costly to export automobiles produced in Japan than to produce them in America.

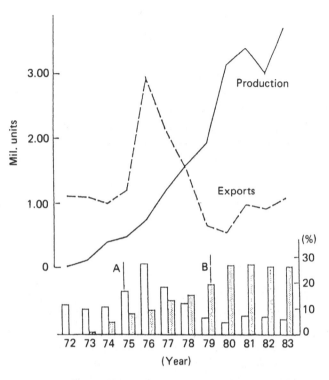

Figure 9.3 The case of color T.V. sets – exports vs. local products. A. Japan's exports to the United States as a percentage of total demand in the United States. B. Japan's local production in the United States as a percentage of total production in the United States. Source: MITI, "Tsusho Hakusho: Annual Report on International Trade," 1985.

Table 9.5. *Production capacity for color television sets: Japanese firms operating in the United States, 1985*

Company	Plant opened	Plant location	Plant history	Capacity (1,000/yr)
Sony	1972	California	New	700
Matsushita	1974	Illinois	Acquisition	800
Sanyo	1977	Arkansas	Acquisition	900
Mitsubishi	1978	California	New	200
Toshiba	1978	Tennessee	New	500
Sharp	1979	Tennessee	New	150
Hitachi	1979	California	New	150

Source: K. Shimada, "Direct Investment Abroad, 1985."

In an interview in 1978, the president of Toyota Motors, Eiji Toyota, stated that his firm did not intend to begin local production in the United States. When asked if he would consider direct investment in the United States as a means of promoting Japan's national interest and lessening trade friction, he replied that Toyota was not in the business of serving the national interest. From the standpoint of private enterprise, he felt that direct investment in America was not in the best interest of Toyota. This reaction may have been due in part to his lack of confidence in using Toyota-style management in America. However, since then import restrictions have been tightened, and even Toyota has begun to manufacture automobiles using American labor.

The example of video cassette recorders (VCRs) should also be mentioned. Since VCRs are not produced in the United States, there is no reason for it to adopt import restrictions in order to protect domestic industries. Nevertheless, in 1985, Matsushita officially announced that its plan to undertake local production of VCRs in the United States was based in part on consideration of Japan–U.S. trade friction. It is not the case that Matsushita placed the national interest ahead of enterprise profit. When European trade barriers were erected against Japanese VCRs, Matsushita was probably encouraged to undertake the investment to ensure continued access to the U.S. market. How the VCR market will evolve in the future is not yet clear. Since Matsushita has decided to continue its operations in the United States, it is likely that seven other companies will follow.[10] If so, they will then compete in direct investment, as well as in profitability.

The primary reason that major industries, such as the automobile and electronics industries, have undertaken direct foreign investment has to do with noneconomic factors. The decision is made from the standpoint of long-term strategy, given the forecasts of possible future changes. However, it cannot be said that all Japanese industries are engaging in direct investment in developed countries.

Research by the Economic Planning Agency (Tables 9.6, 9.7) indicates that most enterprises are looking for other export markets. As a countermeasure to import restrictions, this export market shift is supplemented by local production. However, it is ironic that enterprises overwhelmingly view local production as the primary method of resolving trade friction (see Table 9.8). This tells us that although the shift to local production is the most efficient countermeasure to trade friction from the standpoint of the Japanese government, private enterprises in Japan have little interest in taking such risks.

Of those manufacturers who had invested in the United States before trade friction became a hot issue, many were profit minded. Kikkoman,

Table 9.6. *Measures taken by Japanese companies to avoid import restrictions*

	Present policy[a]	Future policy[a]
Shift exports to countries with fewer import restrictions	50.4	50.5
Local production through joint ventures	31.6	39.3
Local production without joint ventures	26.8	30.5
Voluntary export restraints	30.5	27.4
Shift exports from other countries	11.8	17.2
Export by OEM	11.0	18.6
Other	7.4	5.3

[a] Percentage of companies choosing this policy.
Source: Japanese Economic Planning Agency, "Reports on Company Behavior, 1986."

the soy sauce exporter, started local production in the United States in 1968. According to Tomosaburo Mogi, the managing director of Kikkoman, management talked loudly about the risk of business expansion overseas. However the go-ahead decision was made after it had been confirmed that (1) the American market was big enough to absorb the local production; (2) soy beans, which are the raw material for soy sauce, were produced in America and Canada, and (3) the transportation expense could be drastically reduced compared with the export from Japan.

In the future, local production in America might be undertaken by private enterprises in the simple pursuit of profit. However, this strictly economic justification for direct investment abroad will depend upon future exchange rates. Direct investment in America will also be influenced by the special structure of Japanese industry.

Of the Japanese manufacturers who have recently expanded their business in America, the main ones are in the automobile and the electronics industries. These industries are so-called assembly makers, whose high quality and inexpensive finished goods are made possible by the existence of a wide variety of small subcontractors who provide manufactured inputs. The export of "master enterprises" to the United States therefore requires local production by Japanese subcontractors as well. The Japanese seek to improve not only U.S. value-added but also the quality of

Table 9.7. *Measures proposed by private companies for reducing trade friction*

	Percentage of firms recommending policy
Increase local production	53.0
Increase imports of parts	16.0
Reduce tariffs	38.0
Simplify import procedures	32.0
Raise yen exchange rate	9.0
Expand domestic demand:	
By private sector	47.5
By reducing taxes	33.4
By government sector	28.3
By lower interest rates	23.1
Increase consumer import demand	4.8
Develop cultural exchange	9.0
Others	1.6

Source: Japanese Economic Planning Agency, "Reports on Company Behavior, 1986."

Table 9.8. *Reasons cited for direct investment abroad (to developed countries after 1980)[a]*

	Avoiding trade friction	Market expansion	Follow clients' DIA[b]	Superiority on cost	Others
Business machines	96.7	3.3	–	–	–
Machine tools	77.1	14.3	–	–	8.6
Consumers of electric machines	53.6	13.6	10.7	14.3	7.8
Electronics	30.0	32.1	11.3	10.8	15.6
Automobiles	66.0	24.0	–	–	10.0

[a] Percentage of responses.
[b] Direct investment abroad.
Source: MITI, "Nihon Kigyo no Kaigai Seisan" (Research on foreign local production of Japanese enterprises), 1985.

manufactured inputs. An upward trend is seen in the direct investment undertaken by the small Japanese enterprises geared to the further expansion of major enterprises in America. In this case, the direct investment by small Japanese enterprises should not be motivated by the managerial sense of profit pursuit, but by the sense of compulsion.

5.1   *Necessary conditions for the success of Japanese enterprises
in America*

Once Japanese companies decide to circumvent the barrier of U.S. import restrictions by beginning local production, they will adhere to the decision whether or not local production represents a short-run cost advantage. It is possible that Japanese companies make this decision keeping in mind government policies aimed at relieving trade friction. However, their direct investments must basically be profitable. These enterprises make their decisions after taking into consideration the possibility of adverse shifts in the political or economic environment, such as a reduction in exports to the United States, given current policies; a further tightening of U.S. import restrictions due to increased trade friction; or a continued appreciation of the yen.

In addition, Japanese companies, in spite of their expansion into the United States, which is a country with advanced technology, have not had the same advantages as American companies seeking direct foreign investment in the past (e.g., exclusive technology). Direct foreign investment is defined here as the transfer of managerial and capital resources. With this in mind, the theory was put forth that Japan's primary managerial resource was its superior style of management.

It is clear that the combination of low price, good quality, and high reliability has allowed Japanese automobiles and color televisions to dominate the world market. The participation of labor in managerial decisions through quality control circles has contributed to the success as well. The so-called Japanese style of management is based upon the societal and historical outcome of (1) a life employment system, (2) a wage system based on seniority, (3) the enterprisewide union, and the accompanying social conditions, (4) the emphasis on unanimity in decision making (*nemawashi*), (5) the investment in personnel resources through on-the-job training, and (6) the high morale and willing subordination of the laborer. World opinion indicates that a primary virtue of Japanese management is that more emphasis has been put on humanistic treatment than on scientific personnel administration. This is the fruit of the peculiarities of Japanese society.

Note, however, that when managerial resources are transferred abroad through direct investment, some things cannot be transferred. Although the technology, the capital, and the scientific method of management can be transferred despite the different cultures involved, those characteristics that are an outgrowth of culture and society cannot be transferred. Statistical methods of quality control were created in America. However, in Japan's factories, these techniques have been transformed into the small groups called quality control circles. As such, these groups contribute to

worker morale by increasing a worker's sense of management participation. The laborers belonging to these small groups have discussions,
even if it means giving up their rest time, and submit those proposals that
they expect to be useful in improving product quality, lowering the de-
fect rate, or increasing productivity. Workers are more satisfied when
their suggestions and inventions are used to increase the profit of the
company and improve management's performance. This way of thinking
is not acceptable in the context of American individualism, and therefore
it is not adopted by Japanese companies beginning local production in
America.[11]

It should be emphasized that the direct investment by Japanese companies in America is motivated more strongly by compulsiveness than by
the simple pursuit of profit. Therefore, in order for Japanese companies
to be successful in America, the unique aspects of the Japanese style of
management should be planted in America, in an effort to surmount the
cultural and social gap. That is, this management style must evolve in
America in order to be accepted by American society.

6   Cooperation for revitalization of the American economy

Japanese superiority in specific areas, such as the automobile and semiconductor industries, and superior competitiveness in the U.S. market
have caused a large trade imbalance between the two countries. In order
to work toward reducing the trade deficit, the United States, Japan, the
United Kingdom, France, and Germany (the G5) agreed in September 1985
to intervene in the exchange market and bring up the value of the yen
against the dollar. Prime Minister Nakasone proposed structural adjustment policies to increase the internationalization of the Japanese economy.

Japan's direct investment in the United States and the local production
by Japanese companies provide an opportunity for the transfer of technology to American companies. The so-called Japanese style of management might be difficult to transfer to the American workplace, but the
coexistence of different types of management will be useful in improving
understanding between the two nations.

Trade friction between the two giants may become chronic; it may eventually force America to take the dangerous course of yet stronger protectionism. In order to avoid the deplorable possibility of direct confronta-
tion between these nations, there may be no other alternative for Japan
than to cooperate with U.S. companies in an effort to revitalize U.S. industry through direct investment by Japanese manufacturing companies.[12]

Temporary export curbs, open-door policies for American imports, and
capital transfer by portfolio investment are some useful measures for improving the balance of payments in the short term. In the longer run,

however, both countries need to cooperate more on the production side. Japanese direct investment may play an important role, both by facilitating the transfer of technology to the United States and by providing a model for changing the behavior of American business management.

Notes

1 Economic Planning Agency, "Economic Annual Report 1984," *The Japan Times,* 1985.
2 W. Woodruff, *Impact of Western Man* (Macmillan, 1966), p. 150. The following table provides an indication of direct investment in the United States by affiliates of foreign companies.

1982 investment in the United States by foreign companies

	$US million	Percent
United Kingdom	28,386	23.0
Netherlands	25,994	21.0
Canada	11,435	9.3
West Germany	9,683	7.8
Japan	9,679	7.8
Switzerland	6,391	5.2
Total	123,590	100.0

Source: U.S. Department of Commerce Survey of Current Business.

3 See also *The AMEX Bank Review,* "International Banking Market Shares by Bank Nationality," April 28, 1986.
4 "The Potential of the Japanese Surplus for World Economic Development," Report of a Study Group of the World Institute for Development Economics Research (WIDER) in Helsinki, April 18, 1986.
5 The following is a list of major efforts undertaken by the Ministry of Finance to deregulate financial markets during the period 1983–6.

   a. *January 1983:* Purchase of zero-coupon foreign bonds reopened.
   b. *May 1983:* Post Office Life Insurance managers allowed to purchase foreign bonds up to a limit of 10 percent of total financial assets.
   c. *April 1984:* Ministry of Finance authorizes a new mutual fund specializing in foreign bonds.
   d. *July 1984:* Casualty insurance limit on foreign bond investment increased from 10 to 15 percent.
   e. *November 1984:* Special money fund deregulated.
   f. *June 1985:* College pension fund allowed to invest in dollar-denominated foreign bonds.
   g. *February 1986:* "Loan in trust" reopens foreign bond investment with exchange rate hedge.

h. *March 1986:* Life insurance and casualty insurance foreign investment ceiling increased from 10 to 15 percent.

i. *April 1986:* Seventeen agricultural credit cooperatives (prefecture level) allowed to invest in foreign bonds totaling up to $US300 million.

j. *August 1986:* Life insurance foreign investment ceiling raised to 30 percent.

6 Life insurance companies and trust banks, which manage mainly pension funds, are required by the Ministry of Finance to provide dividends to policyholders or pensioners only from income gains. These banks evaluate investment opportunities only in terms of the interest rate; they ignore capital gains. When the banks suffer a capital loss owing to an appreciation of the yen, they might be able to realize a capital gain by selling Japanese stock in the boom periods of the domestic stock market.

7 MITI, "Japanese Direct Foreign Investment: A New Multidimensional Approach," Report by Committee for Direct Investment Abroad, July 1985.

8 Kiyoshi Kojima, "Direct Foreign Investment" (London: Croom Helm, 1978).

9 Toshio Shishido, "Nihon Kihyou in U.S.A." (Japanese enterprises in the United States), (Tokyo: Toyo Keizai Shimpousha, 1981).

10 Hitachi planned to produce VCRs in an American factory in 1986.

11 Research indicates that only 9 out of 49 companies have introduced the quality control circle system in American subsidiaries. See "Reports on Japanese Enterprises' American Activities and Its Technology Transfer," Japan Association of Overseas Enterprises, May 1981.

12 "Japan's Cooperation for the Revitalization of American Industry," Nikko Research Center, Tokyo, 1981.

CHAPTER 10

The efficiency of U.S. and Japanese stock markets

TOSHIYUKI OTSUKI and NORIYOSHI SHIRAISHI

1   Introduction

The Center for Japan–U.S. Relations at the International University of Japan is currently planning to select, adapt, and develop practical techniques to study the informationally integrated capital markets of the United States and Japan. The analysis of a diversified portfolio of U.S. and Japanese stocks will require a simple, but operationally meaningful, framework in order to test the informational efficiency of capital markets in both countries. Such a framework is also necessary for testing the effectiveness of macroeconomic policies. Defining a testable version of the efficient market hypothesis (EMH) will therefore occupy a central place in the center's initial research effort.

This chapter attempts to illustrate the basic assumptions of the EMH using some empirical evidence on U.S. and Japanese stock markets. These results were generated using a 20-year time series of monthly observations for the holding-period returns of the common stocks listed on the New York Stock Exchange and the Tokyo Stock Exchange. For each of the U.S. and Japanese stocks, we have selected comparable variables and time periods, and have used the same statistical techniques to ensure that the results for the two markets are comparable to the greatest extent possible.

Section 2 points out some theoretical issues raised by the EMH. In Section 3, five models commonly used in testing the EMH are briefly sketched. Section 4 summarizes a few studies on Japanese stocks and our empirical results.

2   An efficient capital market: informal discussion

There are several definitions of market efficiency, each with its own strengths and weaknesses. However, we shall concentrate on the defi-

We are grateful to the Center for Research in Security Prices at the University of Chicago and to the Japan Securities Research Institute for supplying us with the CRSP stock price data and the JSRI common stock rate of return data. We would also like to thank Junko Maru for her helpful comments and suggestions.

nitions advanced by Fama (1970, 1976), Beaver (1981), Latham (1986), and Mishkin (1983). Following a discussion of their definitions of efficiency, we shall look at the critical comments of Grossman (1976) and Grossman and Stiglitz (1980).

Assume that all events of interest take place at discrete points in time, $t-1$, t, $t+1$, and so on. Then define

ϕ_{t-1} = the set of information available at time $t-1$, which is relevant for determining security prices at $t-1$.

ϕ_{t-1}^m = the set of information that the market uses to determine security prices at $t-1$. Thus ϕ_{t-1}^m is a subset of ϕ_{t-1}; ϕ_{t-1}^m contains at most all the information in ϕ_{t-1}, but it could be less.

$P_{j,t-1}$ = the price of security j at time $t-1$, $j=1,2,...,n$, where n is the number of securities in the market.

$P_{j,t+k}$ = the price of security j at time $t+k$, $j=1,2,...,n$, plus any interest or dividend payments at $t+k$, where $k \geq 0$.

The set of information ϕ_{t-1} available at time $t-1$ includes not only the state of the world at time $t-1$, but also the past history of all relevant variables; ϕ_{t-2} is a subset of ϕ_{t-1}, ϕ_{t-3} is a subset of ϕ_{t-2}, and so forth. In addition to current and past values of relevant variables, the set of information ϕ_{t-1} also includes whatever is knowable about the process that describes the evolution of the state of the world through time. Given these definitions, the EMH can be stated as

$$\phi_{t-1}^m = \phi_{t-1}. \tag{1}$$

In other words, market efficiency means that the market is aware of all available information *and* uses it correctly. According to Fama (1976), "This can only be a completely accurate view of the world if all the individual participants in the market (a) have the same information and (b) agree on its implications for the joint distribution of future prices."[1] It is assumed here that one of the things that is knowable about the process describing the evolution of the state of the world through time is the implication of the current state of the world for the joint probability distribution of security prices at future times. Fama admits that "neither of these conditions is completely descriptive. Nor is it completely realistic to presume that when market prices are determined, they result from a conscious assessment of the joint distribution of security prices by all or most or even many investors."[2] He claims that "what we really have in mind, however, is a market where there is indeed disagreement among investors, but where the force of common judgments is sufficient to produce an orderly adjustment of prices to new information."[3] He claims that "such an intuitively appealing statement is, however, too unspecific to be the basis for formal test."[4] What this statement means is that formal tests require formal models, and market efficiency will ultimately be judged on the basis of formal tests.

Beaver (1981) defines market efficiency as follows: "The market is efficient with respect to some specified information system, if and only if security prices act *as if* everyone observes the information system. If the prices have this property, they are said to fully reflect that information."[5] Beaver sees several important attributes in such a definition:

(1) It permits a definition of market efficiency in a world of individuals who are heterogeneous with respect to beliefs and information.

(2) It permits endowments and preferences to play a natural role in influencing prices.

(3) It permits individuals to perceive the market to be inefficient with respect to some information even if it is not.

(4) It gives the term "fully reflect" a well-defined meaning.

(5) It focuses upon prices as opposed to beliefs or actions.

(6) It relates directly to prior allegations of market inefficiency and to the set of empirical research that has been directed at those allegations.

(7) It permits the concept to be as finely partitioned with respect to information as may be desired and it avoids severe definitions of market efficiency.[6]

Latham (1986) extended and refined Beaver's definition as follows: "The market is '(E-) efficient' with respect to an information set if and only if revealing that information to all investors would change neither equilibrium prices nor portfolios."[7] This definition has a useful subset property: Efficiency with respect to an information set implies efficiency with respect to any subset.

Mishkin (1983) proposed a condition of market efficiency analogous to the one advanced by Fama. This condition is presented in more detail in Section 3. Mishkin emphasizes that this condition is also analogous to an arbitrage condition:

Arbitrageurs who are willing to speculate may perceive unexploited profit opportunities and will purchase or sell securities until the price is driven to the point where [the above] condition holds approximately... Transaction and storage costs will [then] be small, while the compensation of arbitrageurs and the cost of collecting information should not be large relative to the total value of securities traded. Thus deviations from the condition...should not be large.... This condition should be a useful approximation even if not all market participants have expectations that are rational. Indeed, even if most market participants were irrational, we would still expect the market to be rational as long as some market participants stand ready to eliminate unexploited profit opportunities.[8]

In general, people trade because of differences in endowments, tastes, or beliefs. Mishkin is fully aware of differences in beliefs, and the importance of the various costs. However, his approach is pragmatic enough so that a testable model may be formulated (see Section 3).

A more detailed analysis of the role of the information and the cost of collecting information in this Hayekian line of reasoning can be found in Grossman (1976) and Grossman and Stiglitz (1980). Grossman (1976) investigated the efficiency of competitive stock markets where traders have diverse information. He focused on the operation of the price system as an aggregator of the different pieces of information. Each "informed" trader gets a "piece of information." He concluded, first, that prices "reveal information to each trader which is of higher quality than his own."[9] That is, "the competitive system aggregates all the market's information in such a way that the equilibrium price summarizes all the information in the market."[10] Second, "informationally efficient price systems aggregate diverse information perfectly, but in doing this the price system eliminates the private incentives for collecting information."[11] The key concepts are the cost of information and the noise in the price system. The implications of this type of analysis may be best summarized in the following statement:

If information is costly, there must be noise in the price system, ... (so that the price system does not aggregate information perfectly), ... so that traders can earn a return on information gathering. If there is no noise and information collection is costly, then a perfect competitive market will break down because no equilibrium exists where information collectors earn a return on their information, and no equilibrium exists where no one collects information.[12]

That is, the price system may be maintained only if it is noisy enough so that information can be costly.

Grossman and Stiglitz (1980) published a rather provocative article entitled "On the Impossibility of Informationally Efficient Markets," in which they focus on a fundamental conflict between the efficiency with which markets spread information and the incentives to acquire information, and derive some implications of such a conflict for the concept of market efficiency. One of the implications Grossman and Stiglitz see is

Efficient markets theorists seem to be aware that costless information is a sufficient condition for prices to fully reflect all available information.... They are not aware that it is a necessary condition. But this is a *reductio ad absurdum,* since price systems and competitive markets are important only when information is costly.[13]

Another implication is "when information is very inexpensive, or when informed traders get very precise information, the equilibrium exists and the market price will reveal most of the informed traders' information.

However, it was argued. . . that such markets are likely to be thin because traders have almost homogeneous beliefs."[14]

Research in efficient markets has maintained a predominantly empirical tradition. From a statistical point of view, much of the recent research has been highly sophisticated. However, from a theoretical point of view, this research has avoided any formal treatment of the subject discussed above. In particular, empirical tests of market efficiency have been concerned with whether prices fully reflect specific subsets of information. Three forms of market efficiency have commonly been considered: the weak form, the semistrong form, and the strong form. A market is efficient in the weak form if prices fully reflect any information in the past sequences of prices. A market is efficient in the semistrong form if prices fully reflect all information publicly available. A market is efficient in the strong form if prices fully reflect all information, including insiders' information. Sources of publicly available information include stock splits, mergers, earnings announcements, a new issue of securities, a switch in accounting methods, and the like.

The weak and semistrong forms of market efficiency have obvious implications for technical analysis and fundamental analysis, respectively. The efficient market hypothesis does not imply that analysts are useless, but it seriously undermines the basic premise of their analyses. This conflict would explain why there has been such an impressive amount of research on the topic of market efficiency. The EMH also has profound implications for accounting, finance, and portfolio management. For recent empirical studies on financial time series and market efficiency, see, for example, Taylor (1986).

3   Selected models of market equilibrium

Any test of market efficiency is simultaneously a test of efficiency and some assumptions about market equilibrium. The following are five commonly used models of market equilibrium. The exposition is based mainly on Fama (1976) and Mishkin (1983).

3.1   *Expected returns are positive*

Define the one-period return on security j from time $t-1$ to t as

$$R_{j,t} = \frac{P_{j,t} - P_{j,t-1}}{P_{j,t-1}}. \tag{2}$$

This model of market equilibrium assumes that the market always sets $P_{j,t-1}$ so that the expected value of $R_{j,t}$, given ϕ_{t-1}^m, is positive:

$$E(R_{j,t} \mid \phi_{t-1}^m) = \frac{E(P_{j,t} \mid \phi_{t-1}^m) - P_{j,t-1}}{P_{j,t-1}} > 0. \tag{3}$$

If the market efficiency holds with respect to ϕ_{t-1}, then $\phi_{t-1}^m = \phi_{t-1}$ by definition, and the market adjusts prices fully and instantaneously whenever new information becomes available. In this case, the best trading strategy for any security is "to buy and hold."

Empirical tests of U.S. capital markets were provided by Alexander (1961) and Fama and Blume (1966). They compared the profitability of a filter rule to a buy-and-hold strategy for daily returns on the individual stocks. The results tend to support the desirability of the buy-and-hold strategy and fail to reject the hypothesis of capital market efficiency. Sato (1985) applied the same filter rule tests to Japanese stock markets. The results are very similar to the results obtained in U.S. capital markets.

3.2   *Expected returns are constant*

From a statistical point of view, the first equilibrium model [(2) and (3)] is difficult to test empirically. More testable is the model in which the expected value of stock returns is assumed to be constant through time:

$$E(R_{j,t} \mid \phi_{t-1}^m) = E(R_{j,t} \mid \phi_{t-1}) = \text{a constant.} \tag{4}$$

Empirical tests based on this model have focused primarily on a subset of ϕ_{t-1}, the sequence of past returns. In this case, market efficiency implies that the autocorrelations of the returns on any security j are zero for all values of lag k. Fama (1965) showed that the autocorrelations of daily returns for each of the 30 Dow-Jones Industrials are not inconsistent with the hypothesis of market efficiency.

3.3   *The market model as an equilibrium model*

The return on a portfolio (R_p) is a linear combination of the returns on the n securities included in the portfolio:

$$R_{p,t} = \sum_{j=1}^{n} w_j R_{j,t}, \tag{5}$$

where w_j represents the proportion of security j in the portfolio.

The "market model" is defined as

$$R_{j,t} = \alpha_j + \beta_j R_{m,t} + \epsilon_{j,t}, \tag{6}$$

where $E[\epsilon_{j,t} \mid R_{m,t}] = 0$, and $\text{var}[\epsilon_{j,t} \mid R_{m,t}] = \text{a constant}$, and $R_{m,t}$ is the return on the portfolio of securities taken to be representative of the market.

From a statistical point of view, the model holds if the joint probability distribution of returns on individual securities is multivariate normal. From an analytic point of view, the market return $R_{m,t}$ presumably reflects marketwide information that affects the returns on all securities. The disturbance $\epsilon_{j,t}$ is presumed to reflect information that is more specific to the prospects of the individual security j. Empirical tests based on this model have focused primarily on the adjustment of returns to a company-specific subset of information, such as stock splits, new issues of securities, earning announcements, and so forth. Thus market efficiency requires that

$$E[\epsilon_{j,t} \mid \phi_{t-1}^m, R_{m,t}] = E[\epsilon_{j,t} \mid \phi_{t-1}, R_{m,t}] = 0. \tag{7}$$

Empirical tests of market efficiency in U.S. capital markets have often failed to reject the null hypothesis in favor of market efficiency. Recent work by Fabozzi and Francis (1978), Sunder (1980), and Hawawini, Levine, and Vora (1984) indicates that the alpha and beta for a market model should be treated as random variables.

3.4   Capital asset pricing model (CAPM)

A portfolio is said to be an "efficient portfolio" if no other portfolio with the same or higher expected return has a lower standard deviation of return. The concept of portfolio efficiency should not be confused with the concept of market efficiency. Under rather restrictive assumptions, market equilibrium requires that the "market portfolio" be an efficient portfolio. One model to represent this market equilibrium is the Capital Asset Pricing Model (CAPM):

$$E(R_{j,t}) = E(R_{z,t}) + [E(R_{m,t}) - E(R_{z,t})]\beta_{jm}, \tag{8}$$

where $E(R_{j,t})$ and $E(R_{m,t})$ are the expected returns on security j and on the market portfolio, respectively; $E(R_{z,t})$ is the expected return on any positive variance security whose return is uncorrelated with the return on the market portfolio; and

$$\beta_{jm} = \frac{\text{cov}(R_{j,t}, R_{m,t})}{\text{var}(R_{m,t})} \tag{9}$$

is taken to be the risk of security j in the market portfolio m measured relative to the risk of m, $\text{var}(R_{m,t})$.

To test the Capital Asset Pricing Model, Fama (1976) proposed the following ex post formulation:[15]

$$R_{j,t} = \gamma_{1,t} + \gamma_{2,t}\beta_{jm} + \gamma_{3,t}\beta_{jm}^2 + \gamma_{4,t}\sigma(\epsilon_j) + \eta_{j,t}, \tag{10}$$

where $j = 1, 2, ..., n$ and n is the number of available securities. The term $\sigma(\epsilon_j)$ is the standard deviation of the disturbance term in the market model in (6), and is meant to be a measure of risk of security j, which is not accounted for in β_{jm}. If the values of β_{jm} and $\sigma(\epsilon_j)$ for each of the securities in the market are estimated from the market model, then the procedure is to run a cross-sectional multiple regression of $R_{j,t}$ on $\hat{\beta}_{jm}$, $\hat{\beta}_{jm}^2$, and $\hat{\sigma}(\epsilon_j)$. The term β_{jm}^2 is included in (10) to test the proposition that the expected risk-return relationship is linear in β_{jm}, and the term $\sigma(\epsilon_j)$ is included to test the proposition that β_{jm} is the only measure of risk required to explain the expected return on security j.

If the market is efficient, and correctly uses all information in assessing the expected returns for time t, then the equilibrium prices are set so that equation (8) holds, where

$$E[R_{j,t} \mid \phi_{t-1}^m] = E[R_{j,t} \mid \phi_{t-1}],$$
$$E[R_{z,t} \mid \phi_{t-1}^m] = E[R_{z,t} \mid \phi_{t-1}], \tag{11}$$

and

$$E[R_{m,t} \mid \phi_{t-1}^m] = E[R_{m,t} \mid \phi_{t-1}]$$

for $j = 1, 2, ..., n$. The general implication of market efficiency is that the information set ϕ_{t-1} available at time $t-1$ cannot be used to predict deviations of the returns on securities at time t from the expected risk-return relationship in equation (8). Therefore, if equation (8) is valid, then the following must be true of equation (10):

$$E(\gamma_{3,t} \mid \phi_{t-1}) = 0,$$
$$E(\gamma_{4,t} \mid \phi_{t-1}) = 0, \tag{12}$$

and

$$E(\eta_{j,t} \mid \phi_{t-1}) = 0.$$

In other words, market efficiency implies that the information set ϕ_{t-1} available at time $t-1$ cannot be used to predict the deviations of $\gamma_{3,t}$, $\gamma_{4,t}$, and $\eta_{j,t}$ from their expected values. If we focus on a subset of ϕ_{t-1}, the sequence of past values of $\gamma_{3,t}$, $\gamma_{4,t}$, and $\eta_{j,t}$, serial correlations are a natural way to test market efficiency. If market efficiency stands up, the autocorrelations of $\gamma_{3,t}$, $\gamma_{4,t}$, and $\eta_{j,t}$ are presumed to be zero for all lags. Fama and MacBeth (1973) have presented empirical evidence in support of market efficiency in line with equation (10), using monthly records of U.S. stock returns.

One of the restrictive assumptions underlying CAPM presented here is that trading does not involve transactions costs broadly defined. Mayshar (1979) has shown that fixed transactions cost imply equilibrium prices substantially different from equation (8). In particular, $\mathrm{var}(R_{j,t})$ enters within the framework described in equation (10).

3.5   *Rational expectation models*

Mishkin (1983) introduced an interesting econometric methodology to test capital market efficiency and macrorational expectations hypotheses. The rational expectations hypothesis central to Mishkin is that, for a variable x,

$$E_m(x_t \mid \phi_{t-1}) = E(x_t \mid \phi_{t-1}), \tag{13}$$

where ϕ_{t-1} = the set of information available at time $t-1$, $E_m(\cdot \mid \phi_{t-1})$ = the subjective expectation assessed by the market, and $E(\cdot \mid \phi_{t-1})$ = the objective expectation conditional on ϕ_{t-1}. The application of this definition of rational expectations for financial markets implies that

$$E\{[R_{j,t} - E_m(R_{j,t} \mid \phi_{t-1})] \mid \phi_{t-1}\} = 0. \tag{14}$$

A model of market equilibrium that relates the subjective expectation of the market to some subset of past information is required to give empirical content to rational expectations:

$$E\{[R_{j,t} - E_m(R_{j,t} \mid \Omega_{t-1})] \mid \phi_{t-1}\} = 0, \tag{15}$$

where Ω_{t-1} is a subset of ϕ_{t-1}.

This condition implies that $R_{j,t} - E_m(R_{j,t} \mid \Omega_{t-1})$ should be uncorrelated with any past information available including the past sequence of $R_{j,t}$. This condition is analogous to, but weaker than, the one advanced by Fama to define capital market efficiency. Mishkin emphasizes that this condition is also analogous to an arbitrage condition, as noted in Section 2.

A model that satisfies the condition in equation (15) is advanced by Mishkin:

$$R_{j,t} = E_m(R_{j,t} \mid \phi_{t-1}) + (x_t - x_t^e)\beta + \epsilon_{j,t}, \tag{16}$$

where $\epsilon_{j,t}$ = a disturbance with the property $E(\epsilon_{j,t} \mid \phi_{t-1}) = 0$; x_t = the vector containing variables relevant to the pricing of the security j at time t; x_t^e = the vector of one-period-ahead rational forecasts of x_t, $x_t^e = E_m(x_t \mid \phi_{t-1}) = E(x_t \mid \phi_{t-1})$; and β = vector of coefficients.

On the basis of this model (16), Mishkin (1983, chapters 4 and 5) has found, using postwar quarterly data, no empirical evidence that interest rate forecasts are irrational in the bond market, and no empirical support for the proposition that increases in money growth are correlated with declines in short- and long-term bond rates. Variables used are the quarterly return from holding a long-term government bond from the beginning to the end of the quarter, the 90-day Treasury Bill rate, quarterly growth rate of money stock, quarterly growth rate of industrial production, and quarterly inflation rate.

4   Empirical evidence

4.1   *Current state of arts*

Empirical tests of the efficiency of U.S. capital markets are numerous. Earlier research seemed to be predominantly in favor of market efficiency in the weak and semistrong forms. More recent research has provided various cases of special deviations from what is predicted by market efficiency, but there are not enough to constitute a general case against the central idea of market efficiency.

Recent evidence indicates that the beta coefficient in the market model [equation (6) in Section 3] is a random variable with various properties depending upon the time unit for which a market model is specified.[16] As long as the beta is independently distributed, the implications of a market model for market efficiency will not be altered, but the implications for the CAPM may be substantial, since the issue involved is the stationarity of market risk. If the beta coefficient is a random variable, it becomes a rather complicated task to estimate a measure of company-specific risk, the variance of the disturbance term in a market model. Misspecification of beta and/or the variance of the disturbance term might significantly affect the interpretation of empirical tests based on equation (10) in Section 3.

Empirical tests of market efficiency and the CAPM within the context of Japanese capital markets are fewer in number, but are not necessarily less sophisticated in approach. Particularly noteworthy is the data file, rates of return on common stocks, developed by the Japan Securities Research Institute. This data file contains, among other things, monthly rates of return since 1952 on all the common stocks listed in the Tokyo Stock Exchange, and is updated annually. The technical paper series published by this institute contains many interesting articles on Japanese capital markets, including some articles on market efficiency (Komine 1975, 1978, 1980) and the application of the CAPM to Japanese markets (Konya, 1978) using the above-mentioned data. Recently two excellent books on Japanese capital markets have been written by the researchers of the institute (Yonezawa and Maru, 1984; Maru, Suto, and Komine, 1986). The books summarize some of the empirical work conducted at the institute, and clarify certain characteristics of Japanese capital markets.

Komine (1975, 1978, 1980) has tested the efficient market hypothesis in a series of three articles. The first article reports her test of market efficiency in the weak form. It is based on a time-series analysis of the daily returns on 80 randomly selected stocks for the period 1969–74. The evidence presented seems to be against the random walk hypothesis [equation (4) in Section 3], but not necessarily against the fair game model if transactions costs are considered.

The second and third articles report her tests of market efficiency in the semistrong form: market efficiency with respect to a specific subset of publicly available information. The second article reports her test of market efficiency with respect to changes in discount rate by the Bank of Japan, based on daily rates of return on a single stock market index for the period 1968–77. The evidence presented seems to be in favor of market efficiency in the semistrong form. The third article reports her test of market efficiency with respect to the gratis issue of common stocks. It is based on monthly returns for an interval of 60 months around the issue date for 282 gratis issues between February 1953 and December 1978. This study uses the market model [equations (6) and (7)] as a basis for a test of market efficiency. The evidence presented does not seem to be in favor of market efficiency.

The idea behind the test of market efficiency in the semistrong form is to examine security returns around the specific dates (for example, the date on which discount rate change is announced) to see if there is any abnormal behavior. In the market model, if a given event is associated with abnormal behavior, this behavior would be reflected in the residuals from the estimated regression model for the time periods surrounding the date when the event has occurred.

Yonezawa and Maru (1984) have checked the validity of the CAPM, in essence, equations (8) and (10) in Section 3. They have used monthly returns on individual stocks listed in the Tokyo Stock Exchange during the period 1953–81. For four out of six subperiods defined to represent growth stages of the Japanese stock market, the systematic risk (the beta) and the unsystematic risk (variance $\sigma^2(\epsilon_j)$) are statistically significant, and the unsystematic risk seems to be gaining in importance in the more recent time period.

Konya (1978) has made a similar test, using the measures of return and risk of 20 portfolios systematically created in accordance with the beta values of individual stocks. The study covers the period 1959–74. The results do not seem to support the CAPM.

Any test of market efficiency is a joint test of efficiency and of a model of market equilibrium. If the tests are unsuccessful, this will reflect either a violation of market efficiency or inappropriateness of a model of market equilibrium. Hence, the evidence on the CAPM presented above alone does not lead to the rejection of market efficiency.

4.2   *Explanatory data analysis needed*

Reviewing the "representative" empirical studies on the efficiency of U.S. and Japanese capital markets, one may be tempted to conjecture that U.S. markets are informationally more efficient than Japanese markets. The empirical studies on Japanese markets cited above have replicated the earlier tests on market efficiency in U.S. capital markets. In many cases, however, a study will often alter focus, statistical method, and the nature of data simultaneously, making it difficult to compare studies. Additional empirical research designed to compare U.S. market efficiency with Japanese market efficiency at the outset seems warranted before conclusions can be drawn about the degree to which U.S. and Japanese markets are efficient. Such empirical research should be based on a simple model and a simple statistical technique, so that interstudy comparison will be made easier.

Experience with the CAPM both in the United States and in Japan seems to indicate that much will be lost if we start with some set of very restrictive assumptions that we cannot check in practice. Confirmatory data analysis is certainly needed, but we need not start with it. The previous tests of market efficiency are typically formulated with market efficiency as the null hypothesis, so that, whenever we cannot reject the null hypothesis of market efficiency, we are at the risk of committing Type II error. In this context, the power of the test seems to be critical. Unless a "powerful test" of market efficiency is available, we believe that much can be gained if we start with explanatory data analysis – looking at data to see what they seem to say.

4.3   *Empirical evidence*

Most of the previous studies use stock returns rather than stock prices, since what really counts, from an investor's point of view, is returns, and stock returns are more likely to conform to the stationarity conditions from a statistical point of view. We follow this conventional approach.

We consider 10 years with 120 observations sufficiently long enough to perform a standard time-series analysis, yet sufficiently short to keep the underlying stochastic structure of a model from being dramatically changed. Major events affecting the world economy occurred around the year 1973 – the emergence of a new international monetary system, a hike in the world petroleum prices, and so forth. Hence two 10-year periods,

January 1964 to December 1973 and January 1974 to December 1983, are selected. We may also divide each period into a set of subperiods, whenever such a division seems to be needed.

The data are monthly stock returns with dividends compiled by the Center for Research in Security Prices at the University of Chicago and the Japan Securities Research Institute. The sample consists of all the common stocks traded continuously from January 1964 to December 1983, 614 from the New York Stock Exchange (NYSE), and 563 from the Tokyo Stock Exchange (TSE). Only those stocks that satisfied a 100 percent data availability requirement (no missing values) over the entire time intervals have been included in the following analysis, 572 from the NYSE and 468 from the TSE. This data requirement may introduce a "survival bias" to the sample used. If the longevity of a firm were systematically related to the beta, a measure of market risk, for example, the statistical results might give us a false picture of the real world.

In order to see how Japanese data are different from U.S. data, the Q statistic and the beta (with the market model) have been computed for each stock for each time period. In fitting a regression model for each stock, we used the value-weighted market portfolio with dividends. The Q statistic has been obtained with the time lags (k in Appendix 1) up to 12, 24, and 36. The Q statistic is used to test whether a series of stock returns is white noise. The Q statistic is explained in more detail in Appendix 1. The frequency of white noise rejections by the Q statistic, the beta values, and the R^2 with the market model are shown in Tables 10.1 to 10.4.

Judging from the summary measures of the distributions of the Q statistic and its frequency distributions (not shown here), the stationarity conditions of the time series of stock returns are, in general, not violated. Table 10.1 shows the number of stocks for which we can reject the null hypothesis that the series of returns is white noise at the .05 level of significance. The null hypothesis of white noise supports market efficiency in the weak form. Relative frequencies of white noise rejections by the Q statistic exceed 5 percent for all the cases shown in Table 10.1, which may suggest that some series are not white noise. If this interpretation is justifiable, it appears that both the U.S. and Japanese markets have been more efficient during the recent period than during the earlier period. It also appears that the U.S. stock market has been slightly more efficient than the Japanese stock market throughout the entire time period. Table 10.2 shows the results of the same type of analysis using the subperiod data, which are not as clear as the results in Table 10.1. Time series data need to be examined further to shed light on market efficiency in the weak form.

Table 10.1. *Frequency of white noise rejections by Q statistic*

	1st period: 1964–73	2nd period: 1974–83
U.S. stocks		
12 lags	68 (0.12)	62 (0.11)
24 lags	87 (0.15)	45 (0.08)
36 lags	96 (0.17)	35 (0.06)
Japanese stocks		
12 lags	91 (0.19)	63 (0.13)
24 lags	91 (0.19)	52 (0.11)
36 lags	86 (0.18)	44 (0.09)

Note: Frequency records the number of stock return series whose test values are significant at the .05 level. Figures in parentheses are relative frequencies; proportion of the non–white-noise stocks in the sample of 572 stocks from the NYSE and of 468 stocks from the TSE, respectively. The test statistic used is the $Q(k)$ statistic, where k is set equal to 12, 24, 36 (see Appendix 1).

Table 10.2. *Frequency of white noise rejections by Q statistic with four subperiods*

	1964–8	1969–73	1974–8	1979–83
U.S. stocks				
12 lags	60 (0.10)	33 (0.06)	74 (0.13)	32 (0.06)
24 lags	76 (0.13)	28 (0.05)	50 (0.09)	41 (0.07)
36 lags	68 (0.12)	33 (0.06)	46 (0.08)	39 (0.07)
Japanese stocks				
12 lags	22 (0.05)	53 (0.11)	43 (0.09)	43 (0.09)
24 lags	33 (0.07)	46 (0.10)	34 (0.07)	40 (0.09)
36 lags	40 (0.09)	36 (0.08)	29 (0.06)	37 (0.08)

Note: Frequency records the number of stock return series whose test values are significant at the .05 level. Figures in parentheses are relative frequencies; proportion of the non–white-noise stocks in the sample of 572 stocks from the NYSE and of 468 stocks from the TSE respectively. The test statistic used is the $Q(k)$ statistic, where k is set equal to 12, 24, and 36 (see Appendix 1).

Table 10.3. *Beta values*

	1st period: 1964–73	2nd period: 1974–83
U.S. stocks		
N	572	572
Mean	1.171	1.004
SD	0.449	0.324
CV	38.3	32.3
Japanese stocks		
N	468	468
Mean	0.957	0.870
SD	0.325	0.447
CV	33.9	51.4

Note: N is the number of stocks, Mean is the arithmetic average, SD is the standard deviation, and CV is the coefficient of variation.

Table 10.3 shows the summary measures of the distributions of the beta. The frequency distribution of the beta for Japanese stocks has become flatter in the more recent period, whereas the one for U.S. stocks has become thinner. In the first period, the frequency distribution of the beta for U.S. stocks is flatter than the frequency distribution of the beta for Japanese stocks. In the second period, the situation is reversed, with Japanese stocks having the flatter frequency distribution of the beta. The frequency distributions are not shown here, but the features of the distributions can be inferred from the relative values of the coefficients of variation (CV).

Table 10.4 provides the summary measures of the distributions of the R^2. The "goodness-of-fit" of the market model for Japanese stock is, on the average, poorer during the entire period. Also note that the frequency distribution of R^2 for Japanese stocks is highly skewed to the right during the second period. For a large number of stocks, the R^2 is much smaller than 0.13.

The Durbin–Watson test of the residuals from the market models at the .05 level of significance indicates that, for a substantial number of both U.S. and Japanese stocks, the residuals are autocorrelated. As shown in Table 10.5, they tend to be negatively correlated, and this tendency is prominent with U.S. stocks. Relative frequencies of autocorrelation rejections exceed 5 percent for all the cases shown in Table 10.5, which may suggest that some residuals are not white noise.

192   Toshiyuki Otsuki and Noriyoshi Shiraishi

Table 10.4. R^2: the coefficient of determination

	1st period: 1964–73	2nd period: 1974–83
U.S. stocks		
N	572	572
Mean	0.296	0.288
SD	0.096	0.105
CV	32.4	36.5
Japanese stocks		
N	468	468
Mean	0.199	0.131
SD	0.101	0.112
CV	50.8	85.5

Note: N is the number of stocks, Mean is the arithmetic average, SD is the standard deviation, and CV is the coefficient of variation.

Table 10.5. *Frequency of zero residual autocorrelation rejections by Durbin–Watson statistic*

	1st period: 1964–73	2nd period: 1974–83
U.S. stocks		
Positive autocorrelation	5	4
Negative autocorrelation	82	71
	87 (0.15)	75 (0.13)
Japanese stocks		
Positive autocorrelation	17	14
Negative autocorrelation	47	71
	64 (0.14)	85 (0.18)

Note: Frequencey records the number of stock return series whose test values are significant at the .05 level. Figures in parentheses are relative frequencies; proportion of the stocks whose residuals calculated from the market model are autocorrelated in the sample of 572 stocks from the NYSE and of 468 stocks from the TSE, respectively. The test statistic used is the Durbin–Watson statistic.

5 Conclusions

Our data analysis has shown similarity and dissimilarity between U.S. and Japanese stock markets. The Q statistic tests reveal that, for both U.S. and Japanese stocks, the greater number of stock return series may be white noise during the more recent time period, suggesting, with reservation, that the U.S. market and Japanese market in particular have become more efficient in the weak form. For both U.S. and Japanese stocks, the explanatory power of the market model is not high in terms of the coefficient of determination – .30 or less on the average. The Durbin-Watson statistic indicates that, when the residuals are autocorrelated in the market model, the correlation tends to be negative. The Japanese stock market during 1974–83 cannot be explained well via the market model – low R^2 and high frequency of autocorrelated residuals. The use of a regression model with random beta might reveal what is wrong with the market model. Work in this direction is in progress at the International University of Japan.

We are convinced that further research is needed on the EMH in the weak form for at least three reasons. First, it is market efficiency with respect to a specific and unambiguous subset of information, so that the empirical results for U.S. and Japanese markets are comparable to the greatest extent possible. Second, it seems to be more consistent with Grossman's view of the price system as an aggregator of different pieces of information. Third, with the recent development of nonlinear and/or nonstationary time-series modeling techniques, more rigorous tests are possible. Furthermore, a useful concept of "near-efficiency" may be developed.

Appendix

Under the null hypothesis that the stationary process x_t is purely random, that is, all autocorrelations for lags 1 through k are zero, the Q statistic (Ljung and Box, 1978)

$$Q(K) = n(n+2) \sum_{k=1}^{K} r_k^2/(n-k) \qquad (A.1)$$

is approximately chi-squared distributed with K degrees of freedom, where n is the number of observations, K is the number of lags used in summation, and r_k is the sample autocorrelation at lag k, defined as

$$r_k = \frac{\sum_{t=1}^{n-k} (x_t - \bar{x})(x_{t+k} - \bar{x})}{\sum_{t=1}^{n} (x_t - \bar{x})^2},$$

where $\bar{x}$ is the sample mean of the stationary series x_t. If the Q statistic is significant, then the null hypothesis should be rejected; that is, the process is not random.

It should be noted that the empirical evidence shows that a nonstationary process tends to yield a very high-valued Q statistic. This is due to the fact that the autocorrelations of a nonstationary process fail to die out quickly and remain nonzero even for large lags. In this case, the transformations of data are necessary to induce stationarity.

Notes

1 Fama (1976), pp. 167–8.
2 Ibid.
3 Ibid.
4 Ibid.
5 Beaver (1981), p. 147.
6 Ibid., p. 148.
7 Latham (1986), p. 50.
8 Mishkin (1983), pp. 10–11.
9 Grossman (1976), p. 573.
10 Ibid., pp. 573–4.
11 Ibid., p. 574.
12 Ibid.
13 Grossman and Stiglitz (1980), p. 404.
14 Ibid.
15 Fama (1976), chap. 9.
16 Fabozzi and Francis (1978), Sunder (1980), and Hawawini et al. (1984).

References

Alexander, S. S. (1961) "Price Movements in Speculative Markets: Trends or Random Walks." *Industrial Management Review,* May.
Beaver, W. H. (1981) *Financial Reporting: An Accounting Revolution.* Prentice-Hall.
Fabozzi, F. J., and J. C. Francis (1978) "Beta as a Random Coefficient." *Journal of Financial and Quantitative Analysis,* March.
Fama, E. F. (1965) "The Behavior of Stock Market Prices." *Journal of Business,* January.
(1970) "Efficient Capital Markets: A Review of Theory and Empirical Work." *The Journal of Finance,* May.
(1976) *Foundations of Finance.* Basic Books.
Fama, E. F., and M. Blume (1966) "Filter Rules and Stock Market Trading Profits." *Journal of Business,* January.
Fama, E. F., and J. MacBeth (1973) "Risk Return and Equilibrium: Empirical Tests." *Journal of Political Economy,* May/June.

Grossman, S. (1976) "On the Efficiency of Competitive Stock Markets Where Trades Have Diverse Information." *Journal of Finance,* May.

Grossman, S., and J. E. Stiglitz (1980) "On the Impossibility of Informationally Efficient Markets." *American Economic Review,* June.

Hawawini, G. A., P. A. Levine, and A. Vora (1984) "Beta as a Random Coefficient: Portfolio and Return Internal Effects." Working Paper Series, no. 329, Salomon Brothers Center for the Study of Financial Institutions, Graduate School of Business Administration, New York University, August.

Komine, M. (1975) "Test of Stock Market Efficiency with Fair Game Model (1)" (in Japanese). Technical Paper of Japan Securities Research Institute, no. 35, July.

(1978) "Test of Stock Market Efficiency with Fair Game Model (2)" (in Japanese). Technical Paper of Japan Securities Research Institute, no. 44, May.

(1980) "Test of Stock Market Efficiency with Fair Game Model (3)" (in Japanese). Technical Paper of Japan Securities Research Institute, no. 51, July.

Konya, N. (1978) "Investor's Behavior and Market Efficiency in the Stock Market: A Test of CAPM" (in Japanese). Technical Paper of Japan Securities Research Institute, no. 44, July.

Latham, M. (1986) "Information Efficiency and Information Subsets." *Journal of Finance,* March.

Ljung, G. M., and G. E. P. Box (1978) "On a Measure of Lack of Fit in Time Series Models." *Biometrika,* vol. 65.

Mayshar, J. (1979) "Transactions Costs in a Model of Capital Market Equilibrium." *Journal of Political Economy,* August.

Maru, J., M. Suto, and M. Komine (1986) *Modern Security Markets Analysis* (in Japanese). Toyo Keizai Shinposha.

Mishkin, F. S. (1983) *A Rational Expectations Approach to Macroeconometrics: Testing Policy Ineffectiveness and Efficient-Market Models.* University of Chicago Press.

Sato, Y. (1985) "Filter Rules and Japanese Stock Market Trading." Student Working Paper Series, no. 4, Center for Japan–U.S. Relations, International University of Japan, November.

Sunder, S. (1980) "Stationarity of Market Risk: Random Coefficients Tests for Individual Stocks." *Journal of Finance,* September.

Taylor, S. (1986) *Modelling Financial Time Series.* John Wiley & Sons.

Yonezawa, Y., and J. Maru (1984) *The Stock Market in Japan* (in Japanese). Toyo Keizai Shinposha.

Index

(Page numbers in italics indicate material in graphs or tables.)